ISLAM AND EDUCATION
MYTHS AND TRUTHS

ISLAM AND EDUCATION
MYTHS AND TRUTHS

EDITED BY WADAD KADI AND VICTOR BILLEH

The University of Chicago Press

The University of Chicago Press, Chicago 60637
The University of Chicago Press, Ltd., London
11   10   09   08   07   5 4 3 2 1

Library of Congress Cataloging-in-Publication Data
Islam and Education : myths and truths / edited by Wadad Kadi and Victor Billeh.
    p. cm.
    Includes bibliographical references and index.
    ISBN 978-0-226-42187-2 (alk. paper)
    1. Islamic education. 2. Muslims—Education. I. Qadi, Wadad. II. Billeh, Victor.

    LC903.E38 2007   2007000215
    371.077—dc22

The paper used in this publication meets the minimum requirements of American National
Standard for Information Sciences—Permanence of Paper for Printed Library Materials,
ANSI Z39.48-1984

ISLAM AND EDUCATION
MYTHS AND TRUTHS

CONTENTS

Preface

DAVID POST, MARK GINSBURG, AND HEIDI ROSS

This volume features nine chapters that first appeared in an expanded issue of the *Comparative Education Review*. In producing the special issue, we benefited from two remarkable colleagues as guest coeditors: Victor Billeh, formerly with the UNESCO office in Beirut, and Wadad Kadi, from the University of Chicago. In what follows, Professor Kadi introduces the articles selected for the issue—manuscripts chosen from a large number of submissions received from every continent after a worldwide call for contributions. As she makes clear, the original scholarship offered by the authors—though focused on education in Islam—should be necessary reading for all humanists and social scientists wishing to understand the nexus between schools and societies, the spiritual dimensions of learning, and the social configuration of learning institutions. Here we want to offer only a few words that are intended to place the efforts culminating in this volume within a larger context.

The *Comparative Education Review* (*CER*) has been sponsored since 1957 by the Comparative and International Education Society (CIES), a cross-disciplinary and international association that includes both academics and practitioners from around the globe. While the roots of this field in China are distinctive,[1] in Western societies the study of comparative education is often traced to Marc-Antoine Jullien, an early advocate of cross-national, scientific investigation who, in 1816, proposed an exhaustive catalog of features and consequences of school systems in the cantons of multicultural Switzerland for the purpose of improving schooling in Europe generally. The French Enlightenment ethos of Jullien's project was one of progressive modernism, and it led to an era of cross-national study and borrowing of pedagogy and educational policy. A counterpoint began to be heard by 1900 in the work of the British Inspector of Education, Michael Sadler, who cautioned against wholesale importation of educational innovation from one society to another. The goal of scholarly study of other nations' education systems, according to Sadler, was mutual understanding of essential differences more than it was the application of techniques or organizational innovations to foreign settings. Influenced by structural-functionalists such as Émile Durkheim, scholars in comparative education began to view the process of education as integral to the operation of whole societies.

This view culminated in the major pre–World War II opus of the field, *Comparative Education*, by Isaac Kandel. An immigrant from Romania and Britain who became the first U.S. professor in this area at Columbia Teachers

---

[1] Mark Bray and Gui Qin, "Comparative Education in Greater China: Contexts, Characteristics, Contrasts, and Contributions," *Comparative Education* 37, no. 4 (2001): 451–73.

College, Kandel took a syncretic view of education in relation to the essential national features of particular societies. One could comprehend a nation's tradition of education, according to Kandel, only through a comprehensive perspective on the history, economy, and culture in that nation. Kandel's text became the standard reference for a generation.

After World War II, as reconstruction and economic development pre-occupied the newly organized UNESCO and other international agencies, progressive modernism again became ascendant. Nation building through education encouraged the cross-national adaptation of forms and techniques, leading to renewed emphasis on planning. National, cultural, and religious differences were acknowledged, but these were viewed as surmountable ob-stacles to international exchange. Scholars during the cold war period iden-tified material progress and the distribution of welfare by nation-states, rather than cultural expression, as the benchmarks for international comparison. Educational planners and scholars of international development adapted to this milieu by institutionalizing cross-national testing, establishing such cen-ters as the International Institute of Educational Planning and incorporating educational research within the aid and loan programs of donor countries and banks. By the early 1960s, human capital theorists had begun to influence comparative education theory and policy by investigating the potential of formal schooling for enhancing economic productivity and poverty allevia-tion. An earlier concern with national culture gave way to a focus on the nation-state as both the object of study and the vehicle for cooperation and assistance.

Since the end of the cold war, two important political processes have broadened the scope of scholarly work in comparative education. First, in-ternational conventions and treaties that view education as a human right rather than merely a civil right acquired saliency and broad acceptance, the best example of which was the 1989 Convention on the Rights of the Child. Human development, rather than national development, became accepted as the proper goal for educators and educational policies. The reduction of clientalist relations between socialist nation-states and the USSR (and, to a lesser extent, the parallel attenuation of clientalism between the United States and some developing countries) ushered in a renewed focus on national aspirations and identity and the questioning by researchers—if not interna-tional agencies—about the capabilities of states to promote human devel-opment. Cultural, linguistic, ethnic, national, and religious expression could be seen not as obstacles to material growth but as manifestations of a more fundamental human development. In that context, there was a renewed con-cern by scholars from many disciplines with the ways that human development was being promoted or stultified by nonmaterial as well as material conditions. The policies and practices surrounding teaching and learning could be stud-ied again as part of the politics of culture.

Nevertheless, the field of comparative and international education has continued to focus on both national similarities and national differences. In part this is the nature of comparative inquiry more generally. Similar or divergent findings may stem from real similarities or differences in the phenomena being investigated, they may reflect similarities or differences in the methods used to study the phenomena, or differences in findings may reflect similarities or differences in the way that people being studied view their social reality.[2]

At present, our field reflects a creative tension between comparisons of unique features of education in particular societies and other research that seeks, while aspiring to scientific method, worldwide generalities and patterns using universal concepts (e.g., stratification) and common measurement tools (e.g., tests of mathematics proficiency). The importance of technical knowledge versus deep expertise in cultural or geographic regions is thus a subject of continuing debate.[3] On the one hand, the welfare needs of children everywhere require that basic preconditions for education must be met with adequate resources and concern. On the other hand, comparative education has learned from history that material welfare is often the least important motive or mover of change in education.

Religion, along with culture and ideology, is relevant in this regard. Although religion figured prominently in work published by earlier generations of comparative educators, including research published in *CER*, it was largely absent from the journal after the 1960s until a special issue dedicated to religion appeared in 1995. More recently, the essentially spiritual and ethical calling of comparative education was highlighted in *CER* by Ruth Hayhoe in her 1999 CIES presidential address.[4]

As the previous account indicates, the antecedents of this volume date back to the concern by comparativists such as Kandel to engage in comprehensive study of the historical and cultural context of schooling in order to explain its features or meet its particular challenges within a particular context. At the same time, this volume might be traced to the frustration felt by

[2] See Melvin Kohn, "Cross-national Research as an Analytic Strategy," *American Sociological Review* 52, no. 6 (1987): 713–31; Piotr Sztompka, "Conceptual Frameworks in Comparative Inquiry: Divergent or Convergent?" *International Sociology* 3, no. 3 (1988): 207–18. In this vein, Joseph Farrell warns comparative and international educators that similarity or dissimilarity "is not something which inheres in the data. It is characteristic of the relationship between the observer and the data" (Joseph Farrell, "The Necessity of Comparisons in the Study of Education: The Salience of Science and the Problem of Comparability," in *New Approaches to Comparative Education*, ed. Philip Altbach and Gail Kelly [Chicago: University of Chicago Press, 1986], 209). Similarly, Edmund King calls our attention to the second and third alternatives when he encourages colleagues to "recognize two inescapably subjective aspects: our own [i.e., scholars'] subjective involvement in the debates about education; and the equally subjective involvement of those [policy makers, educators, citizens] who are trying to arrive at solutions in other countries" (Edmund King, *Other Schools and Ours*, 5th ed. [New York: Holt, 1979], 15).

[3] See "Moderated Discussion: Comparative Education, Area Studies, and the Disciplines," *Comparative Education Review* 50, no. 1 (2006): 125–48.

[4] Ruth Hayhoe, "Presidential Address: Redeeming Modernity," *Comparative Education Review* 44, no. 4 (2000): 423–39, 439.

Heidi Ross, which she recounted in her presidential address to the CIES membership in March 2002.[5] Ross explained how, in the terrible days after September 11, 2001, she was contacted by National Public Radio correspondent Lynn Neary and was asked to comment on how U.S. educators could help the public and U.S. college students better understand and engage world cultures and tensions. In subsequent discussions that Ross had with colleagues, it became clear that, before comparative educators could offer truly generative insights for the general public, we needed better scholarship with the goal of educating ourselves about education in Islam.[6] Such a foundation, it was felt, would be essential before scholars from other spiritual traditions could hope to analyze current educational developments in the Islamic world.

The present volume is a small first step toward that goal, and we are deeply indebted to Victor Billeh and, especially, to Wadad Kadi for their work in making this start. Professor Kadi provided additional leadership by convening a panel of authors at the 2006 meeting of the CIES in Hawaii and by delivering the annual Eggertson lecture to members there. Of course credit must be given to all of the scholars who submitted their work to the *Comparative Education Review* and whose dedication to the understanding of education in Islam should serve as an inspiration to others to illuminate this important topic.

This volume would not have been possible without the diligent efforts of one of our managing editors, Ayman Agbaria. Also, hundreds of volunteer hours were contributed by over sixty scholars who served as anonymous referees for submissions and offered their expert suggestions to the editors and authors. Our colleagues at the University of Chicago Press handled the production and editorial work with their usual efficiency and patience.

The *CER* is produced as a joint effort between the CIES and Penn State University, and we appreciate the support provided by both institutions making this publication possible. Finally, we are grateful to the Spencer Foundation, which early on saw the importance of this project and whose funding made possible the extra costs involved in publishing this volume.

---

[5] Heidi Ross, "The Space between Us: The Relevance of Relational Theories to Comparative and International Education," *Comparative Education Review* 46, no. 4 (2002): 407–32.

[6] For similar issues being raised among social foundations scholars, see Mark Ginsburg and Nagwa Megahed, "What Should We Tell Educators about Terrorism and Islam? Some Considerations in Global Context after September 11," *Educational Studies* 33, no. 3 (2002): 288–310.

Education in Islam—Myths and Truths

WADAD KADI

After announcing a call for papers for a special issue on "Islam and Education—Myths and Truths," *Comparative Education Review* (*CER*) received 34 submissions. This unusually high turnout signals, no doubt, more than scholarly interest in the topic. Noteworthy about these submissions was that many authors mentioned 9/11 directly or indirectly, that several dealt with the madrasas in various parts of the Islamic world today, and that the overwhelming majority of manuscripts treated education in the modern and contemporary Islamic countries. This indicates clearly that the interest in the topic is broad and has a sense of urgency related to the current political situation on the global level and in terms of the relationship between the Islamic world and the West. Another feature of many of these submissions was the authors' sense that there was a great deal of inaccuracy or even sensationalism about Islamic education in the Western media and in the statements by policy makers and journalists. The authors wished, thus, to set the record straight by providing accurate, documented information, based on the use of reliable, scientific methodologies.

It was impossible to publish all these submissions in this issue of *CER* for many reasons, not the least of which was the maximum possible size of any issue of *CER*. Thus, after a lengthy process of vetting and peer review, the nine studies included in this volume were selected by the two guest editors, Wadad Kadi and Victor Billeh. A few others, whose completion could not meet the journal's deadline, will likely appear in later issues of *CER*. We are grateful to the Spencer Foundation for a grant that made possible the extra pages in this issue and allowed us to publish as many articles as we did.

Nine studies obviously cannot satisfy the wide interest in education in Islam, let alone cover the achievements of Muslim scholars and educators over almost a millennium and a half, from the beginning of Islamicate civilization until today. These studies, however, like others published elsewhere, are a start. The studies in this issue touch on education in medieval, modern, and contemporary Islam. They cover different areas of the Islamic world, from the Philippines, Indonesia, and Pakistan to Iraq, Lebanon, Egypt, and Morocco. Their authors discuss both theory and application. The contributions show the great diversity in forms of Islamic education. And they are methodologically quite varied, using censuses, statistics, surveys, field research, historical reconstruction, or a combination thereof. What these studies could not provide is the thread that joins them together and indicates where each of them fits in the larger history of education in Islam. That is what I will attempt to do in this editorial. For that purpose, a periodization has to be created for the topic.

Periodization, any periodization, is risky for any study in any field, as scholars know. It is even riskier when one is dealing with an enormously large geographical area, whose peoples speak different languages, have innumerable cultures, and over the centuries have undergone varied historical experiences. However, the usefulness of periodization is unquestionable. In the particular case of education in Islam, the utility is increased, and periodization becomes an urgent exercise, due to the absence of a comprehensive study of this topic. What will be proposed here, thus, represents a beginning and not by any means a final word on it. In the course of presenting my vision of the development of education in Islamic societies, I will try to elaborate on areas not covered by the articles in this issue and touch more briefly on the areas discussed in depth by contributors, allowing their voices rather than mine to be heard. Since the premodern period is covered only by one article, I shall devote much of this editorial to it.

In a way, education could be envisioned as one of the cornerstones of Islamicate civilization and its backbone, Islam. Although Islam emerged in a largely illiterate society on the Arabian Peninsula, the scripture that lay at its foundation, the Qur'an, called itself, among other things, "The Book," and its study was made incumbent upon Muslims. More generally, seeking knowledge was encouraged in the Qur'an and in numerous traditions (hadiths) of the Prophet of Islam, Muhammad, as well as his actions. As Muslim society grew exponentially as a result of swift conquests and slow but steady conversion, the place of knowledge in that society also grew in a unique way.[1] The result was the foundation of a diversified, vibrant civilization, that acted as an inspiration to a large sector of the inhabitants of the *oikoumene* then, and that made room for the efflorescence of the secular in the midst of the religious. Books, in manuscript form, traveled from Samarqand to Córdoba within months of their publication; whole markets of booksellers emerged in all urban centers; scholars traveled enormous distances and endured real hardships "in search of knowledge"; compilation was viewed almost as a form of worship; and litterateurs sang the praises of books. Because of that, expressions of things educational abounded from the earliest days of Islamicate civilization, beginning thereby the first, and longest, stage of education in Islam, the largely independent, premodern stage that extended from the first years of Islam in the seventh century until the nineteenth century.

In this stage, education was articulated in two forms: institutions and compilations. Both derived their inspiration from indigenous Islamic needs, experiences, and accomplishments. Let me begin with the institutions. By

---

[1] See Franz Rosenthal, *Knowledge Triumphant: The Concept of Knowledge in Medieval Islam* (Leiden: Brill, 1970).

far the most widespread and important of them were the *kuttab*, the mosque, and the madrasa.

The *kuttab* (place of writing; also called a *maktab*) arose in the first Islamic century (or AH, corresponding to the seventh of the Common Era, or CE), providing elementary education in specific quarters outside of the mosque, possibly adjacent to a mosque but also possibly in the open air or in a tent. The subjects taught at the *kuttab* varied from place to place but included memorization and recitation of the Qur'an, reading, writing, spelling, voweling letters, arithmetic, and some basic religious duties, like the rules of ablutions and prayer. The *kuttab* was run by a teacher, called in Arabic a *mu'allim*. The *mu'allim* taught all year round, except for holidays and special occasions. The ages of the pupils varied, since attendance was voluntary, and so a pupil might spend 5 years or more in a *kuttab*. The teacher normally agreed with the pupils' parents on a particular sum of money that would constitute his wages, and, if the number of pupils became large, the teacher might go into partnership with other teachers. The teacher would himself pay for fodder for his mule and also for rent on the place in which he would teach, although he might enter into an agreement with the pupils' parents whereby they would pay that rent. Should the pupils' parents offer the teacher a present on the occasion of one feast or another, like the Prophet's birthday, the teacher could accept it. The teacher's duties included examining the pupils' writing boards and calling their attention to any errors in them. On some evenings, the teacher tested the pupils' mastery of Qur'an memorization one by one, although he might test them in twos or threes if he deemed that appropriate. When the pupil had completed the recitation of the entire Qur'an, he was given an award. The weekly day of recess was Friday. In the Maghreb, however, Thursday was also a holiday, whence its nickname *khamis al-talib* (the pupil's Thursday). Contrary to the scholars who taught at mosques, teachers of the *kuttab* were generally not accorded a high social status, although the usefulness of their profession was universally acknowledged. In modern times, the need for *kuttabs* as a means for elementary education has been severely eclipsed by public and other schools. Many *kuttabs*, however, survived thanks to the generosity of philanthropists, the attempts at reforming the *kuttab's* curriculum and assets, or the desire by various groups to inculcate in the youth an anticolonial spirit. The *kuttab* survived in the form of Qur'anic schools, as seen in this issue of *CER* in the article by Sobhi Tawil.

The mosque (*masjid*, or place of prostration), the quintessential Islamic institution of worship, doubled almost from the start as a place of teaching, thus becoming the oldest and most ubiquitous institution of learning in Islam. Teaching in mosques was normally initiated informally by learned religious scholars who were able to share their knowledge with others. The students (*talib*, pl. *talaba* or *tullab*; Persian *taleban*), always adults, attended classes in study circles (*halqa*, also called *majlis*, sit-up place) created around scholars (*'alim*, pl. *'ulama'*; also *shaykh*, pl. *shuyukh*, masters) specialized in religious knowledge (*'ilm*). This knowledge covered a number of disciplines: the Qur'an and its ancillary disciplines, especially exegesis; hadith, with its sub-disciplines; law and its sources; theology and dogma; the auxiliary disciplines connected with Arabic language, including poetry and oratory; and later also some of the "foreign" sciences, especially logic and later medicine. The circles were open to all, of all ages, and had an informal structure. The students had great freedom in choosing what classes, or circles, they wished to attend, and the choice was often wide, not only in terms of subjects taught but also in terms of educational level. Those who aspired to be leaders in any of the disciplines would attend many circles, work on their own, and "travel in search of knowledge" (*al-rihla fi talab al-'ilm*) for as long as they wished, until they earned sufficient recognition by the leading scholars of their day. In the early period, this recognition was expressed orally; soon, however, it became more formalized and took the form of a written *ijaza*, that is, a license from the professor to the student to teach the materials that he had learned with him. Neither teachers nor students received any regular pay in early Islam, although the teachers were paid in some cases, and this practice eventually became customary. In addition, the students had no residence connected with their studies within the mosque's structure. Mosques could gain lofty reputations and become very influential: often armed with adjunct libraries from gifts and bequests, and illustrious teachers from all over the Islamic world, they attracted scores of bright and dedicated students who eventually became leading men of learning in Islamicate civilization. The oldest mosque to play this role was, as expected, the Prophet's mosque in Medina: it was in there that several Companions of the Prophet taught shortly after his death. Outside of Arabia, the oldest and most well-known mosques were the Aqsa mosque in Jerusalem and Umayyad mosque in Damascus, both founded toward the end of the first Islamic century (seventh century CE). In the Maghreb, the Qarawiyyin mosque in Fez was founded in AH 245/859 CE, while the Zaytuna mosque in Tunis was founded in AH 250/864 CE. But the mosque that was to become the most influential educational institution in Sunni Islam was the Azhar mosque, founded in Cairo in AH 363/972 CE. In the Shi'i world, the most influential mosques include the Imam 'Ali mosque at Najaf, Iraq, founded in AH 368/977 CE.

By the tenth century CE, social and scholarly needs led to the emergence of the third enduring Islamic educational institution, the madrasa (place of study), alongside the mosque. From the eleventh century, madrasas were built by members of the ruling elite and soon became the ubiquitous colleges of Islam, starting most famously with the standard-setting network of Niza-miyya madrasas built by the vizier of the Seljuks, Nizam al-Mulk, first in Baghdad in AH 459/1067 CE, then elsewhere in the Islamic East.

In many ways, madrasas were similar to mosques. Both offered education to adults from the postelementary level to the advanced level, and in both this education was essentially religious. Teachings encompassed law and its subdisciplines but also the usual fields of Qur'an and its sciences, hadith, theology, and dogma, and sometimes Sufism (i.e., Islamic mysticism), in addition to some "foreign" sciences, such as medicine and astronomy. But in almost every other respect, the madrasa differed from the mosque, essentially because it was an institution created expressly for the purpose of education. This difference affected its funding, architecture, organization, staff, faculty, students, and curriculum.

Almost all madrasas in the premodern stage of education in Islam were funded by endowments (*awqaf, ahbas*) provided by their founders, who exerted enormous patronage control over them. Patrons decided whether to open madrasas for the teaching of all legal rites (*madhahb*, pl. *madhahib*) or to restrict them to one, and these patrons were sometimes honored by being buried in mausoleums within the madrasas. The endowments of the madrasas varied considerably in size and educational scope, depending on the wealth and goals of the endower. But, since most madrasas were founded by influential people in power—viziers, sultans and caliphs, albeit sometimes also by wealthy philanthropists, some of them women—most madrasas could depend on substantial revenues that would keep them functioning for a long time. Endowments might consist of shops, mills, houses, baths, pieces of land, or all of these. The proceeds of working or renting these places were used to cover all expenses of the madrasa, from the employees' wages to the cost of replacing the madrasa's furniture and repairing its buildings. Endowments in the form of books sometimes started, or boosted, a madrasa's library, and the libraries of madrasas often vied with, or surpassed, the libraries of mosques. Architecturally, many madrasas were gems of Islamic art, as one can still see today in the Sulaymaniyya complex in Istanbul, the Sultan Hasan madrasa in Cairo, and the Ulug Beg madrasa in Samarqand. In the Shi'ite world, the Hawza complex in Najaf and the sanctuary at Qom, Iran, are perhaps the best known. Unconstrained by the architectural restrictions of the mosque, and constructed at the peak of the self-confidence of Islamicate civilization, madrasas were often showcases for the power of their founders, some having baths, hospitals, kitchens, fountains, running water, lush gardens, magnificent facades, domes, and multiple buildings. One of those buildings would be the madrasa's own mosque, which was in some areas differentiated from the public mosque by the lack of a minaret (as is the case in the Maghreb). If a madrasa did not have its own mosque, it would have a prayer hall.

What made the madrasa unique, architecturally and otherwise, was its identity as an educational institution. In this it was, unlike the mosque in its primary conception, organized, formal, and, above all, residential (although some mosques did later become partially residential). As such, the madrasa had an administrative structure, a defined body of residents, and a distinct curriculum. All madrasas had three basic categories of residents: the staff, the faculty, and the students, each of which had to be accommodated in the madrasa's architecture.

Despite variations between madrasas, the staff of the madrasa, whose wages were provided by the madrasa's endowment, was composed of an imam who led the prayers, a muezzin who was in charge of calling to prayer, a custodian (*qayyim*) who cared for the madrasa's mats, lamps, and general cleanliness, and a gatekeeper (*bawwab*), whose task was opening and closing the madrasa's gate at the appropriate times and granting entry permission to its visitors. Other staff members were the *waqqad* (probably the person in charge of heating), the supervisor of the endowment (*nazir al-waqf*), the cashier (*al-qabid*), and the witness (*shahid*). When the madrasa was large and had a substantial endowment, then it would have several imams, muezzins, custodians, and so on.

The faculty of the madrasa, who could be quite numerous in large madrasas, were, like the scholars teaching in mosques, specialized scholars in the various fields of Islamic and Arabic studies. Unlike the scholars, however, the faculty were salaried right from the early days of the madrasa, with their income supplied by the madrasa's endowment. Some of these faculty were honored by gifts and robes of honor from the political elite. Some, more importantly, had handsomely endowed chairs. Because of that, teaching in a well-endowed madrasa was quite attractive to distinguished scholars, between whom there was often competition. It was not uncommon for sought-after scholars to hold multiple positions simultaneously in several madrasas, especially in madrasas that vied with each other in prestige over the distinction of their faculty. It was also possible for a particularly lucrative professorship to be divided among several scholars, with some holding, for example, "half" a professorship and hence cashing half the salary connected with it. The size of the faculty depended on the size of the madrasa's endowment, so that the larger the endowment, the larger the faculty. When there were many faculty members, the most distinguished among them would be referred to by the term *sadr* (or *ra'is*) *al-mudarrisin* (lead teacher).

But the area in which the madrasa most differed from the mosque was in its students—although the mosque eventually came partly to resemble the madrasa in that respect. The madrasa's students, primarily, were residents of the madrasa, each being housed in a room of his own. The student was expected to use the room for the purpose of study and not rent it out or abuse it in any way. Only in exceptional cases would a madrasa have no student residences. Next, the students received more than a free education: they were also given stipends from the madrasa's endowment. Because this money was provided for the sake of their education, attendance of classes and Qur'an recitation sessions were required of all students, and absences were allowed only when students were ill or had another valid reason. Students were not allowed to take up professions or crafts to earn an income, since they were supposed to devote themselves to their studies full-time. Students who did so risked losing their stipends. Since the madrasa provided post-elementary, specialized, and advanced instruction for adults, the students varied in age, but some sources mention that they should be at least 20 years old when they joined the madrasa. Since no more than 20 students were assigned to a single professor, study in madrasas was more systematic than in mosques. How long students were permitted to stay in the madrasa varied. In the case of some madrasas, we know that if a student had resided there for 10 years and had shown no sign of scholarly accomplishment, he would be expelled from the madrasa by force, since his continuation needlessly drained resources from the madrasa's endowment. In sum, as one jurist noted, the ideal madrasa student was one who possessed a fine natural disposition, intelligence, and discernment and who occupied himself by benefiting from the opportunities presented by the madrasa and by being beneficial to others after the termination of his sojourn at the madrasa.

With regard to the madrasa's curriculum, the books studied there were often the standard books in hadith, such as the *Sahihs* of Bukhari and Muslim; in positive law (*furu'*) and legal thought (*usul*), such as the *Risala* of Shafi'i; in Qur'an exegesis, such as Zamakhshari's *al-Kashshaf*; and in Arabic language and grammar, such as the *Kitab* of Sibawayh and the *Alfiyya* of Ibn Malik. Sufism was also taught in some madrasas in areas where Sufism was not frowned on by the religious establishment. As for Qur'an recitation, its presence in the curriculum was pervasive, being a daily requirement of the students. In the non-Islamic sciences, students read books on logic, such as Ibn Ridwan's *al-Maqalat*, and medicine, such as Avicenna's poem on medicine, written in *rajaz* verse. Abridgments of larger tomes, as well as summae of various disciplines, were often taught by means of poems written in the swift and simple meter of the *rajaz*, which suggests that they were meant to be memorized by the students. Madrasas varied greatly in the matter of when and how different disciplines were taught. A fatwa of a jurist from Tlemcen (in present-day Algeria), is worth citing here as an example of how the academic year fluctuated between vigor and languor. This fatwa says that, during winter, religious scholars taught students exhaustively and meticulously a small number of areas of their expertise, bringing to students' attention previous research on these issues as well as their own evaluation of this research. During this season, the scholars did not permit themselves to be idle or take any time off. Once this season was over, they relaxed and sought recreation. They then started to read the standard books with the students and to guide them in their studies. Covering books from beginning to end and ensuring familiarity with the issues they dealt with were considered best for students. In this way, the students would be well prepared to tackle the thorough scholarly study of the fine issues they are exposed to in winter.

Although it is clear that the madrasa was a complex establishment with a pedagogical, administrative, and financial structure different from that of the mosque, both institutions shared the same modes of instruction. There, reliance on memory was highly prized, repetition was cultivated, and the taking of notes from dictation (*imla'*) was highly valued, given the usefulness of citing materials verbatim during disputation. Discussion of texts was personal and transmission based, focused first on the teacher's commentary on issues, then on his probing of the student's understanding and ability to solve difficult problems. The measure of the student's success was marked in both institutions with the above-mentioned *ijaza*, which recognized the student's qualification to teach all or some of what his professor taught.

The image one gets about the premodern institutions of learning—the applied form of interest in education in Islam—is an extremely lively, diverse, and unmistakably Islamic one, those institutions having been hallmarks of premodern Islamic society where most of the pillars of Islamic thought developed. The theoretical form of that interest, as expressed in various compilations—statements, treatises, and books—is less dynamic or pervasive. Education never actually developed into one of the disciplines of learning that Islamicate civilization nurtured, as it did, for example, in fields such as theology, law, philosophy, and astronomy. But Islamicate civilization did indeed contribute to educational thought. This thought, insofar as the aims, contents, methods, and ethics of teaching and learning are concerned, is the subject of Sebastian Günther's article in this issue. As Günther shows, in past centuries a host of Muslim intellectuals contributed to discussions on educational theory, pedagogy, and didactics, including the ninth-century Iraqi litterateur al-Jahiz and Tunisian jurist Ibn Sahnun, the tenth-century Turkish-born philosopher, social scientist, and musicologist al-Farabi, and the eleventh-century Iranian philosopher Avicenna and towering theologian and Sufi al-Ghazali. Many others continued to feed this tradition. Consequently, Günther asserts, one could certainly talk about a rich, diverse, and sometimes original pedagogical tradition in Islam, one that is not dissimilar to the same tradition in medieval Europe. He concludes his study by emphasizing the importance that we be aware today of the contributions of medieval Islamic educational thought when we evaluate contemporary issues in humanistic education. Which features of premodern Islamic education survived into modern times, and why, is not discussed by Günther. We shall come to this point later.

While tremendous change occurred during Safavid and Ottoman times, it was the integration of the Islamic world into the new world colonial system that most altered the ways in which Muslim intellectuals and educators envisioned Islamic education. With that integration, the second stage of education in Islam began, covering the period from the nineteenth century until the middle of the twentieth. Its hallmarks were the beginning or intensification of the encounter between Islamic lands and the West. Subsequently, most Islamic lands were colonized by various Western powers, especially Britain, France, Holland, Portugal, and Italy. Acting aggressively, these powers caused no less than a seismic transformation in the Islamic world, calling into question norms, practices, and traditions that characterized the Islamic way of life at the political, economic, legal, social, and individual levels. In the process, the colonial powers presented and sometimes enforced alternative, Western ways. It was during this period that the last universal Islamic caliphate, the Ottoman, was ended and new, individual nation-states born, that new government bureaucratic structures were erected, and that Christian missionary schools and colleges were founded, using foreign languages and teaching foreign literatures. Two examples of such colleges are the Syrian Protestant College in Beirut, founded in 1866, and Robert's College in Istanbul, founded in 1872. But the most important change was probably the introduction of secular precollege school systems to the newly formed Islamic countries. Such systems were adopted by most of these countries' national governments, which were working under the calculating eyes of the colonial powers.

Muslim teachers and their students then faced secular schools that not only ignored religion altogether but also that introduced entirely new curricula, school structures, and teaching methods. In addition, they placed the education of women at the same level as that of men. The curricula included new fields of study, including scientific subjects and foreign languages and literatures. Enrollment, promotion, and graduation followed a disciplined, clearly defined process, with age identifications, registration, grades, exams, schedules, and a specific number of years for both elementary and secondary education. The methods of instruction were impersonal and utilitarian, a far cry from the methods that had been used in *kuttabs*, mosques, and madrasas throughout the previous millennium. What made the problem infinitely bigger was the swift success of these schools among Muslims, and the emergence of a plethora of secular schools, both foreign and local, state-sponsored and independent. From the perspective of Muslim educators, it was necessary to keep the Islamic educational institutions relevant, despite the challenging environment. How this could be achieved was the subject of heated debate in this period, with some Muslim intellectuals advocating reform and others refusing it. The rise of nationalism and the important role assigned to educators in nationalist circles complicated the picture even further. The center of this debate was Egypt. Indira Falk Gesink's article in this issue deals with that subject.

According to Gesink, the challenge to the Islamic form of education—financially, administratively, hermeneutically, and pedagogically—began in the first half of the nineteenth century, when Muhammad Ali, the semi-independent ruler of Egypt, undertook sweeping reforms. These brought to Egypt, among other things, a centralized, European-influenced network of civil schools aimed at the creation of officers, technocrats, and administrators. A debate about reforming Islamic education followed, with it modernist advocates, such as Tahtawi, Afghani, Abdu, and Rida, invoking the Islamic principle of *ijtihad* (individual reasoning) and its conservative opponents, such as al-Safti and al-Mahdi, invoking the equally Islamic principle of *taqlid* (following precedents). Gesink traces the partial but steady success of the modernists and the eventual transformation of al-Azhar into a "bureaucratic university," noting, though, the preservation of the Islamic method of teaching there as elsewhere.

The article by Mandy Terc sheds light on another way in which Muslims tried to face the challenge of the West, namely by establishing Western-style schools that differed from the government's secular schools by the addition of a religious, Islamic component to the curriculum. Terc traces this phenomenon in the schools built all over Lebanon by a Sunni private foundation established precisely for that purpose, the Makassed Philanthropic Islamic Association. Terc shows that, from the time of its founding in 1878, the Makassed was conceived as the means for preserving the identity of Lebanese Muslims. Terc carries the discussion further to cover the postindependence period (after 1943), including Lebanon's long civil war (1975–90) and contemporary times, highlighting the ways in which the Makassed stood firmly by the conciliatory formula it had developed to accommodate both its Islamic and national identity.

The issue of national identity and its relation to the government secular school system is also the subject of Orit Bashkin's article, although this article focuses on the government of Iraq between the two world wars. Then a constitutional monarchy under tight British control, the Iraqi government's ministry of education tried to use the secularized school system to forge an Iraqi national identity, with support from many intellectuals who favored pluralistic educational models. Despite some successes, though, the government's efforts were constantly challenged by various segments in Iraqi society divided along confessional, sectarian, and ethnic lines, as well as by resistance to the state's disciplinary power. All this made Iraq's educational system a place where the modern and the premodern would sit uneasily side by side.

The third stage of education in Islam may be called the postindependence stage. It covers the period from the time Islamic countries gained their independence from the colonial powers—around the mid-twentieth century—until today, although it must be kept in mind that clear boundaries between the colonial period and the postcolonial one are often difficult to define. This is a stage in which the issue of Islamic empowerment and identity remain central, in view of the anti-Islamic or un-Islamic nature of the colonial legacy in the area of education and the challenge posed by the nation-states, several of which, from the 1950s to the 1970s, placed mass education at the head of their goals. This stage also, however, has been characterized by creative, bold, and more mature attempts to reshape Islamic educational institutions in such a way that they are both more integrated to government (secular) policies—considered now a fact of life—and more relevant to the issues facing Muslim and non-Muslim societies alike in a globalized world. Some of this creativity derives from local experiences of Muslims. However, it also concerns broader factors, particularly the perceived or real use, for radicalization purposes, of the Islamic madrasas, which have become quite different from their medieval namesakes. For, although the modern madrasas are residential and stipended like their medieval counterparts, modern madrasas, unlike the earlier ones, are precollege educational institutions, offering both elementary and secondary training for the young and teaching a religious curriculum instead of the government's secular or mixed curriculum. In addition, they are funded by politically and religiously motivated governments and groups. This muddied the reputation of Islamic madrasas and prompted many in the media and politics to connect them with terrorism, to exaggerate their negative character, and to associate all Islamic institutions, and sometimes even to associate Islam itself, with terrorism. Overall, then, the picture of education in Islam in this stage is very complex, with truths mixed with myths. One of the articles in this issue (by Tahir Andrabi and his colleagues) tackles the myths surrounding the pervasiveness of madrasas in Pakistan. Another article, by Sobhi Tawil, points out the role that the local economy plays in the state of Qur'anic schools in Morocco. Helen Boyle's article revisits the issue of memorization of the Qur'an in contemporary Islamic schools in three Islamic countries. Articles by Florian Pohl and by Jeffery Milligan present the creative attempts undertaken by a Muslim majority in Indonesia and a Muslim minority in the Philippines, respectively, to make constructive educational Islamic school models by working mostly within government-provided opportunities or by responding favorably to global, Western-supported ideals of civic society.

The article by Tahir Andrabi, Jishnu Das, Asim Ijaz Khwaja, and Tristan Zajonc refutes the myth that enrollment rates in Pakistani madrasas are either high or on the rise. These authors also show there is little correlation between madrasa attendance and poverty. Using field research, published data sources, and analyses of data from censuses and household surveys, the authors apply established statistical methodologies. Their conclusion is that less than 1 percent of Pakistani children are enrolled in madrasas and that this enrollment is not conspicuously rising. Furthermore, school choice by households is determined neither solely by poverty, nor by the religious mindedness of households. As seen in both censuses and surveys, one household could send one of its children to a madrasa, another to a public school, and a third to one of the increasingly common private schools.

Sobhi Tawil highlights in his article the significant role still played by Qur'anic schools in postindependence Morocco, particularly in the northern, mostly rural province of Chechaouen, despite the availability of public schools there. This role, he explains, is shaped by factors relating to the shortcomings of public schools and their relative scarcity in rural areas, resistance to government intrusiveness, and, above all, poverty. It is also related, the author explains, to much of the population's involvement in the increasingly lucrative business of growing, producing, and exporting cannabis, which makes it more profitable for families to send their children to Qur'anic, rather than public schools. The area's rich heritage of religious scholarship further sustains Qur'anic school education in it, as does these schools' tendency to be community based.

Memorization as a method of instruction has been considered in the West as one of the most negative features of traditional Islamic education, fostering passivity in students and making them susceptible to religious and political indoctrination. In her article, Helen Boyle finds this concept, as applied to the Qur'an in particular, to be a mischaracterization resulting from the lack of understanding of the assumptions about memorization, that is, another myth about education in Islam. Relating the concept of memorization to those of understanding, reason, and knowledge, she reexamines the purpose of memorization in light of the ethnographic field research she conducted in Morocco, Yemen, and Nigeria. She concludes that memorization is actually the first, rather than last, step in the learning process in Islamic educational institutions and that the memorization of the Qur'an enables students to "embody" it and hence to make it a constant guide in their spiritual and moral development.

Like Boyle's article, the contribution of Florian Pohl is based on ethnographic field research. Pohl's study is focused on Indonesia's most innovative and successful brand of Islamic boarding schools, the *pesantren*. Pohl frames his research around the issue of secularization. He notes that the assumption that secularization is a precondition for modernity, to the exclusion of religious schooling, is highly questionable—yet another myth. Pohl then examines how the *pesantren* deal with issues of civil society. This examination leads him to conclude that the *pesantren*, despite their being religious schools, do indeed uphold the main principles of civil society, including gender equality, antiviolence, pluralism, and social and economic justice. They do not support terrorism.

Like Pohl, Jeffrey Milligan highlights the ways in which Islamic religious schools, in the Philippines, imaginatively made their institutions a vehicle for advocating the moderate concept of the "good Muslim." After historically contextualizing the issue of Islamic education in the Philippines' colonial past, he notes that the postindependence Philippine governments continued the colonial educational policies of favoring Christians and practically disregarding the needs of a marginalized, restive, and poor Muslim minority in Mindanao in the southern Philippines. When the government allowed educational decentralization and when local autonomy came to Mindanao, Muslim activists, both from within the government and without, took full advantage of this opportunity. They founded, in a somewhat experimental fashion, three Islamic models of educational institutions, each of which sought to integrate secular and Islamic education. Despite potential problems, these models seem to be working to build a peaceful rather than a radicalized society.

There is no doubt that Islamic education in premodern times was successful in transmitting knowledge, for this is the only way to explain the heights reached then by Islamicate civilization. After all, it was in the medieval *kuttabs*, then mosques and madrasas, that the majority of the pillars of that civilization received their training and became educators to successive generations of scholars. This success may be credited to the methods used in education. These methods were genuine and derived from the very nature of the Islamic sciences—highly textual, memorized, personally transmitted— which at that time led the rest of the sciences in a religion-based civilization. Not unexpectedly, some theoretical work on education was produced by these scholars. This work, however, did not go too far beyond the areas of didactics and pedagogy and never developed into a field of specialization in the modern sense. In one sense, this limited development reflected the way that Islamicate civilization viewed specialization as such, which was not as a narrow endeavor that excludes other endeavors but rather as a concentration on one or two areas within a number of other ones. In another sense, it indicates that education was essentially considered an auxiliary science underlying the practice of education: it was considered to underpin all areas of scholarly inquiry, all "knowledge," but was not considered a separate area of inquiry. And this view continued for over a millennium largely because the Islamic way of producing scholarship was the only yardstick by which such scholarship was generated in the wide Islamic world.

When this form of Islamic education faced increasing pressure in the nineteenth century—or earlier in some cases—the very foundations of the production of scholarship were put to the test, threatening to pull down the entire edifice of Islamic education. As the encounter with Europe was transformed into political and economic domination, the alternative model of European education—the secular school—became widespread in all parts of the Islamic world—now recast as nation-states. This led to a great deal of confusion among Muslim scholars and educators, with some advocating reform as a means of survival, while others advocated resilience to change as a means for preserving identity. In the end, the reformists won. In this way the private school was born, with its component of Islamic education, complimentary to the secular public schools. But the puritans did not fail. Appealing to matters of piety, identity, and the marginalization of the Muslims by the West, their efforts—which continue today—created schools meant to replace the secular and national government public schools. These schools take some of their features from the medieval madrasa and discard others, creating a new form of madrasa that teaches the Muslim youth how to be Muslims in the manner of their Muslim predecessors. The fact that they live in environments so different from those of their medieval forebears makes students more rather then less keen on sticking to their Islamic ways. And one of the interesting things this issue shows is how much change occurred within Islamic institutions of education like the madrasa. This mass of Islamically educated Muslims in the modern world made these institutions into a force that could be used by various political powers at work in the Islamic world. In this way, the philanthropist and elitist medieval system of endowment was replaced by a system of political patronage based on exploitative funding, a system in which governments and groups, from the Islamic world as well as from the West, participated. This is how radicalization was wedded to the small but not ineffective madrasa system, in its modern and contemporary configuration.

But this is only one side of the picture. After decades of independence, of debate, of successes and failures, new forms of Islamic institutions of education have emerged in postcolonial Islamic societies. Though they are basically Islamic, they conceive of themselves not as alternatives to the secular public schools of governments, but as complementary to them. In other words, secular education is no longer viewed as an imported, foreign, and illegitimate form of schooling that must be rejected but rather as a legitimate, useful, but deficient system that must be completed. It is in this light that we must understand the fledgling school models being developed in the Philippines, Indonesia, and elsewhere today. Such models indicate that some Muslim intellectuals and educators did not simply react to what the non-Muslims did: they have enough confidence in themselves to experiment in collaboration with the non-Muslims, in the process enriching their circles of interest and engaging with the rest of the world in a dialogue, which is useful to all. This is a very promising turn of events in the world of education in Islam.

Islamic Reformation: A History of *Madrasa* Reform and Legal Change in Egypt

INDIRA FALK GESINK

According to contemporary media opinion, the problem with Islam, and by implication, with Islamic education, is that it never underwent a reformation that freed individual religious inquiry from the control of a religious hierarchy. Thus, it has been assumed that Islam and Islamic education remain bound to rigid seventh-century codes of belief.[1]

This opinion is indicative of Eurocentric assumptions and is subject to considerable scholarly debate.[2] First, Islam was never controlled by a single authoritative hierarchy or body; there existed great diversity of belief from early times, and religious personnel served as repositories of oral literature and as legal advisors rather than as absolute moral authorities. Second, many of the religious practices and legal principles that constitute Islam evolved over time as the product of constant reform and adjustment. One period of reformation occurred in nineteenth-century Egypt. This reformation involved transformative debate over the purpose and methods of Islamic education, accentuating existing traditions of individual religious interpretation and fostering additional sects and splinter groups.

While some central players in this debate, known now as "Islamic modernists," are familiar to most Muslims, their opponents' arguments have languished. I believe it is necessary for both sides of the story to be told. Indeed, modernists' opponents played critical roles in religious educational reform, and at least one of their arguments was predictive of the rise of twentieth-century sectarianism.

In this article I discuss these developments, drawing on archival research conducted in Egypt's Dar al-Kutub and the Azhariyya in 1995–96 and 1998. I employ a theoretical model borrowed from Timothy Mitchell's *Colonising Egypt*, in which the nineteenth-century transformation of educational and legal patterns in Egypt is understood as "enframing," a conceptual colonization that replaces an old "invisible" order with a new order that renders its components and inhabitants visible and quantifiable.[3]

This research was supported by grants from the National Security Education Program and the American Research Center in Egypt.

[1] See, e.g., Salman Rushdie, "The Right Time for an Islamic Reformation," *Washington Post*, August 7, 2005, http://www.washingtonpost.com/wp-dyn/content/article/2005/08/05/AR2005080501483.html; Thomas Friedman, "Breaking the Circle," *New York Times*, November 16, 2001, http://www.nytimes.com/.

[2] See, e.g., Michaelle Browers and Charles Kurzman, eds., *An Islamic Reformation?* (Lanham, MD: Lexington Books, 2004).

[3] Timothy Mitchell, *Colonising Egypt*, rev. ed. (1988; repr., Berkeley: University of California Press, 1991), 142–54.

Origins of the *Madrasa* in Egypt

Since the 1000s, the locus of all formal education in Islamic lands was the *madrasa* (pl. *madaris*), a "place of study" that was usually attached to a mosque, funded by one or several charitable endowments called *awqaf* (sg. *waqf*), and staffed by religious scholars who were provisioned and sometimes housed with funds from the *awqaf*. One of the five basic duties required of a Muslim (the Five Pillars) is almsgiving; one way wealthy people fulfilled this duty was by endowing property as a *waqf*, which protected the property from most taxation and from state seizure, allowed donors to designate some of the property's revenues for their heirs, and also benefited the community through the provision of charitable services. A large *madrasa* might have hundreds of *awqaf* that provided for building maintenance, water fountains, lighting, stables, cash or food payments to staff, bread rations for students living at the *madrasa*, and provisions for indigents, wandering scholars, and refugees.[4]

Education commonly began at a small Qur'an school in Egypt called a *kuttab* (pl. *katatib*), in which students memorized passages of the Qur'an. A few students might progress to a small *madrasa* or regional religious center, such as the Ahmadi Mosque in Tanta, to learn religious principles and reading and writing, often using the Qur'an or dense, rhymed texts that introduced the alphabet and parts of speech. A very few of those students would then pursue the extensive readings needed to become a scholar in one of the four recognized Sunni legal schools, by attaching themselves to a scholar at a regional center such as the Ahmadi Mosque or at a large urban *madrasa*. Al-Azhar *madrasa* in Cairo was the nadir of higher education in northeastern Africa: opened in AD 972, it was one of a few *madaris* to offer training at all levels and in all four Sunni legal schools.

Madrasa education was highly personal. A religious scholar—who might also be a legal counselor (mufti), judge, or prayer leader (imam), or might serve the government in some advisory capacity—would sit with the students around him, ideally in a circle. The scholar would read a text, either one in which he specialized or one students had requested, and comment on its phraseology and meaning. In Egypt, students would memorize or recopy the text from the scholar's recitation, often adding their own comments in the text's margins. Advanced students did not always simply reproduce received knowledge; those marginal commentaries were sometimes themselves worthy of study. Nevertheless, "understanding" a text may not necessarily have entailed the ability to interpret and explain it, because the scholar's primary

---

[4] Al-Maqrizi, summary of al-Hakim bi-Amr Allah's *waqf* charter, 1010 CE, reprinted in Mustafa Muhammad Ramadan, "Dawr al-awqaf fi da'm al-Azhar ka mu'assasa 'ilmiyya islamiyya" (paper presented at the Nadwat al-tatawwur al-tarikhi li-mu'assasat al-awqaf fi al-'alam al-'arabi wa al-islam, Baghdad, April 1983), 37–38.

role was transmitter as opposed to exegete. Understanding was demonstrated, rather, by quoting or otherwise employing its words in social situations.

In general, students were supposed to progress from memorization of the Qur'an and other religious texts to simple treatises on grammar and religious history or principles to the more complicated texts of a juridical specialization, philosophy, theology, theoretical science, or mysticism or commentaries on these texts.[5] Ideally, the teaching scholar ensured that only those students who had truly mastered a text were allowed to read it for others, by issuing them an *ijaza*, a letter listing the chain of transmission of that text that in effect authorized them to become the next links in that chain.

In addition, historically some types of knowledge were sometimes considered dangerous to the state. Texts from certain philosophical or theological perspectives were sometimes banned, and authors wrote carefully, couching their meanings in metaphor and verse. Moreover, writing in Arabic carried higher significance than simple communication of information. In Arabic script, often only the consonants and long vowels are written, so the treatises and commentaries that scholars read were unvowelized. Most Arabic words are based on a trilateral root; the three roots convey different meanings when pronounced with different vowels, prefixes, or suffixes. The meaning of the word is not fixed until it is pronounced aloud, and its pronunciation is to be determined by the reader's perception of the meaning of surrounding words. So because they wrote in unvowelized Arabic, the authors relinquished control of their texts unless they read them themselves. The only way to ensure that subsequent readers derived the correct meaning of the text was to transmit the text orally from author to student. The students would then be authorized to read it to others only when they had sufficiently mastered the text to pass it down faithfully. Thus education—at least in discursive fields—was a process of one-to-one transmission of oral readings.[6]

[5] Jonathan Berkey, *The Transmission of Knowledge in Medieval Cairo: A Social History of Islamic Education* (Princeton, NJ: Princeton University Press, 1992); James Heyworth-Dunne, *An Introduction to the History of Education in Modern Egypt*, rev. ed. (1939; repr., London: Frank Cass, 1968), 42, 66–75; George Makdisi, *The Rise of Colleges* (Edinburgh: Edinburgh University Press, 1981), 128–33. See also Dale F. Eickelman, *Knowledge and Power in Morocco* (Princeton, NJ: Princeton University Press, 1985), on differences in Moroccan context.

[6] Hence the term used to refer to teaching was *qira'a*, "reading," and not *ta'lim*, "teaching" or "instruction," which came into common use in the nineteenth century. Within the religio-historical tradition of Islam, one might understand the oral transmission of knowledge as originating with the oral transmission of Qur'anic verses and *hadith*: from the Prophet to listeners who memorized his words, to those who heard it from them, and so on until they were written down and collected. Although Qur'ans were often vowelized, the meaning of many verses remained obscure except when orally read or interpreted, so the one-to-one transmission was still necessary to ensure that students received the "approved" readings. Mitchell, *Colonising Egypt*, 142–54.

The Challenges to *Madrasa* Education in the Early Nineteenth Century

In nineteenth-century Egypt, educational reforms and borrowed Utilitarian models of instruction threatened this one-to-one transmission of knowledge and with it the authority of the religious scholars and the *madrasa* system. The resulting debate changed the form of *madrasa* education, the function of written Arabic, and the popular understanding of the Islamic legal tradition.

At the beginning of the nineteenth century, Egypt was a semiautonomous province of the Ottoman Empire, recently delivered from Napoleonic occupation. It was governed by local elites, descendants of a Turko-Circassian military caste that had ruled the Mamluk Empire in Egypt from 1249–1517, who were often at war among themselves. Some had resorted to illegal seizure of tax and *waqf* revenues to support their military endeavors, and the religious institutions had consequently suffered.[7] In 1805, the religious scholars of Egypt and the Ottoman sultan colluded in selecting a governor for Egypt who would reimpose central control and stop the predations of the Mamluk elite, Muhammad ʿAli (r. 1805–48).

Muhammad ʿAli's main objective in Egypt was to create a smoothly functioning state and a military capable of defending the empire against the Europeans. In this effort, he followed the example of the Ottoman sultan Mahmud II, who had borrowed extensively from European Utilitarian ideals of military and fiscal discipline. Muhammad ʿAli also corresponded with Jeremy Bentham, father of Utilitarianism.[8] Between 1805 and 1814, he centralized all aspects of the province's financial administration to improve the flow of revenue from taxpayer to state, created monopolies to maximize trade revenues, and established monopsonies over the purchase of agricultural goods to ensure that products needed for the military were available. Muhammad ʿAli also hired European specialists to help train the new military. To wean Egypt from dependency on European-made weapons, he built factories to produce ships, firearms, and uniforms.[9]

At that time, training in technical fields, such as engineering or handicraft, was done via apprenticeships rather than formal schooling. *Madaris* like al-Azhar provided only religious and theoretical training—their alumni were men of the pen, not of the sword or of the crafts. The Ottoman Empire, however, did have a tradition of formal training for officers. Hence between 1810 and 1840, Muhammad ʿAli created an entire network of civil schools

---

[7] See ʿAbd al-Rahman al-Jabarti, *Tarikh ajaʾib al-athar fi al-tarajim wa al-akhbar* (Beirut: Dar al-Jil, n.d.), vols. 1 and 2.

[8] Mitchell, *Colonising Egypt*, x; al-Jabarti, *Tarikh ajaʾib al-athar fi al-tarajim wa al-akhbar*, 1:495, 2:86–87; Afaf Lutfi al-Sayyid Marsot, *Egypt in the Reign of Muhammad ʿAli* (Cambridge: Cambridge University Press, 1984), 67, 140–43; Gabriel Baer, *A History of Land Ownership in Modern Egypt, 1800–1950* (Oxford: Oxford University Press, 1962), 3–5.

[9] Heyworth-Dunne, *Introduction to the History of Education in Modern Egypt*, 72, 75, 157–58; John W. Livingston, "Western Science and Educational Reform in the Thought of Shaykh Rifaʿa al-Tahtawi," *International Journal of Middle East Studies* 28 (November 1996): 551.

intended to train officers, munitions specialists, engineers, medics, veterinarians, translators, factory workers, irrigation specialists, and even buglers for Egypt's new military.[10]

The conflict with religious schools emerged from four aspects of the centralization process. First, smaller religious institutions, whose *awqaf* revenues Muhammad ʿAli judged insufficient, were closed and their revenues remanded temporarily to the state. As a result, students, scholars, and indigents were drawn to the larger *madaris*, such as al-Azhar, swelling their populations and overburdening their resources and administrative structures.[11] Second, while the civil primary schools, a school of language and translation, and a school of law and jurisprudence were populated primarily by staff and students from religious schools, they were intended to create technocrats who would replace *madrasa*-trained scholars as administrators. Thus, a significant percentage of jobs previously open to religious school graduates were now going to civil trainees.[12] Third, although the civil schools were not secular (they did include Islamic principles in their curricula, especially at the primary level), their methods of teaching differed from the *madaris*' one-to-one transmission approach. In particular, Muhammad ʿAli sent students in the 1820s to study in Britain at a Lancaster school, and the first Lancaster model school was established in Cairo in 1843. The Lancaster method involved the more advanced students (rather than the scholar/instructor) teaching and monitoring the progress of the younger students: it was an education factory.[13] Fourth, influenced by European models, Egyptian education ministry staff developed a manual on composition for the War School promoting the use of *insha'*, expository writing that makes the meaning obvious to the reader even without vowels.[14] Such a style of writing, if applied to religious instruction, would undermine the scholars' positions as mediators of texts and sever the necessary oral connection between author and student.

Furthermore, after returning from studying in France, Rifaʿa al-Tahtawi (d. 1873) published a book advocating the French style of education, in which students progress by learning things appropriate to their experiences (e.g.,

---

[10] Heyworth-Dunne, *Introduction to the History of Education in Modern Egypt*, 115–52.

[11] Daniel Crecelius, "The Emergence of the Shaykh al-Azhar as the Pre-eminent Religious Leader in Egypt," in *Colloque international sur l'histoire du Caire* (Cairo: Ministry of Culture of the Arab Republic of Egypt, 1969), 109–123, 117; Ehud R. Toledano, *State and Society in Mid-Nineteenth Century Egypt* (Cambridge: Cambridge University Press, 1990), 199; Edward Lane, *Manners and Customs of the Modern Egyptians*, 2 vols. in one (London: Dent, 1842), 84–85; J. A. St. John, *Egypt and Nubia* (London: Chapman & Hall, 1845), 245–48; A. Chris Eccel, *Egypt, Islam, and Social Change: Al-Azhar in Conflict and Accommodation* (Berlin: Klaus Schwarz, 1984), 232.

[12] Livingston, "Western Science," 551; Eccel, *Social Change*, 158, 162, 165, 173, 205; Heyworth-Dunne, *Introduction to the History of Education in Modern Egypt*, 115–52, 286; Daniel Crecelius, "Nonideological Responses of the Egyptian Ulama to Modernization," in *Scholars, Saints, and Sufis*, ed. Nikki Keddie (Berkeley: University of California Press, 1972), 184–85, 197–98.

[13] Mitchell, *Colonising Egypt*, 69–71.

[14] Al-ʿAttar, *Al-Insha'*, rev. ed. (1835; repr., Cairo: Mahmud Tawfiq, 1936), 101–2, quoted in Peter Gran, *Islamic Roots of Capitalism: Egypt, 1760–1840* (Austin: University of Texas Press, 1979), 156.

"cat" and "canary" for young children) and then moving on to more advanced subjects. This was in explicit contrast to the primary *kuttab* in which religious scholars introduced students first to the Qur'an, despite its archaic phrasing and the inability of most students to comprehend its meaning.

Thus, the initial development of civil schooling, although not secular per se, challenged the *madrasa* system financially, administratively, hermeneutically, and pedagogically. Furthermore, the very method employed to create a centralized industrial-military-education complex with which to resist the Europeans constituted a form of conceptual colonization, a gradual institutionalized penetration of European Utilitarian practices and disciplinary mind-set that tended to disperse the authority of religious interpretation from a cohort of trained scholars into the hands of individual readers.

Promoting Individual Reasoning (*Ijtihad*) versus Following Precedents (*Taqlid*)

During the 1850s, Muhammad 'Ali's successors lost interest in the civil schools. Many were closed, and religious institutions experienced a financial revival while their student populations continued to increase.[15] However, Muhammad 'Ali's grandson Isma'il (r. 1863–79) had attended the Paris model school, was fascinated by European models of instruction, and resolved to reorganize and expand what was left of the civil schools. By the late 1860s, the system included a network of primary schools for every village of 2,000 inhabitants and a statewide code mandating instruction in certain subjects, by a specific timetable, within buildings constructed and classrooms laid out for maximum efficiency, with official registration of students and scheduled examinations.[16]

The Contribution of Rifa'a al-Tahtawi

Rifa'a al-Tahtawi, who was appointed as an education official by Isma'il, promoted the reform of *madrasa* education, emphasizing Utilitarian concepts, such as "useful knowledge" and efficiency, and the reconnection of religious training with science. According to al-Tahtawi, the Prophet Muhammad had approved the acquisition of "knowledge by which one benefits." Scholars had generally defined "benefit" as spiritual and thus "useful knowledge" as reli-

[15] Toledano, *State and Society in Mid-Nineteenth Century Egypt,* 66, 181–88, 197–99, 210, 217; Baer, *History of Land Ownership in Modern Egypt,* 169; Heyworth-Dunne, *Introduction to the History of Education in Modern Egypt,* 28–29, 293, 314, 397–98; Mitchell, *Colonising Egypt,* 85; Eccel, *Social Change,* 232, 236; St. John, *Egypt and Nubia;* 'Ali Mubarak, *Al-Khitat al-tawfiqiyyah al-jadidah li-Misr al-qahirah,* rev. ed. (1887; repr., Cairo: al-Hay'ah al-Misriyyah al-'Ammah lil-Kitab, 1983), 4:40; Michael J. Reimer, "Views of al-Azhar in the Nineteenth Century: Gabriel Charmes and 'Ali Pasha Mubarak, " in *Travellers in Egypt,* ed. Paul Starkey and Janet Starkey (London: Tauris, 1998), 267–68; Bayard Dodge, *Al-Azhar: A Millennium of Muslim Learning* (Washington, DC: Middle East Institute, 1961), 114; Juan R. I. Cole, *Colonialism and Revolution in the Middle East: Social and Cultural Origins of Egypt's 'Urabi Movement* (Princeton, NJ: Princeton University Press, 1993), 38.

[16] Heyworth-Dunne, *Introduction to the History of Education in Modern Egypt,* 253–59; Mitchell, *Colonising Egypt,* 71, 76–77.

gious. Al-Tahtawi argued that "benefit" could also be material: "All knowledge is beneficial to the community [*milla*] of Muslims, even if it be manufacturing. . . . [Also included] are the books of agriculture and commerce and so forth, both as inventions and as complements [to other subjects]."[17] It was incorrect, he wrote, to separate religious from nonreligious subjects, for even legal scholars must be somewhat cognizant of history, administrative practices, military arts, and economics. Indeed, these subjects "benefit and are needed by the state [*dawla*] and the nation [*watan*]."[18] Yet books on such subjects were not read in *madaris*.

Al-Tahtawi argued furthermore that underlying the prejudice against non-religious subjects were legal methodologies practiced by the scholars: *taqlid* and *ittiba'*. *Ittiba'* meant following legal precedent as established by a scholar's legal school (*madhhab*) in an informed manner, having studied the evidence and reasoning process used to derive a particular judgment. *Taqlid*, as al-Tahtawi defined it, meant following precedent, without studying the arguments used in establishing it; the precedents were derived largely from consensus (*ijma'*) as embodied in tomes of rulings reached by individual scholars over the centuries.[19]

Al-Tahtawi's argument was that *madrasa* education inculcated *taqlid* into students' attitudes. He believed, perhaps incorrectly, that students merely memorized and reproduced the texts of old masters and hence that students of jurisprudence would simply memorize and reproduce legal precedents. In turn, this would translate into an attitude that one's forebears had achieved everything that was good and that everything new was suspect or *bida'*—a dangerous innovation that departed from inherited religious truths. *Taqlid* thus was more than a legal methodology; it was a worldview opposed to progress, the cause of social decay, and the main problem preventing Muslims and Egyptians from being able to combat European imperialism.

Al-Tahtawi argued that the educational system must revive *ijtihad*, which meant individual reasoning based on Qur'an and *hadith* texts to reach a novel ruling, possibly exiting the hermeneutics of one's legal school in order to

[17] Rifa'a al-Tahtawi, *Murshid al-amin li al-banat wa al-banin*, in *Al-A'mal al-kamila li Rifa'a Rafi' al-Tahtawi*, ed. Muhammad 'Imarah (Beirut: al-Mu'assasah al-'Arabiyyah li al-Dirasat wa al-Nashr, 1973), 1: 227 (translation mine, here and throughout article). See also Cole, *Colonialism and Revolution in the Middle East*, 42–43; for comparison to Indian *madrasa* reform, see Muhammad Qasim Zaman, "Religious Education and the Rhetoric of Reform: The Madrasah in British India and Pakistan," *Comparative Studies in Society and History* 41 (1999): 294–323.

[18] Rifa'a al-Tahtawi, *Kitab manahij al-albab al-Misriyya fi mabahij al-adab al-'asriyya*, in 'Imarah, *Al-A'mal al-kamila li Rifa'a Rafi' al-Tahtawi*, 228.

[19] In Sunni Islamic legal theory, there are four generally accepted categories of evidence or legal reasoning that a jurist may use in formulating a legal opinion or judgment. Of the evidentiary sources, the Qur'an is the first and most authoritative; the second is sunna, or the normative principles drawn from sayings of the Prophet and his Companions; and the third is *ijma'*, rulings achieved by analogy or other methods but approved by consensus of the community of scholars in a particular legal school. *Qiyas*, analogy based on Qur'an or *hadith* texts, constitutes the fourth source. There are numerous less widely accepted sources, including varieties of customary practice, judgments about common good, etc.; the use of these in part distinguishes one legal school from another.

achieve this. In the early centuries of Islamic legal practice, there were of course always novel situations that had to be resolved by *ijtihad*, and different degrees of *ijtihad* continued to be practiced throughout history.[20] However, if individual jurists have the authority to revisit an issue each time it comes up, and because there are conflicting *hadith* texts and Qur'anic verses that are ambiguous or may have multiple interpretations, there is a problem of inconsistency in application of legal judgments. Recognizing that unbridled *ijtihad* undermines the rule of law, scholars from the fourteenth century on gradually restricted the use of *ijtihad* to high-level jurists and bound lesser scholars to follow the precedents—to practice *taqlid*. By the nineteenth century, it was common for scholars to claim that "the gate of *ijtihad*" was closed.[21]

Al-Tahtawi argued that when *ijtihad* had been practiced widely was the time in which Muslims had been the most advanced civilization on earth, and the most powerful. Without this continuing revitalization of the community through wide reading and investigation into the heart of matters, even scientific matters, the community would languish.[22] Therefore, training students to do *ijtihad* would not be damaging but would actually contribute to the revival of Islamic society and would encourage openness to other nontraditional sources of "useful knowledge," such as applied sciences and European administrative ideas.

The Contributions of Jamal al-Din al-Afghani

Another influential scholar, Shaykh Jamal al-Din al-Afghani (d. 1897), a Persian who had lived in British colonial India and had dedicated his life to the revival of Islamic society and resistance to colonialism, also criticized the *madrasa* system as too *taqlid* bound.[23] However, he took the term *ijtihad* even further from its denotative meaning as a purely legal term and used the term to signify a spirit of intellectual curiosity, which he understood to be the very essence of Islam. "Islam is almost unique among religions in censuring belief without proof, rebuking those who follow suppositions, reproaching those who act randomly in the darkness of ignorance, and chiding them for their conduct. This religion demands that the pious seek proof [for their beliefs]

[20] Wael Hallaq, "Was the Gate of *Ijtihad* Closed?" *International Journal of Middle East Studies* 16 (1984): 3–41, and "On the Origins of the Controversy about the Existence of *Mujtahids* and the Gate of *Ijtihad*," *Studia Islamica* 63 (1986): 134–41.

[21] Muhammad Fadel, "The Social Logic of *Taqlid* and the Rise of the Mukhatasar," *Islamic Law and Society* 3 (June 1996): 193–233.

[22] Rifaʿa al-Tahtawi, "Baqaʾ husn al-dhikr bi istikhdam al-fikr," *Rawdat al-Madaris* 1 (15 Safar AH 1287): 11–15, and *Al-Qawl al-sadid fi al-ijtihad wa al-tajdid* (Cairo: Matbaʿat Wadi al-Nil, 1870), 1–24.

[23] John W. Livingston, "Muhammad ʿAbduh on Science," *Muslim World* 85, nos. 3–4 (1995): 222. Al-Afghani's influence in Egypt was considerable. Although he had no *waqf*-paid position at a *madrasa*, he had a government stipend that allowed him to read texts with students at his own home, and by all reports al-Afghani's private readings attracted many students from al-Azhar *madrasa*, among them men who would become the foremost journalists, jurists, and statesmen of their day.

in the sources of their religion."[24] In contrast, al-Afghani saw *taqlid* as a violation of explicit Qur'anic commandments in which God instructed disbelievers to cease following their forefathers' beliefs, for which they had no evidence of efficacy, in favor of revealed religion:[25]

> The beliefs of the religion should be the first thing engraven on people's souls, built on solid evidence and sound proofs, so that their beliefs do not rest upon the opinions of others. They must disdain contentedness with following [*taqlid*] their forefathers on these matters. If a tenet of faith is held in a person's imagination without proof and without evidence, he may not be convinced, and will not be a believer. Also, the mind of one who accepts beliefs on the basis of supposition becomes accustomed to following suppositions. . . . If they continue like this, ignorance will gradually deceive them.[26]

The key to revival was to teach students to reexamine the primary sources of their religion for themselves, that is, to do *ijtihad* on a simple level. He openly acknowledged that his model for understanding religious revival was derived from the Protestant Reformation: "[The historian Guizot] said that one of the most significant causes influencing Europe in its path to civilization was the appearance of a sect in this country that said: 'we have the right to investigate the sources of our beliefs, and demand proof for them.' . . . And when this sect gained power and its ideas spread, the minds of the Europeans were freed from the malady of ignorance and stupidity, and they were stimulated into an intellectual circuit and returned to [the study of] scientific subjects and worked hard to acquire the elements of civilization."[27] Thus, *ijtihad* applied to personal religious belief would inspire investigation of scientific matters and lead to societal advancement.

Al-Afghani vociferously criticized those who claimed the gate of *ijtihad* was closed and demanded the textual evidence that prohibited individual believers from discovering for themselves the sources of their belief. In this, he was diverging sharply from more traditional scholars such as al-Tahtawi, for al-Afghani taught that *ijtihad* was not to be limited to high-level jurists or to scholars at all. Al-Afghani told his students that anyone could interpret the Qur'an if he or she could read Arabic, was sane, and had a moderate level of religious education (e.g., knew the reliable *hadiths*, the stories of the Companions of the Prophet, the rulings derived from unambiguous verses of the Qur'an or analogies thereof, and the rulings approved by consensus).

Applied to *madrasa* education, the critique of *taqlid* implied that students coerced into accepting their instructors' readings of a text, or the opinions of commentators they studied, were being led progressively away from the

[24] Jamal al-Din al-Afghani, "Al-Radd ʿala al-dahriyyin," in *Al-Aʿmal al-kamila li-Jamal al-Din al-Afghani,* ed. Muhammad ʿImarah (Cairo: al-Muʾassasa al-Misriyya al-ʿAmma li al-Taʾlif wa al-Nashr, n.d.), 1:126–79, quote on 177.

[25] See, e.g., Qurʾan 2:170–71, 5:104–5, 7:70–72.

[26] Al-Afghani, "Al-Radd ʿala al-dahriyin," 176.

[27] Ibid., 176–77.

meaning inherent in the original text rather than preserving the original intent of the author. Furthermore, students' ability and willingness to question would be weaned out of them, and they would learn instead to fear innovative interpretations. Al-Afghani therefore advised the rehabilitation of the *madrasa*, led by a new enlightened cadre of *ijtihad*-practicing scholars who would imbue students with the spirit of intellectual inquiry, the new lay *ijtihad*. In turn, lay *ijtihad* would create a more religiously committed, intellectually curious, scientifically aware, and materially strengthened community, which would be able to resist imperialist incursion.[28]

The Contributions of Muhammad 'Abduh

Muhammad 'Abduh (d. 1905), perhaps the best known of al-Afghani's students, attempted to carry out al-Afghani's plan to reintroduce an *ijtihad* mentality into *madrasa* education. As a student at al-Azhar, 'Abduh "hated the method of instruction. . . . He used to speak of its shortcomings and moan about the students' working with . . . explanation of expressions and useless things with which the students' hours were filled."[29] He wrote articles complaining that the *taqlid* mentality and its consequent mental laziness was causing a crisis of confidence in the scholars: students no longer respected them, they made fun of them, and order suffered.[30] He pleaded with the scholars to offer readings of texts in contemporary subjects, especially European scientific texts. Such subjects were not proscribed by religion, he wrote, but were in fact necessities "especially in times such as these, when people of all religions mingle. It is clear that what is taken from our predecessors and what our relatives told us, if not supported by proofs, will be affected by the sayings of heretics and be refuted by the infidels, and its construction will begin to weaken, and its nature will be destroyed."[31] 'Abduh then accused the *madrasa* scholars of deliberate obstructionism, preferring medieval texts to subjects that would save the community from "ferocious lions" and warning them that they must pursue new fields of knowledge or perish. He asserted that *madrasa* scholars had to become the vanguard in an effort to spread knowledge of science and military technology among the people, particularly because they trained the instructors for the civil school system.[32]

'Abduh, like al-Afghani, explicitly referenced the Protestant Reformation,

[28] Muhammad al-Makhzumi, *Khatirat Sayyid Jamal al-Din al-Afghani al-Husayni* (Beirut: al-Matba'a al-'Ilmiyya li-Yusuf Sadir, 1931), 176–79.

[29] Muhammad Rashid Rida, *Tarikh al-ustadh al-imam Muhammad Abduh* (Cairo: Al-Manar, 1908), 1: 411.

[30] Muhammad 'Abduh, "Al-Ma'arif, " in *Al-A'mal al-kamila li al-Imam al-Shaykh Muhammad 'Abduh*, ed. Muhammad 'Imarah (Beirut: Dar al-Shuruq, 1993), 3:38.

[31] Muhammad 'Abduh, "Al-'Ulum al-kalamiyya wa al-da'wa ila al-'ulum al-'asriyya," in 'Imarah, *Al-A'mal al-kamila li al-Imam al-Shaykh Muhammad 'Abduh*, 3:17.

[32] Ibid., 3:17–22.

noting that the Protestants had acquired a "desire for knowledge" and had resolved to "cut the chains of *taqlid*" and "restrict the authority of the leaders of religion and prevent them from exceeding its counsels and distorting its meanings."[33] Humans have free will and should be empowered to use it: the authority of human reason should be liberated from all chains except submission to God. 'Abduh furthermore claimed that Islam "indicted as stupid and foolish those who accepted the legal dicta of previous scholars"[34] and that "anyone who can read can learn the principles of the discursive fields of knowledge [*'ulum*] from books."[35] This suggested that religious scholars' role as mediators of texts and discursive knowledge would eventually become obsolete.

During his exile (1882–87) for resisting the British occupation of Egypt, 'Abduh lived for a time in Paris, where he crafted a national education policy for Egypt that employed strikingly Spencerian motifs such as "utility" of certain subjects, "practical" education for self-preservation, active learning, moral learning, maternal education, and especially the necessity of scientific expertise for national strength. The plan included a familiar critique of *madrasa* education: that the method of teaching reading through Qur'an memorization taught "words without meaning" and students learned nothing "of benefit," al-Azhar lacked an organized curriculum, the contemporary relevance of the subjects was not made clear, the scholars provided no moral instruction or supervision of the students, and the scholars themselves were "ignorant fanatics." The solution was to impose a European-style administrative system, with registration, examinations, attendance records, moral supervision, practical application of subject material, and state monitoring of the institution.[36]

When 'Abduh returned to Egypt, he offered his plan to the Ottoman viceroy, the khedive Tawfiq. Although Tawfiq did not implement the plan and reportedly even prevented 'Abduh from obtaining a teaching position out of fear that he would have "influence over the young," 'Abduh caught the attention of Egypt's British administrator, Lord Cromer, who helped him gain employment on a council of religious advisors and as a civil court judge. 'Abduh's fortunes continued to improve under Tawfiq's successor, 'Abbas Hilmi II, who appointed 'Abduh in 1895 to lead an administrative council over al-Azhar that had power to enact reform codes, and in 1899 to the top

---

[33] Muhammad 'Abduh, *Risalat al-tawhid*, ed. Mahmud Abu Riyya (Cairo: Dar al-Ma'arif, n.d.), 183–84.

[34] Ibid., 154.

[35] 'Abduh, "Al-Ma'arif," 3:32.

[36] Rida, *Tarikh*, 1:1031, 103; Muhammad 'Abduh, "Mashru' islah al-tarbiya fi Misr" in 'Imarah, *Al-A'mal al-kamila li al-Imam al-Shaykh Muhammad 'Abduh*, 3:106–22; Herbert Spencer, *On Education*, rev. ed. (1854–59; repr., Cambridge: Cambridge University Press, 1932); Wilfred Scawen Blunt, *My Diaries: Being a Personal Narrative of Events, 1888–1914* (New York: Knopf, 1921), 2:66–67.

legal position in the country, that of grand mufti, or chief jurisconsult for the official Hanafi legal school.

As mufti, ʿAbduh authored several controversial fatwas using forms of *ijtihad*.[37] Perhaps the most famous of these was a fatwa ʿAbduh wrote for a private petitioner from the Transvaal in South Africa, where Muslims were a minority. One part of the petition asked whether Muslims could eat meat slaughtered by Christians. According to Qurʾan 5:3, Muslims may not eat animals "killed by strangling, or by a violent blow, or by a fall, or by being gored to death, that which has been eaten by a wild animal, unless you are able to slaughter it in time, that which has been sacrificed to idols, and that which has been used in gambling." The prescribed manner of slaughter was to cut the animal's throat in the name of God. The problem was that the Christians of the Transvaal slaughtered their animals with an ax, and so the question arose of whether a Muslim could conform to the norms of his or her society without violating God's commandments. ʿAbduh's fatwa attempted to minimize the difference between the religious communities and the isolation of the Muslim community in the Christian Transvaal. He cited Qurʾan 5:5, which states that "the food of the People of the Book is lawful for you and your food is lawful for them," and other verses that permitted Muslims to eat the food of Jews and Christians, but warned that the animal should be sacrificed in such a way that priests were permitted to eat it. This novel interpretation focused on the principle of the verse, which was that food animals should be slaughtered humanely and that possibly infected or ritually impure animals should not be eaten, and he ignored the literal restriction against meat killed "by violent blow." Peaceful coexistence among religious groups was to him more important to the good of society than divisive technical details.[38]

Similarly, ʿAbduh reinterpreted verses of the Qurʾan that seemed to permit polygamy. The conventional understanding of Qurʾanic verse 4:3 was that men could marry up to four wives: "If you fear you cannot be equitable to orphan girls, then marry women who are lawful for you, two, three, or four; but if you fear you cannot treat so many with equity, marry only one." But 4:129 stated: "Howsoever you may try, you will never be able to treat your wives equally." ʿAbduh pointed out that if it was not possible to treat multiple wives equally, men were legally limited to one wife. He also stated that animosity among multiple wives spread to their sons and relatives and thus damaged societal amity and that polygamy led to overreproduction, poverty,

---

[37] Fatwas are nonbinding legal opinions on religious matters, usually in response to a petition; by issuing fatwas the chief mufti could set policy for members of his legal school.

[38] Muhammad ʿAbduh, "Lubs al-baranit wa dhabihat ahl al-kitab: Wa salat al-shafiʿi khalf al-hanafi," fatwa no. 625, December 25, 1903, in *Al-Fatawa al-islamiyya min dar al-iftaʾ al-Misriyya* (Cairo: Wizarat al-Awqaf, 1981), 4:1298–99; on modernist use of social good as an operating principle, see Felicitas Opwis, "Changes in Modern Islamic Legal Theory: Reform or Reformation?" in Browers and Kurzman, *An Islamic Reformation?* 38–45.

and crime. ʿAbduh also clarified that, historically speaking, verse 4:3 referred to a situation after the battle of Uhud in 625 CE, when many men were killed, leaving a large number of orphans behind. The concern was that a female orphan's caretaker might become sexually involved with her or appropriate her property. Thus, only in such circumstances when greater principles of chastity and morality were threatened was polygamy even theoretically permitted.[39]

Such rulings appealed to Egypt's British administrators and to the rising class of Egyptian bureaucrats trained in Egypt's civil schools and influenced by European ideals of civilizational progress.[40] But ʿAbduh's apparent coziness with the British and his insistence on employing *ijtihad* in private juristic rulings made him anathema to many *madrasa* scholars.[41] This made his leadership of al-Azhar's administrative council rather turbulent.

For instance, as part of a series of reform codes derived from civil school models that the Egyptian government attempted to impose upon al-Azhar *madrasa*, ʿAbduh led the implementation of a new code in 1896.[42] This code defined and divided subjects into primary, ancillary, and elective; formed committees to examine students for admission; created two degrees that were to be completed within 8 and 12 years (8 or 12 courses), with scheduled annual oral examinations; confirmed ranks of success on exams; and designated for them possible career options. Scholars would teach an approved list of texts rather than reading texts in their specialties or as requested by students. They would have to have the students do drills, and the rules for achievement of a degree implied that a course would have to conclude within the now-defined academic year.[43] The implementation of these codes represented the apogee of modernist reform efforts, and of conceptual colonization of the *madrasa*, in Egypt.

Conservative Critics of "Modernist" Reform

Just as the European Enlightenment had its antiphilosophes, so did the modernist reform movement have its opponents, scholars who called themselves *muhafizun*, "protectors" or "conservatives" in the strictest sense. Mod-

[39] Muhammad ʿAbduh, "Surat al-nisaʾ: Tafsir al-Qurʾan," in ʿImarah, *Al-Aʿmal al-kamila li al-Imam al-Shaykh Muhammad ʿAbduh*, 5:163–64; see also Qasim Amin, *Tahrir al-marʾa*, in *Qasim Amin: Al-Aʿmal al-kamila*, ed. Muhammad ʿImara (Beirut: Dar al-Shuruq, 1989), 393–97.

[40] Lord Cromer, dispatch no. 105 (June 6, 1899), Foreign Office 78/5023.

[41] For example, ʿAbduh was nevertheless roundly criticized for "making permitted that which is forbidden." See Muhammad Abu Shadi, "Raʾy Mufti al-diyar al-misriyya fi lubs al-qubbaʿa wa akl al-lahm al-ghayr al-madhki wa salat al-shafiʿiyya khalf al-hanafiyya," *Al-Zahir*, December 29, 1903, and subsequent issues; Mustafa Kamil, "Masʾalat al-iftaʾ," *Al-Liwaʾ*, January 14, 1904, and subsequent issues.

[42] Successive codes created examinations of candidates who wished licenses to teach and delineated subject areas (1872, 1885, and 1888), implemented formal registration procedures (1881 and 1885), and approved the study of mathematics, geography, and natural sciences (1888).

[43] Lajnat Islah al-Azhar al-Maʿmur, *Mashruʿ muqaddam li-Sahib al-ʿAtufa Muhammad Saʿid Pasha qaʾimmaqam al-hadrat al-khidiwiyya was raʾis al-nuzzar* (Cairo: Al-Matbaʿa al-Amiriyya, 1910).

ernist reformers pilloried the *muhafizun* as mere obstacles in this path of apparent progress. However, conservatives did have practical and ideological objections to aspects of the modernists' objectives and methods. Their objections did not encompass the bureaucratization of *madrasa* education, because the civil school-influenced codes were rendered acceptable by the consequences of al-Azhar's tremendous growth: poor sanitary conditions, overcrowded classes, and inability to personally mentor students. However, they tended to oppose the teaching of mathematics and applied science within the *madrasa*, and they objected to the legal, political, and social implications of modernist *ijtihad* and to the teaching of such *ijtihad* at *madaris*.

For example, one anonymous Azhar scholar wrote that new subjects would distract students from religious studies: "It is the custom for students at al-Azhar to be interested in everything new—so if these subjects were introduced into al-Azhar, they would turn away from us. . . . If this is the case, the desired outcome, which is training of people to be *shariʿa* judges or *muftis* or *imams* of mosques or professors, would be lost."[44] A scholar who was responsible for supervising student housing at al-Azhar, Muhammad Sulayman al-Safti, further commented: "The circumstances do not permit other than the current subjects. . . . If we were to require the student to acquire mathematical subjects, as is now the plan, without increasing the time . . . the matter would end in abandoning important parts of the *shariʿa*. . . . Thus would the *shariʿa* of the Messenger of God, peace be upon him, be annihilated. All of this for the sake of mathematical sciences and the fruits of progress, which . . . cause the spread of skepticism." True reform, al-Safti claimed, did not require the addition of new subjects but simply the imposition of order and the supervision of student learning and morality.[45]

Another al-Azhar scholar, Muhammad al-Hifni al-Mahdi, argued that the religious scholars should not become generalists; they fulfilled a specific function for society by performing a *fard kifaʾi*, an obligation that could be fulfilled by some on behalf of all. The preservation of religious knowledge was such an obligation. If religious scholars were forced outside their specialties, they "would not work to achieve the degree of completion that is the goal itself, and they will be limited to the minimal edges of each art."[46] This was a novel argument, since specialization of knowledge was not recognized as such in the *madrasa* context: all knowledge was regarded as connected to religion.

The argument for specialization also had a financial basis. Hasan Husni al-Tuwayrani, editor of the literary journal *Al-Nil*, pointed out that al-Azhar was still partly financially dependent on its *awqaf* endowments. A *waqf* theoretically endured in perpetuity—"until God inherits the earth"—so the *ma-*

---

[44] Reprinted in ʿAli Yusuf, "Taʿmim al-taʿlim," *Al-Adab* 3 (November 22, 1889): 485–87.

[45] Muhammad Sulayman al-Safti, "Al-Azhar," *Al-Islam* 1 (January 27, 1895): 267–71.

[46] Muhammad al-Hifni al-Mahdi, "Adab al-ʿilm wa al-ʿulama," *Al-Islam* 2 (October 20, 1895): 206–7.

drasa would be perpetually bound to the study of religion, ensuring the continuity of God's guidance on earth. Also, *awqaf* endowers often set out in excruciating detail exactly what was to be funded, including what scholars who received stipends from the *waqf* could teach. *Awqaf* were used in the building and maintenance of the *madrasa* and its surrounding student housing, and the assumption of a *waqf* was that its funds would be used for religious purposes. Therefore, any change in that purpose or in the subject matter taught might violate the legal stipulations of hundreds of *waqf* charters. Al-Tuwayrani also implied that the new subjects should be excluded because they were European in origin. They were being proposed "under the pretext that they are among the causes of advancement and progress," but in his view they were vectors of colonization intended to sever the Muslims from religious guidance.[47]

Such arguments did not prevent the introduction of mathematics and sciences. The government circumvented the *awqaf* by funding grants and student incentive packages for the new subjects. However, the protests did lead a committee of scholars to reject 'Abduh's suggestion that the students study literature, which he said would help them better understand the Arabic language. The scholars replied that the mission of the *madrasa* was to teach religious studies and that the subjects the students already had to study according to the new curriculum left no time for literature. Studies in literature were thus judged "commendable but unnecessary."[48] But in general, although some leading *muhafizun* stalled the effectuation of reforms, they still organized committees to define subject areas, select textbooks, and prepare the ground for implementation.[49]

The most virulent protests were reserved for the proposed introduction of *ijtihad* and its potential effects. When Muhammad Rashid Rida, an associate of 'Abduh's, wrote in their influential journal *Al-Manar* that al-Azhar's curriculum and pedagogical traditions should incorporate the new emphasis on *ijtihad*, some religious scholars reacted in horror.[50] *Taqlid* was the foundation of the rule of law within Islamic societies. If, as these reformers suggested, it was replaced with *ijtihad* as independent legal reasoning, judges would no longer be constrained to give similar rulings for similar legal cases, and petitioners for legal advice could go from one mufti to another until they received a ruling they liked. Furthermore, since the reformers saw *ijtihad* as something all individuals could do for themselves, they would theoretically be able to resolve their own legal questions. Legal authority on religious

[47] Hasan Husni al-Tuwayrani, "Al-Azhar fi Misr," *Al-Nil* 4 (January 31, 1895): 4; see also Ramadan, "Dawr al-awqaf," 37–38.

[48] Ibrahim al-Muwailihi, "Mustahsan ghayr lazim," *Misbah al-sharq*, November 2, 1899.

[49] 'Abd al-Rahman Salman, *A'mal majlis idarat al-Azhar: Min ibtida' ta'sisihi sanat 1312 ila ghayat sanat 1322*, rev. ed. (AH 1322; repr., Cairo: Matba'at al-Manar, 1905), 19, 60–62.

[50] Muhammad Rashid Rida, "Al-Muhawarat bayna al-muslih wa al-muqallid: Al-Muhawara al-sadisa; Al-ijtihad wa al-taqlid," *Al-Manar* 4 (May 5, 1901): 166–67.

questions would no longer reside in the hands of the scholars, but would be possessed by ordinary individuals. One anonymous defender of *taqlid* said that what the reformers "imagined to be religious reform" would undermine public trust in the law and confuse laymen.[51] He protested: "My heart constricts from hearing your argument for abandoning *taqlid*. . . for I anticipate anarchy in religion for the common Muslims."[52] Revival of unbridled *ijtihad* would only result in further divisions in the religious community: "I think this reform is nothing but a hellish fire that will spread chaos on the earth and a great corruption."[53]

Muhammad ʿIlish, the chief mufti of the Maliki legal school in Egypt (1854–82), also expressed in many fatwas such concerns that the spread of *ijtihad* would undermine the rule of law. He warned against the dangers of *ijtihad*, specifically by leaders of reform groups such as the Sanusiyya in Libya or the Wahhabis in Arabia. ʿIlish asserted that many Qurʾanic verses were ambiguous and that interpreters must be familiar with the related histories and prophetic sayings in order to understand them; otherwise, interpretations could even be blasphemous. If *ijtihad* was to be practiced at all, it should only be done within the confines of the legal school's methods and only by the highly trained. Untrained practitioners of even limited *ijtihad* could lead themselves and others into error, threatening their chances of salvation.

Furthermore, a mufti had to confine himself to a single legal school, or he could pick and choose rulings based on his client's desires, leading to corruption, conflicting rulings on criminal cases, and confusion. This would undermine public confidence in the authority and legitimacy of the law and the educational system training legal specialists. Further, ʿIlish, a Shadhili Sufi, argued that only those close to the Prophet, either through personal or mystical contact, could have the perfect understanding necessary to interpret without error. Ideally, then, in order to preserve public confidence in religion and law, all contemporary Muslims were bound to follow precedents laid down by the founders of the legal schools, whom he claimed had mystical contact with the Prophet Muhammad.[54]

ʿIlish once confronted the then student Muhammad ʿAbduh for teaching a book of Muʿtazili thought (the *Sharh al-ʾaqaʾid al-nasafiyya*), which advocated reason as well as revelation as a source of true knowledge. When ʿAbduh postured, claiming that he was prepared to "abandon *taqlid* altogether and use only the evidence," ʿIlish sneered that the likes of him were not prepared

[51] Muhammad Rashid Rida, "Al-Muhawara al-sabiʿa bayna al-muslih wa al-muqallid—al-ijtihad wa al-wahda al-islamiyya," *Al-Manar* 4 (May 19, 1901): 212.

[52] Muhammad Rashid Rida, "Al-Muhawara al-tasiʿa bayna al-muslih wa al-muqallid—al-taqlid wa al-talfiq al-ijma," *Al-Manar* 4 (July 17, 1901): 369–70.

[53] Rida, "Al-Muhawara al-sabiʿa," 212–13.

[54] Muhammad ʿIlish, *Fath al-ʿali al-malik fi al-fatwa ʿala madhhab al-Imam Malik*, rev. ed. (1882; repr., Cairo: Sharikat Maktaba wa Matbaʿa al-Babi al-Halabi wa Awladihi, 1958), 1:67–68, 70–71, 77, 89–93, 95–96, 104.

to understand such books and forbade him from teaching it.[55] In this case, as with the position he articulated in fatwas, 'Ilish stressed that those who are not trained—who are not approved transmitters in an oral chain of certainty—are not capable of independently interpreting texts. Whether the text is the *Sharh al-'aqa'id* or the Qur'an, the argument is the same: *ijtihad* (here, unguided interpretation of a text) challenges the integrity of knowledge as transmitted truth.[56]

From a juristic perspective, the modernist use of *ijtihad* simply did not make sense, so many of the conservative critics believed that the modernists had other motivations than their claimed focus on the revival of education.[57] Muhammad 'Abduh was the chief victim of their invective. For example, some pilloried *ijtihad* as a cover for reinterpreting the law in accord with British wishes, using as examples 'Abduh's Transvaal fatwa and others that legitimated the giving of interest on bank deposits.[58] Muhammad Tawfiq, the editor of the muckraking *Humarat Munyati*, attacked 'Abduh's *ijtihad* proposals as doing the will of foreigners at the expense of the people.[59] Likewise, Tawfiq refuted 'Abduh's argument for free will with quotations from the Qur'an that suggested humans' fates were to some extent determined and accused 'Abduh of European-inspired heresy.[60] *Al-Zahir*, a newspaper that many viewed as speaking for the khedive, argued that 'Abduh's role as a chief mufti was to deliver fatwas according to the principles and rulings of the Hanafi school; thus, issuing fatwas that included the words "I think" and "my opinion is" (e.g., his Transvaal fatwa) just confused the public. How would people be able to tell the difference between law and educated opinion? Therefore, 'Abduh's belief that he had "the right to *ijtihad*" was unjustified.[61]

Al-Zahir also worried openly about 'Abduh's influence over al-Azhar *madrasa*.[62] So did the top-ranking al-Azhar administrator, the scholar 'Abd al-

[55] 'Abduh's autobiography as reported by Rashid Rida in *Al-Manar* 8 (July 19, 1905): 391.

[56] For 'Ilish, a ruling was regarded as epistemologically certain if the community, represented by its scholars, achieved consensus on it, and acceptance of consensus was one of the fundamental principles that defined the Sunni community. Thus, someone who rejected rulings achieved by consensus was in effect excusing himself from the community and therefore a heretic. 'Ilish, *Fath al-'ali*, 92; Wael B. Hallaq, *A History of Islamic Legal Theories: An Introduction to Sunni* usul al-fiqh (Cambridge: Cambridge University Press, 1997), 207–9.

[57] Ibrahim al-Muwailihi, "Al-Im'an fi al-tafarnuj," *Misbah al-sharq*, October 4, 1901; Muhammad Abu Shadi, "Hukm Allah fi ra'y al-Mufti" *Al-Zahir*, January 2, 1904.

[58] Muhammad 'Abduh, "Sharikat mudaraba," fatwa no. 436, in *Al-Fatawa al-islamiyya*, 3:879–85.

[59] Muhammad Tawfiq, "Darwish wa abu hashish wa ghayr keda ma fish," *Humarat Munyati* 3 (January 8, 1901): 502–5.

[60] Muhammad Tawfiq, "Wa hadha al-ustadh al-'allama al-shaykh Muhammad 'Abduh mufti al-diyar al-Misriyya," *Humarat Munyati* 4 (July 28, 1901): 142–44.

[61] Abu Shadi, "Hukm Allah fi ra'y al-Mufti," 1, "Hukm Allah fi fatwa al-Mufti . . . rabbuna Allah la ghayruhu," *Al-Zahir*, January 6, 1904, and "Rabbuna Allah la ghayruhu: Mas'alat al-fatwa," *Al-Zahir*, January 7, 1904; "A-la yakhjalu al-muhawwasun" *Al-Zahir*, January 6, 1904.

[62] Abu Shadi, "Rabbuna Allah," 1.

Rahman al-Shirbini.[63] He claimed that ʿAbduh's *ijtihad* meant teaching students to value "Spencer's philosophy" over the authority of the legal scholars and that this would lead to a loss of respect for religion and its scholars. The purpose of the *madrasa* was to perpetuate religious guidance for the community, so the guidance offered by "principles of philosophy" and "the new high sciences" should be left to the civil schools. According to al-Shirbini, ʿAbduh's reforms would only turn the *madrasa* away from its mission and into "a school of philosophy and literature to put out Islam's light."[64]

Discussion

ʿAbduh's ally Rashid Rida tried to explain that ʿAbduh had not completely rejected *taqlid*: ʿAbduh only wanted believers to read for themselves the Qurʾan and the *hadith* rather than relying totally on the rulings of jurists. However, Rida's statement that ʿAbduh believed that an individual's interpretation of the sources could override the opinions of medieval jurists, at least in matters of personal belief, confirmed some of the fears of those who defended *taqlid*.[65]

The outcomes of these debates over religious education in Egypt were varied. On the one hand, the "modernist" reformers did not really fail in bringing change to Egypt's *madaris*. On the other hand, they initiated an extended period of negotiation that ultimately resulted in *madrasa* scholars' enfranchisement in the process of reform. Scholars sat on committees, wrote codes, and decided on texts. In 1904, a student of the *muhafizun* party, Muhammad al-Ahmadi al-Zawahiri, who returned as teacher and later as chief administrator, reported that he admired Muhammad ʿAbduh and embraced *ijtihad*-based teaching.[66] By 1908, Utilitarian modes of order and discipline had almost entirely colonized the *madrasa*. A council of high-ranking scholars pronounced that there was nothing entailed in such reforms that contradicted Islamic principles, and there were student demonstrations in which students

[63] Such public criticisms of ʿAbduh also affected his relations with al-Azhar students, as one reported: "Our professors, may God forgive them, used to constantly criticize the Shaykh [ʿAbduh] in our presence and represent him as being dangerous for religion and for the religious—subtly dangerous. As a consequence, . . . I used to flee from encountering the professor, for the sake of my religion, and to flee from listening to his lessons, even though he was a friend of my father." ʿAbd al-Baqi al-Surur, quoted in Eccel, *Social Change*, 177.

[64] ʿAbd al-Rahman al-Shirbini, "Al-Azhar al-sharif wa al-gharad min islah turuq al-taʿlim fihi," in Rida, *Tarikh*, 1:502–4.

[65] Muhammad Rashid Rida, "Irad[a] ʿala tark al-taqlid," *Al-Manar* 8 (June 19, 1905): 294–97.

[66] Muhammad al-Ahmadi al-Zawahiri, *Al-ʿlim wa al-ulama wa al-nizam al-taʿlim*, rev. ed. (1904; repr., n.p., 1955), 27, 43, 233, and "Raʾy al-tawasut fi masʾalat islah al-azhar al-sharif: Kitab maftuh ila sumuww mawlana al-khediw al-muʾazzam," *Al-Muʾayyad*, March 11, 1905.

named themselves Partisans of the New Order.[67] The 1911 Reorganization Code, which is generally held to have been the first irrevocable step in the transformation of al-Azhar *madrasa* into a bureaucratic university, was devised with significant input from both scholars and students and included many elements from previous administrative codes.

At the same time, the 1911 code also preserved an element of the old system that would remain outside bureaucratic regulation, the Corps of the Distinguished Scholars. This was an elected body of senior scholars, whose members gave public lectures in traditional fashion three times a week, in their areas of specialty. The Corps was created deliberately to preserve the method of teaching via close textual analysis and discussion with the audience and the unbroken oral transmission of the old texts. These lectures were open to the public and routinely attracted large audiences of students and other scholars. In 1923, a higher degree was added in which students would study 4 years exclusively with the scholars of the Corps in one of the religious specializations. Only these students were licensed to teach at al-Azhar, ensuring that the continuous oral link between authors and recipients, and thus the integrity of religious knowledge, was maintained.[68]

While ultimately the indirect colonization of Islamic education in Egypt resulted in a negotiated compromise, the modernists, unwitting agents of conceptual colonization, succeeded in other, more potent venues. Since many of Jamal al-Din al-Afghani's students had followed his encouragements to found journals, it was al-Afghani's vision of *ijtihad* that was broadcast to the public via emergent Arabic media sources, to officials of the occupation, and to visiting orientalists. European administrators and scholars tended to see in the new *ijtihad* something akin to their ideologies of progressive social change and to write of the reformers' ideas with great enthusiasm while simultaneously denigrating the practitioners of *taqlid* and the denizens of the *madrasa*.[69] Thus did the new definitions of *taqlid* and *ijtihad*, and the concomitant criticisms of *madrasa* education, pass down into authoritative bodies of Euro-American scholarship—as if the terms' new connotations had always

---

[67] Ahmad Shafiq, *Mudhakkirati fi nisf qarn* (Cairo: Sharikat Musahima Misriyya, 1934–36), 2, bk. 2: 138, and "Al-Azhariyyun wa mutalabatuhum," *Al-Mu'ayyad*, January 25, 1909. These demonstrations have often been misconstrued as demonstrations against reform; a simple reading of newspapers from the time shows that students supported the principle of the 1908 bureaucratic reforms and were demonstrating because their implementation was not planned well (e.g., some subjects required for degrees were not being taught).

[68] Lajnat Islah al-Azhar al-Ma'mur, "Mashru' qanun al-Azhar," in *Mashru' muqaddam li-Sahib al-'Atufa Muhammad Sa'id Pasha qa'immaqam al-hadrat al-khidiwiyya was ra'is al-nuzzar*, 36–39; 'Abd al-Mit'al al-Sa'idi, *Tarikh al-islah fil-Azhar wa safahat min al-jihad fil-islah* (Cairo: Matba'at al-I'timad, 1951), 84–85, 88–89, 90, 94. Nevertheless, some students felt that the bureaucratization of the *madrasa* severed the spiritual connection between teacher and student, the sense that the act of reading itself was sacred, and as a result the students became increasingly motivated by material concerns. Mohamed Abdulla 'Enan, foreword to *Tarikh al-Azhar* (Cairo: Lajnet al-Ta'lif, 1958).

[69] For example, see comments on 'Abduh in Evelyn Baring Cromer, *Modern Egypt* (New York: Macmillan, 1908); and Charles Adams, *Islam and Modernism in Egypt: A Study of the Modern Reform Movement Inaugurated by Muhammad 'Abduh*, rev. ed. (1933; repr., New York: Russell & Russell, 1968).

existed and the refusal by some to accept the spread of lay *ijtihad* was simply unreasoning refusal to progress.

Also, the Arabic journals, such as *Al-Manar*, which first broadcast the new *ijtihad*, came to dominate the emerging global market for Arabic print journalism. The early issues were reprinted multiple times, quoted and requoted, and so passed into authoritative Arabic and Islamic scholarship. The new *ijtihad* became an iconic element of the nation-building efforts of the early twentieth century, Muhammad 'Abduh a hero of modernist Islam, and *taqlid* a much-maligned signifier of intellectual and cultural stagnation. To a great extent the chains of one-to-one transmission of texts, in which authorial intent was passed down via oral readings, were broken. In a few of the great *madaris* that retain their religious orientations, such as al-Azhar, there are still professors who studied with so-and-so who read such-and-such a text with someone whose teacher was in a direct line of transmission with the author. Some of the more recent *madaris* trace their intellectual heritages to more recent reform movements and the *ijtihad* of their leaders, such as Deoband *madaris* in India and Pakistan. Some civil *madaris*, such as the public schools of Egypt, retain the faults of one-to-one transmission, such as use of textbook interpretations in place of primary sources, while simultaneously promoting *ijtihad* as justifying scientific "confirmation" of religious truths.[70] Thus, there exists a tension between an intellectual culture promoting *ijtihad* and a bureaucratic demand for acceptance of hierarchical authority.

Ijtihad can be understood as a solitary pursuit of truth for personal understanding of one's religion—as self-education, which might, as the modernist reformers intended, lead one to become grounded in personal understandings of universal truths and curious about other sources of truth, such as science. Mass civil education programs have improved literacy rates and replaced the understanding of "knowledge as transmitted" with "knowledge as contained within books and available at face value to readers."[71] However, it can also be defined as the individual derivation of religious rulings from the Qur'an and sunna for personal practice, eschewing communally approved norms of interpretation passed down to legal scholars through the *madrasa* system. Because many Qur'anic verses and *hadiths* are ambiguous, and many are artifacts of particular historical circumstances, readers with little knowledge of the contexts may arrive at vastly differing interpretations. Indeed, even within the books of rulings accreted over centuries within one legal school, there were contradictory rulings. As has been said before, Islam

---

[70] Gregory Starrett, *Putting Islam to Work: Education, Politics, and Religious Transformation in Egypt* (Berkeley: University of California Press, 1998), 137–42.

[71] Eickelman, *Knowledge and Power*, 168, "The Art of Memory: Islamic Education and Its Social Reproduction," in *Comparing Muslim Societies: Knowledge and the State in a World Civilization*, ed. Juan R. I. Cole, 121–22, 125, and "Who Speaks for Islam? Inside the Islamic Reformation," in Browers and Kurzman, *An Islamic Reformation?* 23.

is no monolith. The potential richness of interpretation is one of its great strengths.

The disinheritance of the hermeneutic tradition—the disintegration of oral links to past interpretive structures—has had negative effects as well. For instance, Shukri Mustafa, leader of the militant group that assassinated President Anwar al-Sadat of Egypt in 1981, once stated that the Qur'an was written in "clear Arabic" and that anyone with a good dictionary could interpret it— hence militants interpreted Qur'anic verses that permit fighting oppression as abrogating those that command believers not to kill Muslims or innocents.[72] Osama bin Ladin, who has degrees in business and engineering, but no formal religious training, issues fatwas declaring it a duty of all capable Muslims to attack Americans.[73] More incredible, thousands of believers accept fatwas issued by laymen as legitimate legal opinions. How far this is from al-Afghani's judgment that a practitioner of *ijtihad* would need to know *hadith*, the early history of the Prophet's life, and books of rulings derived from Qur'an, analogy, or consensus, and be sane!

In conclusion, Islam is now adapted continuously by individual believers and is in a state of perpetual reformation. This, in both its personally inspirational and communally divisive aspects, was due in part to reform of the *madrasa* in Egypt.

---

[72] Quoted in Giles Kepel, *Muslim Extremism in Egypt*, trans. Jon Rothschild, rev. ed. (1984; repr., Berkeley: University of California Press, 1993), 79. See also Starrett, *Putting Islam to Work*, 231.

[73] Osama bin Ladin, interview by Peter Arnett, CNN, March 20, 1997.

"When Mu'awiya Entered the Curriculum"—Some Comments on the Iraqi Education System in the Interwar Period

ORIT BASHKIN

In this essay I explore the nationalization and secularization of the Iraqi educational system during the period between the two world wars, while demonstrating how various intellectuals championed pluralist educational models. Iraqi social and intellectual history has focused on education as an important prism reflecting approaches to discipline and power and emphasized the role of educators as agents of socialization and Arab nationalism.[1] These studies, however, neglected educational theorists who were part of the opposition and relied on essays, textbooks, and plans produced by the Ministry of Education.[2] Therefore, I examine new sources on Iraqi education—

This essay is based on two chapters from my PhD dissertation. I thank Robert L. Tignor and Samah Selim, and Mark Ginsburg, David Post, and Wadad Kadi for their helpful advice, as well as the anonymous readers of this essay for their useful comments.

[1] On the changes in the studies of Arab nationalism and their effects on the field, see Israel Gershoni, "Rethinking the Formation of Arab Nationalism in the Middle East, 1920–1945: Old and New Narratives," in *Rethinking Nationalisms in the Arab Middle East*, ed. Israel Gershoni and James Jankowski (New York: Columbia University Press, 1997), 3–25. For studies of Iraq's education, see William L. Cleveland, *The Making of an Arab Nationalist: Ottomanism and Arabism in the Life and Thought of Sati' al-Husri* (Princeton, NJ: Princeton University Press, 1971); Reeva Simon, *Iraq between Two World Wars: The Creation and Implementation of a Nationalist Ideology* (New York: Columbia University Press, 1986); Phebe Marr, "The Development of Nationalist Ideology in Iraq, 1921–1941," *Muslim World* 75 (1985): 85–99. On the British policies to Iraqi education, see Peter Sluglett, *Britain in Iraq, 1914–1932* (London: Ithaca Press for the Middle East Centre, 1976), 273–95; on textbooks, see Ernest C. Dawn, "The Formation of Pan-Arab Ideology in the Inter-war Years," *International Journal of Middle Eastern Studies* 20 (1988): 67–91. Studies in Arabic based on state publications are 'Abd al-Razzaq al-Hilali, *Ta'rikh al-ta'lim fi'l Iraq* (Baghdad: n.p., 1959); Ibrahim Khalil Ahmad, *Tatawwur al-ta'lim al-watani fi'l 'Iraq* (1869–1932) (Basra: Markaz Dirasat al-Khalij al-'Arabi, 1982). On Iraqi nationalism, see Cleveland, *Making of an Arab Nationalist*; Dawn, "Formation of Pan-Arab Ideology"; Simon, *Iraq between Two World Wars*; Eric Davis, *Memories of State: Politics, History, and Collective Identity in Modern Iraq* (Berkeley: University of California Press, 2005); Phebe Marr, *The Modern History of Iraq* (Boulder, CO: Westview, 1985); Liora Lukitz, *Iraq: The Search for National Identity* (London: Frank Cass, 1994); Michael Eppel, *The Palestine Conflict in the History of Modern Iraq: The Dynamics of Involvement, 1928–1948* (London: Frank Cass, 1994).

[2] The recommendations of the Monroe Commission, an American board that inspected Iraqi education; the prolific pedagogical works of intellectuals such as Sati' al-Husri and Fadhil al-Jamali; British material on educational policies; and textbooks published by the Iraqi Ministry of Education were used to examine Iraq's education. On the Monroe Commission, see Paul Monroe, *Report of the Education Inquiry Commission* (Baghdad: Government Press, 1932); for books on educational and pedagogical theories produced by the ministry executives, see Sati' al-Husri, *Naqd taqrir lajnat Monroe: Rasa'il muwajjaha ila al-ustadh Paul Monroe hawla al-taqrir alladhi qaddamahu ila wizarat al-ma'arif al-'Iraqiyya* (Baghdad: Matba'at al-Najah, 1932), *Fenn-i Terbiye* (Istanbul: Kitaphane-yi Askeri, 1911–12), and *Ahadith fi'l tarbiyya wa'l ta'lim* (Beirut: Dar al-'ilm li'l Malayin, 1962); Fadhil al-Jamali, *Durus fi'l tarbiyya wa'l ta'lim* (Baghdad: n.p., 1931), and *The New Iraq: Its Problem of Bedouin Education* (New York: Teachers College, Columbia University, 1934); Matta Akrawi, "Curriculum Construction in the Public Primary Schools of Iraq in the Light of a Study of the Political, Economic, Social, Hygienic and Educational Conditions and Problems of the Country, with Some Reference to the Education of Teachers: A Preliminary In-

such as newspaper articles, novels, and short stories—to document the opposition to many plans proposed by the Ministry of Education and the unsuccessful implementation of these plans. Such accounts illustrate the resistance to the state's disciplinary power and point to the hybrid nature of Iraqi
education in which the modern and the premodern intertwined.[3]

The Iraqi education system was neither a British nor an Arab creation.
Ottoman educational models also informed the collective mentality of Iraqi
statesmen trained as Ottoman officers and bureaucrats, as Reeva Simon and
Phebe Marr observed in their pioneering works.[4] Benjamin Fortna recently
underlined the Ottoman endeavor during the late nineteenth century to
"ward off Western encroachment by adapting Western style education to suit
Ottoman needs."[5] While Simon and Marr highlighted the role of German
educational themes in the military academies, France provided ample paradigms in the fields of literature, as well as in social and political thought.[6]
Through the production of textbooks and curricula, the state strove to provide proper preadolescent education and to cultivate such values as cleanliness, discipline, self-reliance, and obedience.[7] Iraqis, as well as other Arab
educators, were therefore reconfiguring previous notions of education within
the new Arab state. Nevertheless, in the Ottoman context, Fortna illustrated
how the state's power dissipated in local contexts. While his study focused
on archival documents dealing with students and their teachers, I argue that
sources like literary works, memoirs, and the contemporary press lead us to
similar conclusions concerning the state's limited power and the ability of
both students and teachers to resist and subvert it.

---

vestigation" (PhD thesis, Columbia University, 1942); Sami Shawkat, *Hadhihi Ahdafuna* (Baghdad: Ma-
jallat al-Muʻallim al-Jadid, 1939). For studies that relied on these sources, see Cleveland, *Making of an
Arab Nationalist;* Simon, *Iraq between Two World Wars*, chap. 4; and Marr, "Development of Nationalist
Ideology in Iraq."

[3] Timothy Mitchell's study of disciplinary institutions and their relationship to both the state's
power and colonization in nineteenth-century Egypt sheds significant light on Iraqi education. Despite
the differences between the Iraqi and Egyptian nation-states, the Egyptian and Iraqi case studies share
similar features, since both experienced the formation of disciplinary institutions within a colonial
context, and, in both, the state utilized the language of reform to represent the changes in their
respective military and education systems. See Timothy Mitchell, *Colonising Egypt* (Berkeley: University
of California Press, 1988).

[4] Marr, "Development of Nationalist Ideology in Iraq"; Simon, *Iraq between Two World Wars*, and
"The Education of an Iraqi Ottoman Army Officer," in *The Origins of Arab Nationalism*, ed. Lisa Anderson,
Muhammad Muslim, and Reeva Simon (New York: Columbia University Press, 1991), 151–66.

[5] Benjamin Fortna, *Imperial Classroom: Islam, the State, and Education in the Late Ottoman Empire* (New
York: Oxford University Press, 2002), 12.

[6] Ibid., 14–18. A cursory look at the writings of the Iraqi intellectual and poet Jamil Sidqi al-
Zahawi, who taught in Istanbul, shows the effects of the debates on science, positivism, and Darwinism
on young Iraqis residing in Istanbul. See ʻAbd al-Hamid Rushdi, *Al-Zahawi: Dirasat wa-nusus* (Beirut:
Dar al-hayah, 1966). On Ottoman education, see also Selçuk Akşin Somel, *The Modernization of Public
Education in the Ottoman Empire, 1839–1908: Islamization, Autocracy, and Discipline* (Leiden: Brill, 2001),
in particular, chap. 5, "Professional Schools or Public Education: Curricular Issues," and chap. 7, "Children's Impressions of School and the Process of Early Socialization (1869–1908)."

[7] Fortna, *Imperial Classroom*, 215, 229.

State's Education—Secularizing and Modernizing

During the interwar period, Iraq was a constitutional monarchy ruled by the Hashemite dynasty, whose first king, Faysal I (1921–33), was supported by the British as a leader sympathetic to their colonial concerns. A British mandate was imposed on Iraq, ending in 1931. The Hashemites were supported by the Sherifians, a group of mostly Sunni officers, who took part in the Arab revolt or collaborated with Faysal in his short-lived Syrian government, established after the collapse of the Ottoman Empire. The mostly Sunni political elite of Iraq were received with reservations and qualms by Iraq's Shi'i population, especially the tribes in the south. However, many Shi'i sheikhs who desired to maintain large land tracts in their possession integrated into the new political system during the 1930s, in particular as parliament members.

In Hashemite Iraq, education became a primary disciplinary institution, equaled, perhaps, only by the army. As the number of students in elementary schools increased from 12,226 in 1921 to 29,644 in 1931, the Ministry of Education became an employer of writers, journalists, and poets who worked as teachers and educational supervisors. Although teachers were forbidden to engage in political activities, many wrote about education and politics in the press.[8] Students, concurrently, became a valuable sociopolitical factor as the clients of new schools and members of new political parties. Student demonstrations, often organized by politicians, became part of the Baghdadi urban scene in the 1930s, thus making students a power to consider in national politics.[9]

The new Iraqi state suffered from tribal revolts and ethnic tensions. Many teachers and bureaucrats thus hoped that proper national education would obliterate differences between sects and religions. Officially, Iraqi governments and the Hashemite monarchy proclaimed that all Iraqis belonged to the same nation-state, regardless of their race, religion, or ethnicity.[10] In private correspondence, however, King Faysal pinpointed the diversity in races and religions as the factors that halted the emergence of an independent

---

[8] Simon, *Iraq between Two World Wars*, 76; For further data, see Monroe, *Report of the Education Inquiry Commission*, 97–100. In 1932 Iraq had 276 elementary schools for boys and 49 for girls, in comparison to 124 schools for boys and 27 for girls in 1921. Baghdad, Basra, and Mosul each had one public high school. For accounts of the intellectuals who served as teachers in Iraq, see, e.g., Muhammad Mahdi al-Jawahiri, *Dhirkrayati* (Damascus: Dar al-Rafidayn, 1988), 141–72; Anwar Sha'ul, *Qissat hayati fi wadi al-rafidayn* (Jerusalem: Manshurat rabitat al-jami'iyyin al-yahud al-nazihin min al-'Iraq, 1984), 61–80; Rufa'il Butti, *Dhakira 'Iraqiyya, 1900–1956* (Damascus: al-Mada, 2000), 48–60.

[9] On the demonstrations in favor of the teacher Anis al-Nusuli, the demonstrations against British-Zionist Alfred Mond, and the series of protests that occurred following the signing of the Anglo-Iraqi treaty, see Nur al-Din Masalha, "Faysal's Pan-Arabism, 1921–1932," *Middle Eastern Studies* 27, no. 4 (1991): 683; Hasan Salman, *Safahat min hayat* (Beirut: al-Dar al-'Arabiyya li'l mawsu'at, 1985), 22–24; Nissim Kazzaz, *The Jews of Iraq in the Twentieth Century* [in Hebrew] (Jerusalem: Yad Ben-Tzvi, 1991), 189–91.

[10] Faysal argued that the national principle made obsolete the distinctions between "Muslim," "Christian," and "Jew." On Faysal's speeches on national unity, see Faysal ibn al-Husayn, *Faysal ibn al-Husayn, fi khutubihi wa aqwalihi* (Baghdad: Mudiriyyat al-Di'aya al-'amma, 1946), 247–49; 256–57.

Iraqi nation. "Iraq is a kingdom ruled by an Arab, Sunni government," yet threatened by ignorant Kurdish, Yazidi and Shi'i tribes, which tended to disdain organized government and resented the fact that while they suffered from taxation, leadership positions were reserved for the Sunnis.[11] Sectarian and ethnic differences became visible in the capital because the immigration of poor Shi'is from the south to Baghdad created new slums and caused these populations to be classified as a social problem.[12]

In this context, religious education was associated with perilous sectarianism. The works of the two most influential Iraqi educators, Fadhil al-Jamali (1902–97) and Sati' al-Husri (1862–1968) clarify this attitude.[13] Although they disagreed on a variety of issues, both Jamali and Husri called for the secularization of the education system. Jamali censored the "fundamentalists," namely, the men of religion who objected to modern reforms in education. He viewed the fundamentalists as sectarian and a threat to the very existence of national solidarity because of their loyalty to the literary interpretation of the Qur'an and the *hadith*, as well as their hostility to modern science.[14] Sati' al-Husri constantly called for measures to prevent religious parents from intervening in their children's education and celebrated the secularizing efforts of philosophers like Rousseau, Voltaire, and Diderot.[15]

The modern education system was viewed by Faysal and others as contributing to the formation of a national consciousness among diverse Iraqi populations.[16] Thus, Faysal had sought to minimize *Mujtahids'* power during the 1920s, and Sati' al-Husri attempted to limit sectarian education. Ironically, Husri, whose mother tongue was Turkish and whose vast knowledge of philosophy and political thought was a product of an Ottoman cosmopolitan milieu, underscored the adherence to a stricter national model that emphasized Arab language and history as the sole characteristics of national identity.

---

[11] Muhammad Anis and Muhammad Husayn al-Zubaydi, eds., *Awraq Naji Shawkat* (Baghdad: n.p., 1977), 71–76, 79–80, 93, 100. See also Masalha, "Faysal's Pan-Arabism," 679–93.

[12] On the immigration of Shi'is to Baghdad, see Marion Farouk-Sluglett and Peter Sluglett, *Iraq since 1958: From Revolution to Dictatorship* (London: I. B. Tauris, 2001), 191–93.

[13] Jamali was born in Kazimiyya to a Shiite family. He studied in Najaf and at Baghdad's Teachers Training College (*Dar al-Mu'allimin al-'Aliya*) and later at the American University in Beirut and Columbia University, New York, where he earned a PhD in education. During the interwar period, Jamali served as director general of education (1934, 1940), inspector general of education (1935–36), and director general of public instruction (1937–40). See Simon, *Iraq between Two World Wars*, 84–89, 93–95, 112–14; Yitzhak Nakash, *Shi'is of Iraq* (Princeton, NJ: Princeton University Press, 1994), 112, 125–27; Harry J. Almond, *Iraqi Statesman: A Portrait of Mohammad Fadhel Jamali* (Salem, OR: Grosvenor, 1993). Husri was born in Yemen to a family of Syrian origins. After graduating from the *Mülikiye-mektebi* in Istanbul, he worked as a teacher and administrator in the Balkans and later became the director of Darülmuallimin in Istanbul (1909–12). In Iraq, Husri served as the director general of the Ministry of Education (1921–27) as well as a director of the Ministry of Antiquities (1935–41) and taught at the Teachers Training College (1927–37). See Cleveland, *Making of an Arab Nationalist;* Albert Hourani, *Arabic Thought in the Liberal Age* (London: Oxford University Press, 1962), 312–14; Sylvia Haim, *Arab Nationalism: An Anthology* (Berkeley: University of California Press, 1976), 42–44.

[14] Fadhil al-Jamali, *The New Iraq*, 9, 21–25.

[15] Husri, *Ahadith*, 155–58, 237–57.

[16] Anis and al-Zubaydi, *Awraq*, 71–76; Faysal, *Faysal ibn al-Husayn*, 317–21.

Nevertheless, the fact that Husri was constantly confronted by such Shiʻi intellectuals who worked in the Ministry of Education, like Jamali, Muhammad Madhi al-Jawahiri, and Fahmi al-Mudarrris shows that his views were never universally accepted.[17]

The dual move of secularizing and modernizing the education system occurred in various domains. The first feature of the state's secular education was the emphasis it put on the bodies of the students. In the mid-1930s, clinics were built inside school, and physical education became part of the curriculum as a means for combating moral and physical illness.[18] This move to safeguard the bodies of Iraqi boys and girls was based on Iraqi and British concerns that "the standard of physical fitness in Iraq is regrettably low," which was seen as both contributing to high rates of infant mortality and having "an important [negative] bearing on the moral character of the student."[19] It became commonly accepted that the state should supervise the development of the healthy bodies of students, but differences of opinion remained as to who had the mandate for this—the British, the army, or the Iraqi government—and which institutions should teach Iraqis about health and physical education—the school system, the army, or after-school youth organizations.

The preoccupation with the body was linked to the desire to produce soldiers for the nation's army.[20] In May 1939, the ministry introduced new regulations intended to develop masculine ideals through military training.[21] Each official in the ministry received military titles, and it became mandatory for teachers and students to wear uniforms in schools.[22] The Ministry of Education's bulletin, the New Teacher (Majallat al-Muʻallim al-Jadid), reported on the collaboration between the paramilitary youth organizations, teachers,

---

[17] Husri objected to the attempts of the *mujtahid* Hibbat al-Din al-Sharastani to open a rural school for children of the tribal sheikhs; acted against the Shiʻi theological college, Jamiʻat al al-bayt, headed by the Shiʻi intellectual Fahmi al-Mudarris; fired the Shiʻi poet Muhammad Mahdi al-Jawahiri from the Ministry of Education; and sabotaged the establishment of training colleges in Mosul, fearing that its students would be mostly Christians. See Nakash, *Shiʻis of Iraq*, 112, 251; Simon, *Iraq between Two World Wars*, 85; Sami Zubaida, "The Fragments Imagine the Nation: The Case of Iraq," *International Journal of Middle Eastern Studies* 32 (2002): 205–15.

[18] Salman, *Safahat min hayat*, 34–36.

[19] Memorandum by England's Royal College of Medicine, PRO, FO 624/8/293, no. 2, February 24, 1937; Shawkat, *Ahdafuna*, 79, 56.

[20] Simon (chap. 4) has argued that these practices were influenced by educational models developed in Nazi Germany and Fascist Italy. Both Marr ("Development of Nationalist Ideology in Iraq," 85–87) and Simon (chap. 4) pointed out that Iraqi Sherifians were prone to such ideas because they absorbed German militaristic concepts in Ottoman military academies, like Carl von Clausewitz's glorification of a strong state that educates its soldiers, and Colmar von der Golz's perception of the army as a school fitted for the nation.

[21] On youth movements and health, see Saʻadi Khalil, "General Review of Boys Scouts and Boys[' Education] under Military and Physical Education," *al-Muʻallim al-Jadid* 2 (May 1937): 235–42.

[22] From Houston Boswell (Baghdad) to Halifax (London), PRO, FO 371/23217 no. 246, May 31, 1939.

professors, and students in the performance of public parades, which ex-pressed a feeling of unity and encouraged the students' healthy physiques.[23]

A second feature of Iraq's modern education was the secularization of the educational theories to which teachers were exposed. Texts produced by the Ministry of Education often ignored medieval Islamic theory. Instead, they focused on educational projects in China, Turkey, and especially Mexico, which expanded the basis of its rural education.[24] Sati' al-Husri advocated the works of Pestalozzi, Tolstoy, and Rousseau.[25] Similarly, Fadhil al-Jamali often quoted the educational theories of American educators such as Paul Monroe and John Dewey and attempted to popularize the theory of prag-matism among teachers.[26]

A third feature of the secularized education system was professionalization and specialization (*ikhtisas*). Islamic education was viewed as promoting too broad and unprofessional modes of instruction, while modern education was viewed as divided into particular branches of knowledge. Iraqi officials often regretted the absence of a trained and professional cadre and therefore called for professional instruction.[27]

The fourth element of secularization entailed a new reading of the Islamic past. An attempt was made to present many of the modernizing features of Iraqi education as "Islamic." When women's education became a vital issue, Faysal asserted that Eastern women lagged far behind their American or Anglo-Saxon sisters and, consequently, were in need of education. At the same time, however, he emphasized that the Islamic tradition encouraged women's education.[28]

The ideals of nationalism were likewise presented as belonging to Islamic tradition. The nationalization of the past began with textbooks.[29] Sati' al-Husri maintained that Arabic history books were respectful of other cultures and nations whereas in the West, the few books that did mention Islamic

[23] Nahid 'Abd al-Majid, "General Parade of Boy Scouts and Sportsmanship," *al-Mu'allim al-Jadid* 3 (June 1938): 224–31.

[24] See, e.g., the articles on Mexican education that quoted such books as Saenz Moises and Herbert J. Priestley's *Some Mexican Problems and Lectures on the Harris Foundation* (Chicago: University of Chicago Press, 1926); Frank Tennenbaum, *The Mexican Agrarian Revolution* (Washington, DC: Brookings Insti-tution, 1929). See Najla 'Aqrawi, trans., "The House of the People in Mexico," *al-Mu'allim al-Jadid* 2, no. 1 (February 1937): 69–89; 2, no. 2 (May 1937): 188–201; 2, no. 3–4 (December 1937): 271–79; and 3, no. 2 (April 1938), 115–25.

[25] On Tolstoy, see Husri, *Ahadith*, 283–309; on Pestalozzi, see ibid., 185–218; on Rousseau, see ibid., 219–82.

[26] Fadhil al-Jamali, "John Dewey, the Philosopher Educator," *Middle East Forum* 45 (1969): 75–89.

[27] See Jamali, *The New Iraq*. An essay published in the cultural magazine *al-Yaqin*, e.g., championed a professional study of history. It elucidated that medieval historians like Muhammad ibn Jarir al-Tabari (d. AH 310/AD 922) viewed history as a sequence of events, pieced together without any particular order. It was only in the nineteenth century that the rational study of history excluded myths from historical writings and gave birth to the science of history (*'ilm al-ta'rikh*); *al-Yaqin*, no. 17 (February 17, 1923).

[28] Faysal, *Faysal ibn al-Husayn*, 332–33.

[29] On textbooks, see Dawn, "Formation of Pan-Arab Ideology."

history did it only in passing and usually condescendingly. He therefore objected to the supervision of the League of Nations or the British on Iraqi textbooks and claimed that Iraqi teachers could not use French or British textbooks, since these reflected the disparaging outlook of these colonizing nations.[30] The Ministry of Education sponsored the writing of Iraqi textbooks and imported similar texts from other Arab countries.[31] Moreover, Iraqi as well as Palestinian and Syrian educators gave prominence to what Ernest Dawn termed the "Semito-Arab nation," as they portrayed the struggles between the Arab-Muslims and their enemies (the Sassanians or the Byzantines) as a battle between the Semites and Aryans and between the East and the West.[32] The physician Sami Shawkat, who served as a director general of education (1931–33, 1940–42) and minister of education (1940) highlighted the period of the *futuhat*, namely, the period of the Arab occupation of the Middle East, and celebrated the heroic deeds of its military commanders. Shakwat likewise emphasized that the empire created by the Arabs thrived by granting equality and full rights to whoever adopted the Arabic language.[33]

Although these narratives presented a nationalized, Arabized version of Islamic history, they synthesized colonial perceptions as well. Sami Shawkat referred to Disraeli as a great imperial administrator, equal to the Caliph 'Umar ibn al-Khattab (who ruled 634–44 CE); he drew parallels between the fine character of Englishman and Arab; and he concluded a collection of essays published by the Ministry of Education with a translation of Rudyard Kipling's (1865–1936) "If."[34] Semitic/Aryan, East/West binaries were fused with Kipling's poems and the history of the *futuhat* into a national Iraqi historiography of a glorious Islamic past that fitted both global politics and the internal needs of Iraq. During this period the British and France dominated the Arab Middle East (whether directly or indirectly), while Germany, Japan, and Italy began their own imperial campaigns. These narratives demonstrated to Iraqi students that the Arabs, just like their colonizers, once had an empire of their own—an empire that had been far superior to modern-day Western empires.

In producing and conveying national identities, educators and other officials paid special attention to groups deemed unaware of being part of the Iraqi community, such as Iraq's tribesmen and Bedouins, who were mainly Shi'i. Although both the national elites and the British viewed the Bedouins

---

[30] Sati' al-Husri, *Abhath mukhtara fi'l qawmiyya al-'Arabiyya* (Beirut: Dar al-Quds, 1974), 386–409.

[31] For example, the textbook *Our History in a Narrative Form* [Ta'rikhuna fi uslub qisasi] defined its goal as creating young Arab nationalists by the teaching of a simplified version of the past. See Akram Zu'aytar and Darwish al-Miqdadi, *Tarikhuna bi-uslub qasasi* (Beirut: Maktabat al-Kashshaf, 1939). A review of the book in *Istiqlal* praised the textbook, which was taught in Iraq, as being both inspiring and accurate. See *Istiqlal*, no. 3512, November 24, 1939, 2.

[32] Dawn, "Formation of Pan-Arab Ideology," 67–91.

[33] Shawkat, *Ahdafuna*, 5–6, 34–35, 58; on the virtues of the Arab conquerors in comparison to other empires, see "Editorial," *Istiqlal*, no. 3345, September 4, 1939, 4.

[34] Shawkat, *Ahdafuna*, 16, 78, 101.

as ignorant and hostile to political order, educators sought to discipline the tribes, both nomads and settled peasants, so that they would become part of the nation and its army.[35] This led to a renewed interest in the Bedouins and their history and inspired a new literature that examined the formation of tribal communities in Iraq. Tribal revolts and the immigration of tribal members to Baghdad produced rather negative stereotypes of the tribesmen as criminal, fatalistic, emotional, and illiterate. In many cases, such depictions reproduced orientalist images, emphasizing the unchanging nature of the tribesman. These narratives depicted the immigration of the tribesmen to Baghdad as harmful and underscored the urgent need to educate these populations in their local habitat. Jamali referred to Ibn Khaldun's (1332–1406) theory that introducing the Bedouins to city life led to their degeneracy and corruption; Jamali himself, however, held that if they were educated first, these negative side effects could be averted.[36]

Iraqi educators, however, did not adopt the negative colonial stance in its entirety. As nationalists, they felt that their mission was also to pinpoint and herald the remarkable qualities of the tribes, such as bravery, loyalty, and generosity. Their illiteracy, for instance, made them closer to the desert culture of pre-Islamic Arabia, as epitomized in their capacity to memorize poetry and Qur'anic verses.[37] When postulating various options for the education of the tribesmen, many writers, most notably Jamali, devised teaching programs that would capitalize on these extraordinary merits. Unlike Sunni educators, Jamali saw the Shi'i background of the majority of the tribes as advantageous. He celebrated the religious schools in Najaf that allowed students the freedom to choose their professors and cultivated a learning atmosphere centered on discussion and personal bonds between pupil and instructor. The Shi'i legal doctrine, in whose tradition the gates of independent jurisprudence (*ijtihad*) remained unlocked, allowed for a religious approach that was "harmonious with the changing times."[38] Although many positive assertions concerning the tribes were backed by updated studies from the Western academia, Islamic medieval literature was also used to construct these positive images. The Islamic past was thus synthesized into the colonial present in order to identify the fine character of Iraq's tribes and the ways to discipline them.

---

[35] On peasants and tribes in Iraq, see "Resolutions of the Rural Education Conference in Lebanon (2–7/September/1937)," *al-Mu'allim al-Jadid* 3–4 (December 1937): 362–64; 'Abd al-Majid Mahmud, "The School and Rural Reform," *al-Mu'allim al-Jadid* 1, no. 2 (June 1935): 221–24. On the formation of tribal communities, see Abbas 'Azzawi, *'Asha'ir al-'Iraq*, vol. 1 (Baghdad: Matba'at Baghdad); vol. 2 (Baghdad: Matba'at al-Ma'arif); vols. 3–4 (Baghdad: Sharikat al-Tijara wa'l tiba'a, 1937–57), and see also his *Ta'rikh al-Yazidiyya wa-asl 'aqidatihim* (Baghdad: Matba'at Baghdad, 1935).

[36] Jamali, *The New Iraq*, 95; see also Ibn Khaldun, *The Muqaddimah: An Introduction to History*, trans. from the Arabic by Franz Rosenthal; abridged and ed. N. J. Dawood (Princeton, NJ: Princeton University Press, 1989).

[37] Jamali, *The New Iraq*, 47.

[38] Ibid., 88–89.

Iraqi educators firmly believed that education was crucial in order to impress upon various segments of the population—tribesmen and city dwellers, Shi'i and Sunni—the existence of the Iraqi nation and its importance. As the irrationality of the colonized served to justify the historical necessity of the civilizing mission, educators acknowledged that certain Iraqi traditions were indeed archaic, yet at the same time they highlighted the positive aspects of Islamic and Iraqi culture.[39] They utilized the Islamic past in order to produce a romantic national history and a romanticized vision of Iraq's tribes. Although the national understanding of the past was profoundly affected by colonial ideas, these concepts were often used to strengthen the objectives of Arab and Iraqi nationalism. This hybridized national synthesis, which was assembled from various sources, sustained modern disciplinary institutions, bequeathed the Iraqis with a past, and afforded them the potential for a bright future.

Challenges to the Education System—Maintaining Disorder

Educators faced many challenges in the newly constructed Iraqi education system. To begin with, their students possessed the power to interpret the Islamic past in their own unique ways. Novelist Mahmud Ahmad al-Sayyid depicts an educator's experience in one of his short stories:

> From all the sciences [offered] in his elementary school, [the teacher] elected to teach history and geography. He defied the ordinary practices of the Ministry of Education when he taught these subjects. When he spoke to his students, he would, for example, blend the ancient Islamic glory with the new Arab and Islamic grandeur that, in his mind, should follow the Arab Revolt. . . . He was mistaken. He imagined he would create students according to his desires, but he found them to be neglectful, thinking he was recounting tales for their amusement, killing their time. When the day of examination came, few of them succeeded in his classes. . . . He appeared not to know that students were children, who could not envisage what he had conceived, and were inept to long for what he had desired.[40]

The teacher, despite his desire to connect the Islamic past to the present, discovers that his students are less than enthusiastic about such stories.

Similarly, Sati' al-Husri describes how his son, Khaldun, returned from school to inform his father that he learned how the angel Gabriel came to the prophet Muhammad in the form of a dog. Further inquiry revealed that the child misunderstood the name "Dihya al-Kalbi," the man who narrated the story about Gabriel, to be *ha'yat al-kalabi* (form of dog). This episode caused Husri to conclude that regardless of the teachers' aims, the imagination of children, as well as their interpretations of texts based on their

---

[39] I am paraphrasing here Partha Chatterjee, *The Nation and Its Fragments: Colonial and Postcolonial Histories* (Princeton, NJ: Princeton University Press, 1993), 55.

[40] Mahmud Ahmad al-Sayyid, *Al-A'mal al-kamila li Mahmud Ahmad al-Sayyid* (Baghdad: Dar al-hurriyya, 1978), 352.

perception of language, remained more powerful and significant than the narratives and interpretations offered to them by their teachers.[41] 'Ali Tantawi, a Syrian professor of literature in the Teachers Training College, also cautioned literature teachers not to assume that their profession had specific rules. Good teachers accepted ideas from students and did not force upon them prescribed notions of aesthetics. He recalled that as a child, his teachers assigned him poor grades in composition because they felt that he should describe a garden according to familiar patterns and frowned on his own independent descriptions.[42] All three intellectuals—al-Sayyid, Husri, and Tantawi—thus emphasize the importance of students' interpretations rather than those of their teachers.

Another challenge was the lack of a unified and cohesive vision of reform or agreement as to the ways to nationalize the Islamic past. Although the director general of the Ministry of Education was usually Sunni (Husri for most of the period), the minister was often Shi'i. At times, this created a clash of interests on certain issues leading to very slow implementation of policies.[43] An additional challenge arose because many educators were not always willing to accept a unified nationalized version of their past. The focus on the Arab empire and the *futuhat* was problematic in the Shi'i context because the list of imperial Arab heroes included the Umayyads as well as individuals like 'Amr ibn al-As or the Caliph Mu'awiya (who ruled 661–80 CE), who were depicted in a very negative light in Shi'i history. The choice of this period, which signified the most important division between Sunnis and 'Alids, made the creation of a unified past impossible. The Umayyads, for instance, served as the perfect example of an Arab empire, yet at the same time, their glorification aroused the anger of the Shi'is. In 1928, Anis al-Nusuli, a Syrian teacher, published a book in Baghdad on the history of the Umayyads. The account was very pro-Umayyad, with little sympathy for the Prophet's slain grandson, Husayn, and this provoked much anger among Iraqi intellectuals, mostly Shi'is. Interestingly, many educators invoked the notion of freedom of speech in Nusuli's defense, while the Shi'is and Sunnis who attacked the publication argued that the work was not scientific and ignored important historical evidence. Therefore, although this debate could have been sectarian at its core, it was framed in terms of the modern concepts of scientific research and rights of free speech.[44]

The presence of Egyptian professors in the Teachers Training College

[41] Husri, "*Ahadith*," 143–44.

[42] 'Ali Tantawi, "Arabic Literature in the Iraqi Schools," *al-Mu'allim al-Jadid* 2 (May 1937): 201–8.

[43] For example, while Jamali and Husri accepted Ibn Khaldun as a theoretical basis for some of their research and arguments, Shawkat rejected his inclusion in the curriculum. Whereas Shawkat advocated martyrdom for the sake of the nation, Husri rejected such ideas and was especially disgusted by these ideas coming from a physician such as Shawkat. On the debates within the ministry, see Simon, *Iraq between Two World Wars*, 112–14.

[44] Nakash, *Shi'is of Iraq*, 114; Masalha, "Faysal's Pan-Arabism," 683; Salman, *Safahat*, 22–24.

further complicated the nature of instruction. A liberal, antifascist agenda was promulgated by the Egyptian literary critics Zaki Mubarak and Ahmad Hasan al-Zayyat and the legal theorist 'Abd al-Razzaq al-Sanhuri, who all lived in Iraq during this period.[45] Zayyat opposed the introduction of militarism into the Iraqi school system and specifically the introduction of uniforms into classrooms.[46] Mubarak criticized the idea of knowledge specialization, which was a major domain of Iraqi modernization of education. He believed that although specialized education aimed at producing professionals like doctors, mathematicians, and lawyers, it encouraged narrow-mindedness, as "an engineer should consider esthetics in his work, and a lawmaker should take into account mathematics and medicine." Mubarak argued that the scholars of the Middle Ages (e.g., Aristotle, Plato, Ibn Sina, and al-Jahiz), as well as such modern luminaries as the reformer Muhammad 'Abduh (1849–1905), dealt with numerous fields of knowledge and were not specialists.[47] Although Iraq and Egypt faced different problems concerning their national identities, both Egyptians and Iraqis were part of the same community of discourse. Iraqis published essays in Egyptian magazines, and intellectuals like Husri and al-Jamali were very attentive to the views of their Egyptian peers.

The diversity in teachers and educational methods often produced a diversity of students. During the interwar period, the Teachers Training College (established 1927) was one of the few academic venues in which students interested in the humanities could obtain a higher degree.[48] For this reason, middle-class men, influenced by communism and socialism, were trained as teachers. Although those teachers were supposed to implement the schemes of the Ministry of Education in their classrooms, they often reversed, transformed, and reformed official discourses.[49] Sasson Somekh, a former student of the Jewish high school, Shammash, recalls his Shi'i teacher in the late

[45] On the anti-Fascist camp in Egypt, see Israel Gershoni, "Beyond Anti-Semitism: Egyptian Responses to German Nazism and Italian Fascism in the 1930s," EIU Working Papers, Mediterranean Programme Series, RSS no. 32 (2001). On the life of Egyptian intellectuals in Iraq, see Zaki Mubarak, *Layla al-mardia fi'l 'Iraq: Ta'rikh yufassil Waqa'i' Layla bayna al-Qahira wa-Baghdad min sanat 1926 ila sanat 1938* (Beirut: al-Maktaba al-'asriyya, 1976), *Wahy Baghdad* (Cairo: al-Maktaba al-'asriyya, 1938), and *Malamih al-mujtama' al-'Iraqi: Kiaab yusawwiru al-'Iraq fi madhahibih al-adabiyya wa'l-qawmiyya wa'l-ijtima'iyya* (Cairo: Matba'at Amin 'Abd al-Rahman, 1942).

[46] *Risala*, August 28, 1935.

[47] Mubarak, *Wahy Baghdad*, 101–6.

[48] During the interwar period, Iraqis could attend a number of higher institutions: the Law College (established 1908), the Medical College (1927), the Pharmacy College (1936), and the College for Engineering (1942). Marr, *The Modern History of Iraq*, 137–38.

[49] The communist Husayn al-Shabibi, the social-democrat 'Abd al-Fattah Ibrahim, as well as some founding members of the Communist Party ('Abd al-Hamid al-Khatib, Nuri Rufa'il, Madhi Hashim, and Sami Nadir Mustafa), were all employed as teachers by the state during the 1930s and 1940s. The social democrat Muhammad Hadid was a professor at the Teachers Training College, and Jewish liberal intellectuals like Anuwar Sha'ul, Murad Mikha'il, and Ezra Haddad worked as teachers during the 1930s. See Hanna Batatu, *The Old Social Classes and the Revolutionary Movements of Iraq* (Princeton, NJ: Princeton University Press, 1978), 416–21; Sha'ul, *Qissat*, 61–80.

1940s: "We were given a sort of civics class called 'the conditions of Iraq' (*Ahwal al-'Iraq*). . . . The instructor of this subject was Muhammad Sharara, . . . Sharara, however, was not a disciplined teacher. . . . He lectured his explicit leftist opinions to us and in every class, we would hear expressions like 'imperialism,' 'class exploitation', 'fake parliament'. He frequently talked about our cultural backwardness and the great gaps between the wealthy, on the one hand, and the millions of peasants and workers, on the other."[50]

More generally, the intellectuals associated with the Left argued that the state focused on the glorious Islamic past or the positive characters of the tribes in order to avoid discussing the troubled present in which the landed elites manipulated Iraq's resources. The newspaper of Iraq's social-democratic party, *al-Ahali* (founded in 1932), promoted a Fabian, social-democratic agenda that extolled education as a mechanism capable of engendering social change. *Al-Ahali*'s secularism initially positioned the group in support of the state's secularizing efforts. The Iraqi teaching methodologies, they argued, were still rooted in the previous centuries and in the religious education system. As such it was a system based on memorization that was not relevant to the milieu or lifestyle of the students.[51] Nevertheless, many writers opposed the view that education should serve as a preparatory institution for the military or to the participation of students in demonstrations organized by the government.[52] In 1933, *al-Ahali* established the Society for Combating Illiteracy (*Jam'iyat mukafahat al-'umiyya*) that intended to mimic educational attempts conducted in Turkey, Russia, Italy, Mexico, and China, in which intellectuals cooperated with the government to provide better rural education. The society included social democrats, as well as nationalists, politicians, and famous journalists, actors, and writers.[53]

'Abd al-Fattah Ibrahim, a young socialist affiliated with *al-Ahali*, who held a master's degree from Columbia University, indirectly attacked the ways in which the past was taught in schools. Ibrahim characterized romanticized nationalism as subordinated to a narrative form (*uslub qisasi*) and felt that the notion of history as the outcome of the deeds performed by great men was terribly outmoded. This narrative stance, he believed, was rooted in European individualism and laissez-faire ideology, portraying individuals as striving to achieve economic and political independence while still being tied to their nations. Based on his reading of historical materialism, albeit without

---

[50] Sassom Somekh, *Baghdad, Yesterday* [in Hebrew] (Tel Aviv: Ha-Kibutz ha-Me'uhad, 2004), chap. 10.

[51] On *Ahali*, see Muzaffar 'Abd Allah al-Amin, *Jama'at al-Ahali: Nushu'ha, 'aqidatuha, wa-dawruha fi'l siyasa al-'Iraqiyya, 1932–1946* (Beirut: al-Mu'assasa al-'Arabiyya li'l Dirasat wa'l nashr; Amman: Dar al-faris, 2001), 383–86; Fu'ad Husayn al-Wakil, *Jam'at al-ahali fi'l 'Iraq, 1932–1937*, 2nd ed. (Baghdad: al-Jumhuriyya al-'Iraqiyya,Wizarat al-Thaqafa wa'l I'lam, 1980).

[52] *Al-Ahali*, nos. 1–2, January 2, 1932. Regarding students in demonstrations organized by the government, see *al-Ahali*, March 3, 1932, discussed at Wakil, *Jam'at al-ahali fi'l 'Iraq*, 383–286.

[53] On the need to battle illiteracy, see *al-Ahali*, no. 39, February 26, 1932, 1; see also Wakil, *Jam'at al-ahali fi'l 'Iraq*, 125–27. On the society, see Wakil, *Jam'at al-ahali fi'l 'Iraq*, 124–35, 150–51; Amin, *Jama'at al-Ahali*, no. 86, 200–209.

mentioning Marx's name, Ibrahim criticized the Ministry of Education for producing histories that emphasized historical heroes and were nothing more than dated, nationalized literary narratives.[54]

The communists likewise critiqued Iraqi education. They, too, called for a secular system that would discount sectarian and economic differences. Following the training of the party's leader, Yusuf Salman Yusuf (Fahd) (1901–49) in the Soviet Union, the communists adopted the perception of the educator as a Leninist revolutionary, since education to them was a means to both organize and revolutionize the masses.[55] The essays of one of the party's leading intellectuals, Husayn Muhammad al-Shabibi (1914–49), illustrate this approach. Shabibi viewed the educational activities of the "Brothers of Purity" (Ikhwan al-safa') as an example of an intellectual group that was able to peacefully revolutionize society and teach its unorthodox dogma through an encyclopedia of their philosophical beliefs. The secretive propagation of knowledge appealed to the image of the Iraqi communist educator striving to challenge orthodoxies. The Shi'i communist thus appropriated the historical accounts of the Brothers of Purity but used them to challenge, not support, the national perception of the past.[56]

The nationalists dominated the educational field in the interwar period, yet the new literati classes affiliated with the Left, although members of small groups, were highly significant. Their criticism of the education system was as sophisticated as Husri's or Jamali's, as exemplified in the writings of 'Abd al-Fattah Ibrahim. After 1941, and in particular in the 1950s, many Iraqi intellectuals were inspired by the views of social democrats and communists, who published their early works already during the 1930s and 1940s.[57]

Dhu Nun Ayyub: The Uneducated Educator

Through his short stories and novels, the teacher Dhu Nun Ayyub (1908–88) criticized the programs of the education ministry and encouraged resistance to the state's modernizing attempts. Ayyub was born in Mosul, where he received his elementary and secondary education. He later moved to Baghdad to study math in the Teachers Training College. Despite his excellent school record, his requests to be included in educational missions abroad were repeatedly rejected—officially, due to his poor health. Ayyub,

[54] 'Abd al-Fattah Ibrahim, "The Scope and the Philosophy of History," *al-Mu'allim al-Jadid* 3 (April 1938): 94–94, and "Aims and Methods of History," *al-Mu'allim al-Jadid* 3 (June 1938): 179–86.

[55] On Fahd's views, see Yusuf Salman Yusuf (Fahd), *Kitabat al-Rafiq Fahd* (Baghdad: al-Tariq al-Jadid, 1976).

[56] Sabah 'Ali al-Shahir, "On the Role of the Party in Iraqi Literature," *al-Thaqafa al-Jadida* 103 (1978): 96–101.

[57] Batatu, *Old Social Classes*, 389–403; Leftist novelists like Mahmud Ahmad al-Sayyid, who addressed educational themes in their writings, were revered by later generations for their pioneering thinking. On al-Sayyid, see 'Ali Jawad al-Tahir, *Mahmud Ahmad al-Sayyid: Ra'id al-qissa al-haditha fi'l 'Iraq* (Beirut: Dar al-Adab, 1969).

however, felt that the rejections stemmed from his affiliation with the Left and his unorthodox views. Upon graduation from the Teachers Training College, he worked as a math teacher in various districts. He was initially affiliated with the Iraqi Communist Party but was banished from its ranks in 1942 due to disagreements with its leader, Fahd. In the years 1937–39, he published a few collections of short stories. In 1939, his first novel, *Doctor Ibrahim* (Duktur Ibrahim), was published.[58]

Doctor Ibrahim tells the story of Ibrahim, a son of rural *'alim*, who obtains a PhD in agriculture from London University. Ruthless yet astute, Ibrahim becomes a high-ranking official and the most sought-after persona in Baghdadi salons and political gatherings. The novel, whose chapters were first serialized in *al-Majalla*, created an uproar at the time of its publication. It was published after Ayyub was punished and demoted from his position as a Baghdadi teacher and ordered to work in the provinces, following the publication of his collection of short stories, *The Tower of Babylon*, which was officially condemned by the Ministry of Education. Literary critics, as well as contemporary readers, have suggested that Ibrahim's character was modeled on that of Fadhil al-Jamali.[59]

The novel criticizes several aspects of Iraqi education. First, it shows that the attempts of the system to secularize its students were unsuccessful. Ibrahim's father initially objects to his son studying in the city, the center of heresy, but Ibrahim does manage to study in Mosul where, under the guidance of his mostly Turkish teaching staff, he learns to question the religious beliefs of his father. Nevertheless, when Ibrahim returns to his village, he recognizes that his father, who worked at a local shrine, would loose his livelihood if the villagers abandon religion. Ibrahim, therefore, prefers to conceal his own secularism.[60] *Doctor Ibrahim*, then, does not present the secularizing effects of education as a positive change, since Ibrahim's generation cynically sanctifies religion, recognizing that it is the power that secures capital and sociopolitical hegemony.

The text also criticizes the division of knowledge into specific branches acquired through professional training. Ibrahim's diploma is frequently mentioned in the novel and is included in its title. The degree ensures Ibrahim

---

[58] On Ayyub, see Dhu Nun Ayyub, *Qissat hayatihi bi-qalamihi* (Vienna: n.p., 1980), his autobiography; 'Aziz al-Hajj, *Abu Hurayra al-Mawsili* (London: Riyad al-Rayyis, 1990); 'Abd al-Ilah Ahmed, *Nash'at al-qissa wa-tatawwuruha fi'l 'Iraq, 1908–1939* (Baghdad: Matba'at Shafiq, 1969), 257–87, and *al-Adab al-'Iraqi mundhu al-harb al-'alamiyya al-thaniyya* (Damascus: Itihad al-kuttab al-'Arab, 2001), 271–307; 'Umar Talib, *Al-Fann al-Qasai fi'l 'Iraq al-hadith* (Baghdad: Maktabat al-Andalus, 1971), 281–318. For an insightful and innovative reading of *Doctor Ibrahim*, see Mushin J. Musawi, *Reading Iraq: Culture and Power in Conflict* (London: I. B. Tauris, 2006), 6, 19, 62, 72, 99, 116–77, 120–21, 136.

[59] 'Abd al-Ilah Ahmed, *Nash'at al-qissa wa-tatawwuruha fi'l 'Iraq*, 287–88; Talib, *Al-Fann al-Qasai fi'l 'Iraq al-hadith*, 282–83. These literary critics noted the following similarities: both Ibrahim and Jamali studied abroad, both married foreign wives, both championed professionalism, and both had links to the Shi'i communities of the south.

[60] Dhu Nun Ayyub, *Al-Athar al-kamila li-adab Dhi al-Nun Ayyub* (Baghdad: Wizarat al-i'lam, 1978), 3:87.

the esteem of colleagues, and he uses it to portray himself as a professional who is capable of devising important plans for the future of Iraq. Ibrahim's critics fault him for lacking any real knowledge of the country's social conditions and insinuate that he does not possess the essential qualities of a thinking man, namely, desire to work for the community as well as curiosity and inquisitiveness.[61] The criticism implied here is that Ibrahim and his cohorts abuse their academic expertise to perpetuate corrupt norms, rather than using their education and knowledge to better Iraq's social and political realities.

The nationalization of the Islamic past is satirized in the novel. From his historical inquiries, Ibrahim learns to admire the Umayyad Caliph Mu'awiya. The Prophet Muhammad, Ibrahim contends, was a spiritual leader who battled barbarism, exploitation, and egoism. His followers, like Khalid ibn al-Walid, felt obligated to wage war against tyranny and destroyed thrones that supported injustice. Mu'awiya, however, patiently anticipated the opportunity to assume political power and to exploit the empire's economic resources. Moreover, he was not above such nefarious means as bribery and murder to consolidate his power, means that he employed in the name of Islam—even though Islam emerged in reaction to such reprehensible norms.[62] While Iraqi-Sunni educators emphasized the positive features of the Umayyad dynasty to highlight the virtues of an early Arab empire, Ibrahim portrayed Mu'awiya as the sort of Machiavellian genius who justified in the name of Islam those very actions against which the founders of Islam rebelled.

Another feature of Iraqi education parodied in the novel is its racism. Referring to an actual club called al-Muthanna (named after al-Muthanna ibn Haritha), the text describes a club that was created by figures in the Ministry of Education who wished to solve the problems of the Arab nation. These individuals "believed in the themes of race [literally, damm (blood)], which Hitler had established, and applied their principles to discriminate between a genuine Arab and a false one." This obsession with race initially alarms Ibrahim, predominantly because his father has Persian origins and his wife holds British citizenship. His fears evaporate, however, once he comprehends that most of club members who tout the "Arab race doctrine" are sons of former Ottoman bureaucrats and themselves are not pure Arabs but even of mixed Turkish descent.[63] He thus becomes an Arab nationalist:

> In my turn, I asked to join the club, and began my service in the national field by delivering a splendid lecture on the fine virtues of the Arab race, and its destruction by assimilation with other races. I explicated racist and chauvinistic theories, affirming that, presently, they have scientific value. I exemplified this with Hitler's categorization of nations according to their races and capacities. I verified this with

[61] Ayyub, *Al-Athar al-kamila li-adab Dhi al-Nun Ayyub*, 3:140, 141–46.
[62] Ibid., 3:81–82.
[63] Ibid., 3:161–62.

the actions of Hitler and Mussolini and [demonstrated] how these two leaders revived their countries in a short period of time, and brought such a revival to its utmost power. The room was shaken by applause and the newspapers cited this speech, interpreted it, and pointed out my excellent nationalism and warm patriotism. Some even added that I belonged to the tribes of northern Iraq that are the purest of Arabs, that my father was one of the sheikhs of the genuine Arab tribes of Shamar; and that I was a *sayyid*, with the pedigree of the prophet, and subsequently, there should be no wonder as to my zealous support of Arabism.[64]

Mocking the nationalist spirit of the Ministry of Education, the text unmasks the ease with which the title "Arab" is bestowed, to suggest that Iraq's ethnic differences were constructed linguistically in a particular sociopolitical context. Ayyub felt that Iraq, a nation and a crossroad of three peoples—Turks, Arabs, and Persians—must reject the hideous concepts of racism and racial purity, which were created by the Nazis to battle the Jews and the opposition.[65] Ayyub's perception of diversity in society is very different from that of nationalist educators, who advocated national unity through discipline. Ayyub, on the contrary, celebrated the diversity of the Iraqi nation and thought that this diversity should be represented in the education system.

Another important feature of Ayyub's writings is preoccupation with the body, but his message differs from the ministry's goal of cultivating the body to create strong soldiers and families blessed with many healthy children. Ayyub, however, places the fostering of a healthy physique in a homosocial context in which men (friends, pupils, and comrades) admire each other's bodies. For instance, Ayyub's collection of short stories entitled *My Friend* (Sadiqi) portrays the various friends of the narrator and his complicated relationship with them. His ideal man is blessed with a muscular and strong body yet is unmarried, perhaps to denote his resistance to social norms (Ayyub himself also never married). The hero of the story "The Anthem of the Eagles" (Nashid al-nusur) is attracted both to his friend, who is a pilot, and to the pilot's wife, who is despondent by her husband's long absence from home due to his patriotic duties. In their youth, the pilot's physical strength and beauty caused his classmates to gaze at his body "with a combination of adoration and jealousy" during physical education classes.[66] The adulation of the strong body, however, succeeds only partially. It has indeed given rise to a national hero who battles the enemy for the motherland. Yet the adoration of the body by the pilot's friend triggers a relationship that endangers the heterosexual family. The story, nevertheless, ends when the pilot's airplane crashes and his beautiful body is burned and charred. The text, quite tellingly, identifies the inherent contradiction of the education system that, on the

---

[64] Ibid., 3:162.

[65] See, e.g., Ayyub's positions as depicted in the story "At the Top of the Tower," in ibid., 1:427–35.

[66] Ibid., 1:189–96.

one hand, promotes the human body yet, on the other hand, leads to its annihilation in war.[67]

For Ayyub, one of the important elements of challenging the education system is located in the students themselves and in their ability to reinterpret the practices of the Ministry of Education. In the autobiographical short story, "The Fools' Conspiracy" (Mu'amarat al-aghbiya), Ayyub narrates the educational odyssey of a young Iraqi intellectual, Nuh, whom we meet in the fourth grade and accompany until he begins writing stories. At 10 years of age, Nuh is attracted to stories told in coffeehouses and imagines himself a hero equal to such popular figures as 'Antra or Abu Zayd al-Hilali. Nuh and his friend 'Adnan use such stories as a refuge from their tedious history lessons: "While the history teacher was insipidly delivering the lesson, Nuh and 'Andnan hid their heads behind a corpulent student and began discussing the stories they had heard the previous night, protected from the evil of the teacher whose terrorizing eyes oversaw the classroom, as they might find a mischievous student."[68]

Another student tells Nuh about handwritten manuscripts in his house, and the friends meet daily to read them. Nuh deciphers the handwriting while mimicking the narration techniques of the storytellers. Obsessed with reading, Nuh nonetheless fails in his studies. His teacher, however, gives him a historical novel by Jurji Zaydan (1861–1914), titled *The Maidens of Quraysh* ('Adhra' Quraysh), promising him that this book will be far superior to anything he had read previously. The teacher promises Nuh that he will supply him with such texts if he passes his exams. Further deals take place, and Nuh becomes an excellent student. Nevertheless, when a local religious scholar discovers Nuh's books and grumbles, This is how teachers spoil our students! They accustom them to contemptible practices instead of reading the Qur'an, tales about righteous men and religious sciences. Had Nuh read more about saints in place of these foolish books and utterances of such heretics, he would have been a righteous man by now! The conspiracy to destroy Nuh's happiness, plotted by this "turban-wearing monkey," is reinforced by Nuh's father, who shouts at his wife: "The fault is on your head, corrupt woman. Had you not accustomed him from his youth to hear such stories, he would have become a righteous man by now!"[69] Nuh's schoolmaster, however, convinces the father not to squash his son's inquisitive spirit on the advice of an ignorant man. Nuh now turns to reading novels by Doyle,

[67] Similar approaches were conveyed in Ayyub's memoirs. He recalls that as a child, he was so emaciated and weak that his physician was convinced he would not survive beyond age 20. In the classroom, the frail Ayyub found refuge from his sickness in friendship with children who did not look like him. He fell in love with one of his friends, "a handsome green-eyed youth." This platonic, asexual love was the "spiritual delicacy" of his childhood. He confesses that he had a friend like this in every school he attended. See Hajj, *Abu Hurayra al-Mawsili*, 43.

[68] Ayyub, *Al-Athar al-kamila li-adab Dhi al-Nun Ayyub*, 295.

[69] Ibid., 300–301.

Foe, Dumas, Scott, and Haggard; he finds additional friends in the likes of Sherlock Holmes, Tarzan, and the Count of Monte Cristo. As he grows older, the texts change and he turns to Ibn Khaldun, Marx and Freud. He discovers that he enjoys reading any text, "even a children's tale," not for amusement and the passing of time but for the pleasure of researching it.[70] Upon graduating his academic studies he is appointed as a clerk in one of the government offices, where his love of reading saves him once more from the monotony entailed in his position, yet it makes him realize that "patriotism is a meaningless noun, nationalism means constructing a few ornamented buildings for a small number of people, and *shu'ubiyya*, populism (*sha'biyya*), and communism (*shuyu'iyya*) all signify the same meaning."[71]

The importance of independent inquiry by students as an alternative to state-produced texts is prominent in this coming-of-age story. For Ayyub, writing and reading outside the classroom caused students to become independent thinkers. Nuh favors popular tales like *Sirat Sayf bin Dhi Yazan*, *Sirat Bani Hilal*, or *The Arabian Nights*. Such stories were told by musicians, poets, and storytellers who enjoyed the freedom to change a classical, well-known plot a little, as opposed to the authority of the written text.[72] In Nuh's mind, these stories connote family and warmth, as they are associated with stories he heard from his mother and from the women in the house. Most important, the popular texts are presented as an interesting alternative to the dreary history lesson, suggesting that storytellers offered a more imaginative perception of history and sparked the imagination of their young listeners. Islamic history, then, is not mediated through the schools and textbooks, but rather through local and popular institutions.

The story portrays different kinds of teachers: while the history professor is dull and violent, the schoolmaster and the teacher who gives Nuh the novels are depicted as Nuh's liberators. The historical novels of Jurji Zaydan, the renowned Lebanese intellectual, publisher, and historian, included stories from the *Arabian Nights* as well as historical accounts from such sources as the writings of Tabari and Ibn Khaldun. Ayyub suggests that teachers utilize such novels as educational means. The historical novels of Zaydan were popular in Iraq and led to a series of local imitators. However, they also provoked much opposition not only in Iraq but also in Egypt for their secular and disrespectful approach to Islamic history.[73] The opposition between the "pro-

---

[70] For the texts Ayyub read as a child, see Hajj, *Abu Hurayra al-Mawsili*, 50–51; Talib, *Al-Fann al-Qasai fi'l 'Iraq al-hadith*, 261.

[71] Ayyub refers here to the fact that three very different concepts (*shu'ubiyya/sha'biyya/shuyu'iyya*) sound the same. The association in sound may indicate also an association in content, because in the Iraqi public sphere ideas tend to be emptied from their meanings. See Ayyub, *Al-Athar al-kamila li-adab Dhi al-Nun Ayyub*, 1:289–318.

[72] On popular narrative, see Bridget Connelly, *Arab Folk Epic and Identity* (Berkeley: University of California Press, 1986); Harry Norris, "Introduction," in *The Adventures of Sayf ben Dhi Yazan: An Arab Folk Epic*, ed. and trans. Lena Jayyusi (Bloomington: Indiana University Press, 1996).

[73] On Zaydan, see Thomas Philipp, *Ğurği Zaidan, His Life and Thought* (Wiesbaden: Steiner, 1979).

Zaydan" teacher and the religious man thus bestows upon the teacher the secularizing role of narrating history in a nonreligious manner. Nevertheless, the antitheses in the story are not between secular teachers and religious students but rather between people who read/write/narrate interesting narratives (Nuh, his mother, his teacher, the schoolmaster, the storytellers, Zaydan) and people who either produce boring narratives or seek to eliminate narration altogether (the history professor, the father, the religious man). The teacher who introduces Zaydan to Nuh seems to be a mediator between the stories of Nuh's mother, the storytellers, and the history books. Just as the teacher in Najaf became a part of the society to which he initially felt ill at ease, the teacher here understood Nuh's storytelling background and offered Nuh a textual world that combined both types of stories so as not to obliterate one form (storytelling) over the other (novel).

I have highlighted here some of Ayyub's positions concerning the Iraqi education system. In his texts, Ayyub portrays a structure that seeks to speak the language of progress and nationalism, the language of the twentieth century, yet preserves the old. The education system, according to Ayyub, aspired to form the minds and bodies of both the Iraqi teachers and their students. Yet, Ayyub offered modes that enabled students and teachers to question the values and doctrines the state attempted to promote. He underscored the power of the relationship of the individual teacher with his students rather than his status as a supervisor. He likewise underlined the possibility of independent readings of, and listening to, texts that are different from the ones supplied in lessons. Ayyub did not offer a unified educational theory, yet his stories signal the failure of the education system to discipline its teachers and students alike.

Expressing criticism of the system, however, was possible, since Ayyub himself managed to publish texts that voiced his denunciation of the state's education ministry, while working as its employee. Ayyub did not take the trouble to hide his views concerning his supervisors, the policies of the administrators in the ministry, and the educational theories of the ministers. Left-leaning, unmarried, and attracted to both men and women, his lifestyle undoubtedly contradicted every possible value a teacher was supposed to introduce to his students—especially the family values championed by the ministry's educators, who called for the creation of healthy and productive families. Yet despite the fact that he was punished by the system by being transferred from one place to the other, he persevered, continued to publish and remained within the system.

Conclusions

It has now become a matter of conventional wisdom to depict the secularized Iraqi education system as anti-British, Pan-Arab, and often pro-Nazi. These assumptions, however, should be questioned. First, the secularization of the education system was also inspired by British and American models. The variety of educational models, moreover, indicates that Iraq's state-controlled education was part of a larger process of regulation that was not necessarily "German" or "Iraqi" but could also be simply viewed as "modern." The variety of backgrounds—Ottoman, Egyptian, American, and British—to which teachers were exposed produced a more pluralistic view of education and prevented the existence of a unified historical narrative. There was a consensus that Islamic history should serve as a national model but little agreement as to which historical narratives best represented the Iraqi and Islamic pasts.

It is very tempting to adopt a Foucauldian model to explicate features of Iraqi education, whose officials assumed the position of fashioning the bodies and minds of their students.[74] Yet we must not fall into the trap of relying solely on the texts produced by the Ministry of Education. Short stories and autobiographical material by writers like Ayyub, as well as evidence provided by the ministry's executives themselves, reveal the power of an important subaltern group, namely, the pupils themselves, to resist the propositions of their teachers. Popular storytelling, coffeehouses, as well as strong emotional bonds with other students, offered a variety of ways to challenge and resist. Different historical narratives assumed different meanings according to each student's ideology, socioeconomic class, and religious sect. In addition, students like Somekh or Ayyub reported about the ways in which teachers subverted dreary and boring curricula and regulations. While many of us might have been mesmerized by a charismatic teacher or, more likely, bored by our classes, these accounts have important political implications since the tedious curricula and textbooks are identified with the state, while the teachers' readings are identified with the opposition.

Finally, scholars of Iraqi history (most notably Michael Epple) identified the relationship between the traditional and landed elites of Iraq (Sunni notables, the Sherifians, Shi'i tribal leaders), and a nascent middle class. Composed of young men, mostly students in secondary schools and colleges, the budding middle class was dependent on the state apparatus. This significant factor substantially weakened their potential to pose as an alternative to the old Iraqi landed elites or to challenge the socioeconomic status quo.[75] Nevertheless, the younger generation was able to express harsh criticism of the state's apparatus in the pages of newspapers like al-Ahali. Not all educators, in other words, wholeheartedly accepted state patronage. Their texts call our attention not to the distinguished intellectuals of the era or the powerful

[74] In particular, the models suggested in Michel Foucault, *Discipline and Punish: The Birth of the Prison*, trans. Alan Sheridan (New York: Vintage Books, 1979).

[75] See Michael Eppel's thoughtful essay, "The Elite, the Effendiyya, and the Growth of Nationalism and Pan-Arabism in Hashemite Iraq, 1921–1958," *International Journal of Middle East Studies* 30 (1998): 227–50.

bureaucrats but to those teachers who read Egyptian magazines and were aware of contemporary leftist and Marxist literature, with which they sought to radically alter the status quo. These educators, in a sense, refused to be educated.

Be Masters in That You Teach and Continue to Learn: Medieval Muslim Thinkers on Educational Theory

SEBASTIAN GÜNTHER

Insufficient awareness of the educational achievements of the past bears the risk of not recognizing what is genuine progress in the field of education and what is mere repetition. In other words, without knowledge of the history of education, we may fail to achieve the level of understanding and reasoning reached by former generations while, at the same time, keeping ourselves busy with self-postulated problems, the solutions to which have long been available in the stores of historical knowledge.

Part of the issue is that there is a tendency in contemporary Western research on education to neglect theories, philosophies, and intellectual movements originating from cultures and civilizations other than the occidental one. For instance, studies in education in the West are often concerned with the Greco-Roman and Judeo-Christian foundations of a European-centered history of learning, while educational concepts and practices of other cultures and civilizations are not given adequate consideration. This is somewhat surprising in view of the complex challenges Western societies are facing at the beginning of the third millennium. In fact, the increasing ethnic and religious diversity of the population in nearly every large city in North America and Europe (and in most institutions of primary, secondary, and higher learning) seems to call rather urgently for a change in the approach toward education, both nationally and internationally. At the same time, it seems necessary to recognize fully that the study of educational thought is a key tool for a better understanding of cultures, civilizations, and religions other than "our own."

For more than one reason, this latter point is particularly true of Islam: a critical, unbiased, and systematic study in the West of Islam's diverse values, concepts, and beliefs—especially those relating to the educational theories and philosophies developed by Muslim scholars—is a pressing and real need. Thus, this article is dedicated to shedding light on a spectrum of issues in educational thought in Islam, which may—due to their universal relevance— be of interest not only to specialists but also to a wider readership. This article aims to accomplish the following. First, it will provide an idea of the edu-

---

The title makes reference to chap. 3, verse 79, of the Qur'an, "Be you masters in that you teach the Scripture and in that you yourselves study [it]." This article presents some initial results from research for my book, tentatively entitled "Medieval Muslim Thinkers on Education: Insights into Islam's Classical Pedagogical Theories," planned to be completed in 2007. Sections I and II of the present article revisit certain topics also discussed in a previous article (see n. 6 below). All dates are given in Common Era (CE). Arabic expressions use a simplified transliteration. Different diacritic marks serve to distinguish between the Arabic consonants hamza ('), a voiceless glottal stop, and ʿayn (ʿ), a laryngeal voiced fricative. All translations from the Arabic are my own, unless otherwise specified.

cational views and philosophies advocated by some great medieval Muslim thinkers. These offer insight into the foundations of educational thought in Islam and show that medieval Muslim scholars have made significant, original contributions to various fields of pedagogy and didactics. Second, it will draw attention to the fact that many "classical Islamic" views on education can only be understood properly if due consideration is given to both the specifics of their development within the framework of Islam and to their place within the general course of the history of ideas in the ancient and medieval Mediterranean world. Finally, it is hoped this article will help reveal the richness, sophistication, and diversity of scholarly discussion in Islam on educational theory and practice, and indicate how "current" and "modern" certain of the educational ideas advanced by medieval Muslim scholars are.

A lifelong pursuit of learning is a characteristic ideal of Islamic piety and underlies the concept of "Islamic" education. While the primary focus of this concept was the nurturing of religious belief in the individual, its scope broadened to incorporate various secular disciplines, literary and scientific, as it aimed at developing within the Muslim community fully integrated personalities, grounded in the virtues of Islam. This general notion relates to the theory and practice of both basic and higher education in Islam. It is evident in the Qur'an and the literature of prophetic tradition (*hadith*), with the latter including, for example, such sayings attributed to the Prophet Muhammad as "To acquire knowledge is an obligation on every Muslim, male or female"; "Seek knowledge from the day of your birth until the day of your death"; and "Seek knowledge, even if it were in China."[1] Likewise, 'Ali ibn Abi Talib, the Prophet Muhammad's son-in-law and a particularly important figure for the Shiites, is quoted as having said: "Learning is the glory of mankind, and the wise are beacons on the road to truth. . . . Knowledge is man's hope of life immortal. Man may die but wisdom liveth ever."[2]

The high esteem that knowledge and education are granted in Islam is no less evident in countless proverbs, aphorisms, and wisdom sayings, in addition to poetry and prose texts of the Middle Eastern literatures.[3] It is especially prominent, of course, in the numerous medieval Arabic works devoted to pedagogical and didactic issues. Based on directions provided in the Qur'an and the literature of the prophetic tradition, these works explain and analyze teaching methods, the ways in which learning does or should take place, the

---

[1] The prophetic tradition, i.e., the authoritative religious literature in Islam, owes much of its vital educational potential to the "model character" of the events and messages included in reports believed to preserve what the Prophet Muhammad said, did, or condoned. For concepts of learning in the Qur'an, see P. E. Walker, "Knowledge and Learning," in *The Encyclopaedia of the Qur'an*, ed. Jane D. McAuliffe, 5 vols. (Leiden: Brill, 2001–5), 3:1–5; and Sebastian Günther, "Teaching," ibid., 5:200–205.

[2] Cited by al-Ghazali in his *The Revival of the Sciences of Religion* (*Ihya' 'ulum al-din*); cf. *The Book of Knowledge, Being a Translation with Notes of the Kitab al-'ilm of al-Ghazzali's* (*sic*) *Ihya' 'ulum al-din*, trans. Nabih Amin Faris (Lahore: S. M. Ashraf, 1962), 14.

[3] See Franz Rosenthal, *Knowledge Triumphant: The Concept of Knowledge in Medieval Islam* (Leiden: Brill, 1970).

aims of education, and how educational goals are to be achieved. These include the actions and behavior of both students and teachers, their (moral) qualities, their relationship with one another in the process of education, didactics (including the organization and contents of learning as well as the curriculum), and the means and methods of imparting and acquiring knowledge.

Two general observations can be made about these medieval Arabic texts on education in Islam. First, elements of ancient Arab and Persian culture and, very importantly, the Greco-Hellenistic heritage were creatively adapted and incorporated into Islamic educational theory. This is particularly evident in the works of Muslim philosophers who dealt with the various stages in the development of the human character and personality, child education, and higher learning. Second, from the eighth century to the sixteenth, there was a continuous tradition of Arabic-Islamic scholarship dealing with pedagogical and didactic issues, reflecting a range of individual scholars' theological stances, ethnic origins, or geographical affiliations. Medieval Muslim scholars writing on education included theologians, philosophers, jurists, littérateurs, *hadith* scholars, and scientists. Although many of them taught, none of them were specialists in education. Nonetheless, their ideas and philosophies on education contributed much to what can be called Islam's classical pedagogical tradition.

Teaching and Curriculum Development in Early Islam: Ibn Sahnun (817–70)

Apparently, the very first Muslim scholar to write a "handbook" for teachers was the ninth-century Arab jurist and chief judge (*qadi*) of the Malikites, Muhammad ibn Sahnun.[4] He was born and lived most of his life in Kairouan (al-Qayrawan), a town in north-central Tunisia and one of the holy cities of Islam, which was, at Ibn Sahnun's time, a flourishing economic, administrative, cultural, and intellectual center of the western lands (Maghreb) of the Islamic empire.

Ibn Sahnun's book on education is entitled *Rules of Conduct for Teachers* (*Adab al-mu'allimin*).[5] It is a legal treatise that deals, from the viewpoint of a (conservative) Maliki scholar, with issues teachers at elementary schools may have encountered while teaching. Composed over a thousand years ago, this work is a document of remarkable significance for the history of pedagogy. It provides us with an idea of the beginnings of educational theory and

[4] Malikites, also called Malikis, are the adherents of one of the four law schools (singular: *madhhab*) in Sunni Islam, named after their principal imam, the legal expert Malik ibn Anas (ca. 715–96) from the city of Medina. This school stresses what was practiced by the local community of Medina. It prefers a strict reliance on the prophetic tradition (*hadith*) to traditional opinions and deduction by "analogy" (*qiyas*). The remaining three law schools are the Hanafi (named after, and developed from, the teachings of Abu Hanifa, ca. 700–767), Shafi'i (derived from the teachings of its founder Abu 'Abdallah al-Shafi'i, 767–820), and Hanbali (named after, and based on, the teachings of Ahmad ibn Hanbal, 780–855).

[5] Muhammad ibn Sahnun, *Adab al-mu'allimin*, ed. Muhammad al-'Arusi al-Matwi, reprinted in 'Abd al-Rahman 'Uthman Hijazi, *Al-Madhhab al-tarbawi 'inda Ibn Sahnun* (Beirut: Mu'assasat al-Risala, 1986), 111–28; the French translation is by Gérard Lecomte, "Le livre des règles de conduite des maîtres d'école par Ibn Sahnun," *Revue des études Islamiques* 21 (1953): 77–105.

curriculum development in Islam while at the same time showing that certain problems relating to the ninth century continue to concern us today. The first four chapters of *Rules of Conduct for Teachers* are based on Islamic prophetic traditions that deal with the merits and advantages of teaching and learning the Qur'an and with the fair treatment of pupils by their teacher. The remaining six chapters present questions that Ibn Sahnun asked and the answers given to him by his father, Sahnun—a widely respected jurist at the time and still considered a major authority on Maliki law today. Ibn Sahnun provides to (medieval) elementary-school teachers a number of specific instructions and rules that range from aspects of the curriculum and examinations to practical legal advice in such matters as the appointment and payment of the teacher, the organization of teaching and the teacher's work with the pupils at school, the supervision of pupils at school and the teacher's responsibilities when the pupils are on their way home, the just treatment of pupils (including, e.g., how to handle trouble between pupils), classroom and teaching equipment, and the pupils' graduation.[6]

The curriculum Ibn Sahnun refers to is representative to some degree of the medieval Islamic elementary school (admitting children at 6 or 7 years of age). It includes obligatory topics to be taught, such as the precise articulation and memorization of the Qur'an; the duties of worship; knowledge of reading and writing; and good manners, since these are obligations toward God. Furthermore, there are recommended topics, such as the basics of Arabic language and grammar; good handwriting; arithmetic; poetry, provided the verses are morally decent; and proverbs, historical reports and legends (of the ancient Arabs), and speeches. Ibn Sahnun cites maxims attributed to the Prophet Muhammad that highlight the crucial significance that religiously oriented schooling in Islam grants to the learning and memorization of the Qur'an (just like medieval Europe stressed the study of the Bible):

> The best of you is the one who learns the Qur'an and teaches it.
>
> For he who learns the Qur'an in his youth, the Qur'an will mix with his flesh and blood. [However,] he who learns it in old age and does not give up on it, even when it escapes [his memory], will receive double the reward.
>
> You must [occupy yourselves with and] make use of the Qur'an, for it eliminates hypocrisy in the same way that fire eliminates rust from iron.[7]

At several places in his book, Ibn Sahnun stresses that modesty, patience, and passion for working with children are indispensable qualifications for teachers, basing these views again on maxims from the Islamic prophetic tradition. Yet, he makes it also clear that physical punishment was part of

---

[6] Sebastian Günther, "Advice for Teachers: The 9th Century Muslim Scholars Ibn Sahnun and al-Jahiz on Pedagogy and Didactics," in *Ideas, Images, and Methods of Portrayal: Insights into Classical Arabic Literature and Islam*, ed. Sebastian Günther (Leiden: Brill, 2005): 95–110.

[7] Ibn Sahnun, *Adab al-muʿallimin*, 113–14; see also Günther, "Advice," 101.

rectifying a child's behavior in Islam in the Middle Ages, leaving no doubt, however, that punishment should not cross the line and that the child should not be seriously harmed.

As for the practical sides of teaching and learning, Ibn Sahnun advises teachers to encourage pupils to study individually and with others but also to create situations to challenge their minds. He suggests, for example, that pupils dictate to each other and that advanced pupils would profit from writing letters for adults. Fair competition between the pupils is expressly favored, as the author tells us, since it contributes to the formation of the pupils' character and to their general intellectual development.

Other rules and regulations concern a variety of matters. Muslim teachers are advised, for example, not to instruct young girls together with boys, because mixed classes corrupt young people. This statement seems to imply, first, that education was not restricted to boys and, second, that coeducation was conducted at elementary schools to a certain extent. Furthermore, Ibn Sahnun, citing his father, says that teachers must not teach the Qur'an to the children of Christians. This seems to indicate that (*a*) Muslim and Christian children were attending the same classes together and (*b*) Ibn Sahnun took literally the Qur'anic injunction: "There is no compulsion in matters of faith" (Qur'an 2, 256).[8]

Deduction and Reasoning versus Memorization as Techniques of Learning: Al-Jahiz (ca. 776–868)

A book about teachers quite different from Ibn Sahnun's was written by al-Jahiz, a celebrated man of letters and Mu'tazili theologian.[9] Al-Jahiz, probably of Ethiopian descent, was born in Basra, Iraq, the ethnically and intellectually diverse city that shaped his mind and inspired him throughout his life and scholarly career.

In contrast to Ibn Sahnun's legal text for elementary school teachers, much of al-Jahiz's *The Book of Teachers* (*Kitab al-Mu'allimin*) deals, from a literary-philosophical point of view, with questions of learning and teaching

---

[8] It is of note that, although throughout the Middle Ages most educational texts by Muslim scholars deal exclusively with the instruction of boys and male students, there is clear evidence, especially in historical and biographical sources, that girls and women were at no time completely excluded from elementary or higher learning, nor were girls always confined to moral education provided within their families.

[9] Mu'tazila is the name of one of the earliest and most important schools of speculative theology (*kalam*). It had the support of the ruling 'Abbasid dynasty (750–1258) during the caliphates of al-Ma'mun, al-Mu'tasim, and al-Wathiq (813–47) but lost this support during the caliphate of al-Mutawakkil (847–61). It continued, however, to be theologically creative, though gradually losing its dominance to the Ash'arite school of theology. The Mu'tazila is noted for placing reasoning and dialectics at the center of its doctrine. At the beginning of the twentieth century, Mu'tazilism was "rediscovered," especially in Egypt. See Daniel Gimaret, "Mu'tazila," in *Encyclopaedia of Islam*, new ed. (Leiden: Brill, 1954–), 7:783–93.

at the more advanced levels.[10] In this essay, al-Jahiz not only defends school-teachers but actually champions them and stresses their superiority over all other categories of educators and tutors—an appreciation not evident in society as a whole, where the status of schoolteachers was actually quite low. Al-Jahiz depicts teachers as knowledgeable, diligent, and hardworking people, who are passionate about their profession and suffer with their students when the students do not progress as expected. Parents, therefore, should not blame the teachers when a child is slow in school; instead, they should consider the mental capabilities of their offspring.

Interestingly, al-Jahiz highlights the significance of the teachers' work by emphasizing the fundamental impact that writing has had on human civilization and by speaking of writing and recording data—along with calculation—as "the pillars" on which rest the present and the future of civilization and "the welfare of this world." He states that the great independent thinkers and researchers of the past disliked memorization, which makes "the mind disregard distinction" and rely simply on what their predecessors achieved, without making attempts to reach conclusions of their own. Still, al-Jahiz says, a good memory is needed and valuable for learning as a process; otherwise, the results of any study would not last. He states:

> The leading sages, masters of the art of deductive reasoning and [independent] thinking, were averse to excellence in memorization, because of [one's] dependence on it and [its rendering] the mind negligent of rational judgment, so [much so] that they said: "Memorization inhibits the intellect." [They were averse to it] because the one engaged in memorization is only an imitator, whereas deductive reasoning is that which brings the one engaged in it to calculated certainty and great confidence.
>
> The true proposition and the praiseworthy judgment is that, when [a student] learns only by memorization, this harms deductive reasoning; and when he uses only deductive reasoning, this harms learning by memorization—even if memorization has a more honorable rank than [deductive reasoning]. So, when he neglects rational reflection, ideas do not come quickly to him, and when he neglects memorization, [these ideas] do not stick in his mind or remain long in his heart.
>
> The nature of memorization is other than that of deductive reasoning. [However,] what both [memorization and deductive reasoning] are concerned with and support is something agreed upon: it is to free the mind and to [make the student] desire only one thing [that is, learning]. By means of these two (i.e., freeing the mind and desiring only to learn), perfection comes to be and virtue appears.[11]

Al-Jahiz enumerates the major topics for pupils to learn in the following

---

[10] 'Amr ibn Bahr al-Basri al-Jahiz, *Kitab al-Mu'allimin*, in *Kitaban li-l-Jahiz: Kitab al-Mu'allimin wa-Kitab fi l-radd 'ala al-mushabbiha* [Two essays by al-Jahiz: "On Schoolmasters" and "Refutation of Anthropomorphists"], annotated, with an introductory study, and ed. Ibrahim Geries (Ibrahim Jiryis), 1st ed. (Tel Aviv: Department of Arabic Language and Literature, Tel Aviv University [also 'Akka: Matba'at al-Suruji], 1980), 57–87.

[11] Ibid., 62–63. See also Günther, "Advice," 122.

sequence: writing, arithmetic, law, the pillars of religion, the Qur'an, grammar, prosody, and poetry. Further subjects that are to be taught include logical argumentation for all situations in life as well as polo, archery, horsemanship, music, chess, and other games. Al-Jahiz also suggests making the students familiar with the arguments of famous writers, their elegant style of writing and measured use of vocabulary. Moreover, the students need to be taught how to express themselves in a way that people can understand, without any need for additional interpretation and comment. They should also understand that content has priority over style. Teachers are, therefore, advised to provide a good example and choose ideas for their classes that are not shrouded in complexities or scattered throughout a long discourse.

As for the actual process of teaching and education, al-Jahiz advises teachers in particular to take the mental ability of students into account; thus, teachers should use a language understandable to the students. Furthermore, teachers are to treat their students gently and in a most loving way and attempt to reach their students' hearts when it comes to the subject matter taught. Al-Jahiz concludes his book on teachers with an inspiring passage on the merits of treating students gently, advising readers to treat students with great care, gentleness, and kindness, not to force them so as not to make them dislike good manners, and not to neglect them, for students, as al-Jahiz says, "deserve your care and hard efforts."[12]

Student-Centered Learning and the Art of Instruction: Al-Farabi (d. 950)

Abu Nasr al-Farabi (known as Alfarabius or Avennasar in medieval Europe) is considered to be one of the most influential philosophers and, perhaps, the first truly eminent logician in Islam.[13] Medieval Muslim thinkers refer to him as the "second teacher," with the first being Aristotle. Al-Farabi was of Turkish origin. He was born in Turkestan, but lived many years in Baghdad, Iraq, and in Aleppo, Syria. He died in Damascus at the age of 80 years or more.

Al-Farabi was among the first Muslim scholars to suggest an integrated curriculum for the higher learning of both the "foreign" and "religious" sciences, with the foreign being those grounded in Greek philosophy and science and the religious being those based on the Qur'an and its interpre-

[12] Al-Jahiz, *Kitab al-Mu'allimin*, 86–87. See also Sebastian Günther, "Al-Jahiz and the Poetics of Teaching," in *Al-Jahiz: A Humanist for Our Time*, ed. Tarif Khalidi (Beirut: Orient-Institute, 2006, forthcoming), and "*Praise to the Book!* Al-Jahiz and Ibn Qutayba on the Excellence of the Written Word in Medieval Islam," *Jerusalem Studies in Arabic and Islam (Franz Rosenthal Memorial Volume)* 31 (2006), forthcoming.

[13] Al-Farabi believed that "human reason is superior to religious faith, and hence assigned only a secondary place to the different revealed religions which provide, in his view, an approach to truth for non-philosophers through symbols." In his view, "philosophical truth is universally valid whereas these symbols vary from nation to nation," being the work of philosopher-prophets, of whom Muhammad, the Prophet of Islam, was one. See R. Walzer, "Al-Farabi," in *Encyclopaedia of Islam*, 2:778–81.

tation.[14] The curriculum al-Farabi envisioned "depicted the hierarchical structure of the universe and affirmed the distinction between human and divine knowledge."[15] This approach toward studying, however, did not become an integral component of formal higher learning in Islam; yet, it did have an impact on the philosophers who—in their private studies and in study circles—followed it to some extent.[16]

Certain ideas of al-Farabi's theory of instruction are included in his treatise *The Demonstration* (*al-Burhan*); they are part of his discussions on logic.[17] He begins his treatment of this topic by stating that Arabic terms such as *ta'lim* and *talqin* (both basically meaning "teaching" and "instruction") are often used imprecisely, and sometimes interchangeably, with what could be called "[general] education" and "refinement of character" (*ta'dib*), or "accustoming" (*ta'wid*). Al-Farabi then specifies that *ta'lim* results in understanding, or in an aptitude for acquiring understanding, while *talqin*, however, whose aim is not the acquisition of knowledge, results in a strengthened character that produces action. The imprecise use of these terms prevents people from discriminating correctly between the different methods necessary for acquiring knowledge, habits, skills, or strong traits of character. Al-Farabi stresses, moreover, that terminological precision is a basic prerequisite of learning in general, for clarity in expression promotes clarity in ideas and, thus, learning.[18]

These are reasons enough for al-Farabi to define "instruction" more precisely. He states that although there is divine and human instruction, he is

[14] This view is particularly evident in al-Farabi's *Enumeration of the Sciences*; see Abu Nasr Muhammad ibn Muhammad al-Farabi, *Ihsa' al-'ulum*, ed. 'Uthman Amin, 3rd ed. (Cairo: Maktabat al-Anglu al-Misriyya, 1968); a German translation (based on a twelfth-century Latin translation of the *Ihsa'*) was published by E. Wiedemann, "Über al-Farabis Aufzählung der Wissenschaften (De Scientiis)," in *Aufsätze zur arabischen Wissenschaftsgeschichte: Mit einem Vorwort und Indices herausgegeben von Wolfdietrich Fischer*, by Eilhard Wiedemann, 2 vols. (Hildesheim: Olms, 1970), 1:323–50. A summary is given by Seyyed Hossein Nasr, *Science and Civilization in Islam*, with a preface by Giorgio de Santillana (Cambridge, MA: Harvard University Press, 1968), 60–62.

[15] Charles Michael Stanton, *Higher Learning in Islam: The Classical Period, A.D. 700–1300* (Savage, MD: Rowman & Littlefield, 1990), 84.

[16] Ibid., 84. See also David C. Reisman, "Al-Farabi and the Philosophical Curriculum," in *The Cambridge Companion to Arabic Philosophy*, ed. Peter Adamson and Richard C. Taylor (Cambridge: Cambridge University Press, 2005), 52–71. Sebastian Günther, "Education: Islamic Education," in *New Dictionary of the History of Ideas*, ed. Maryanne Cline Horowitz (Detroit: Scribner's, 2005), 2:640–45; and the insightful article by Asma Afsaruddin, "Muslim Views on Education: Parameters, Purviews, and Possibilities," *Journal of Catholic Legal Studies* 44, no. 1 (2005): 143–78.

[17] *Al-Burhan* is the Arabic equivalent of *Analytica Posteriora* or *Apodeictica*, as Aristotle's work *Posterior Analytics* was known in the medieval Arabic sources. Of Aristotle's works, it was one of the most frequently commented on or paraphrased by medieval Muslim scholars. Al-Farabi's *al-Burhan* is one of the earliest of such paraphrases. Compare M. Fakhry, in *Al-Mantiq 'inda al-Farabi: Kitab al-Burhan wa-Kitab Shara'it al-yaqin ma'a ta'aliq Ibn Bajja 'ala l-Burhan*, ed. Majid Fakhry (Beirut: Dar al-Mashriq, 1987), 1 (introduction). See also Michael E. Marmura, "The Fortuna of the *Posterior Analytics* in the Arabic Middle East," in *Probing in Islamic Philosophy: Studies in the Philosophies of Ibn Sina, al-Ghazali and Other Major Muslim Thinkers* (Binghamton, NY: Global Academic Publishing, 2005), 355–73.

[18] Abu Nasr Muhammad ibn Muhammad al-Farabi, *Kitab al-Burhan*, in Fakhry, *Al-Mantiq 'inda al-Farabi*, 17–96, esp. 77–78. See also Fuad Said Haddad, *Alfarabi's Theory of Communication* (Beirut: American University of Beirut Press, 1989), 123–24, 126–27.

only concerned with human instruction.[19] According to al-Farabi, human instruction (*a*) is a human activity, (*b*) deals with human intelligibles, and, therefore, (*c*) should be examined within the parameters of philosophy, whereas divine instruction is not. Furthermore, for al-Farabi human instruction is a purposeful activity that aims to achieve a certain end, that is, the understanding (*ma'rifa*) of things not known before; requires a kind of previous or initial knowledge for instruction to build upon; builds on the fact that the increase in knowledge is a natural desire in humans; takes into account that the realization of the desire to learn implies the learner's awareness of his ignorance; and acknowledges that ignorance is a necessary condition or component of instruction, for it is the level at which instruction starts.[20] However, making a person recall previously acquired knowledge that he is no longer aware of is not to be called "instruction." As for the process of instruction, al-Farabi generally notes that

> teaching can take place verbally or through providing an example. The verbal [method of teaching] is the one in which the teacher uses articulate statements; this is what Aristotle calls "aural teaching" (*al-ta'lim al-masmu'*). The [other] one, the one [conducted] through example, takes place when the student observes the teacher [engaged] in an action or the like, so that [the student] will imitate him in this regard or act as he does, and thus attains the capacity [to do] the same thing or [perform the] same act.[21]

Furthermore, he specifies:

> Every instruction is composed of two things: (a) making what is being studied comprehensible and causing its idea to be established in the soul [of the student], and (b) causing others to assent to what is comprehended and established in the soul. There are two ways of making a thing comprehensible: first, by causing its essence to be perceived by the intellect, and second, by causing it to be imagined through the similitude that imitates it. Assent, too, is brought about by one of two methods, either by . . . [conclusive] demonstration or by . . . persuasion.[22]

As can be seen, instruction is expressly conceived of here as an interactive process that involves both the teacher and the student. While it is the teacher's responsibility to introduce new knowledge to the student in ways that he can understand, it is the student's responsibility to work actively with new facts until he can use them in contexts different from those demonstrated to him. Furthermore, an effective method of instruction ensures that both teacher and student participate actively in the process. This interactive element in

---

[19] Al-Farabi, *Kitab al-Burhan*, 82; see also Haddad, *Alfarabi's Theory of Communication*, 125.

[20] Al-Farabi, *Kitab al-Burhan*, 79–80; see also Haddad, *Alfarabi's Theory of Communication*,126.

[21] Abu Nasr al-Farabi, *Kitab al-Alfaz al-musta'mala fi l-mantiq: The Utterances Employed in Logic*, Arabic text, ed., with introduction and notes, Muhsin Mahdi (Beirut: Dar al-Mashriq [Imprimerie Catholique], 1968), 86, par. 40.

[22] *Alfarabi's Philosophy of Plato and Aristotle* [*Tahsil al-sa'ada*], translated and with an introduction by Muhsin Mahdi (New York: Free Press of Glencoe, 1962), 44.

the learning process allows the instruction to be student-centered since the aim is for the teacher to facilitate the student's own voyage of discovery.

Al-Farabi stresses that the teacher needs to facilitate the students' comprehension and conceptualization. He offers several pieces of advice in this regard. For example, he recommends that the teacher should describe and define the matter to be taught, using various methods of explanation. It is also helpful to name the various aspects and individual qualities of the object of study or to refer to a correspondence in kind or quality or similitude of it. Teachers may rely in this regard on methods and techniques such as arrangement and classification, induction, analogy, and syllogisms; these help to familiarize the students with the subject matter to be taught, facilitate their comprehension, and, thus, assist in imparting knowledge or conviction of something to them. Hence, the use of a variety of teaching techniques facilitates the teachers' efforts at creating in the students' minds an image or an idea of something not previously known, which assists them in their learning. Additionally, this makes it easier for the students to retain new information. However, this kind of instruction should be used only until the students are experienced and strong enough to be taught "directly" so that the teacher can instruct the students in the matter or subject itself, without needing to draw anymore on elaborate explanations and comments.

Al-Farabi relies here again expressly on Aristotle, who, al-Farabi says, discredited teaching that involved substituting nonessential qualities or accidents of a given thing or matter for the thing or matter itself, since this bore the risk of getting too far away from the actual teaching subject. As a result, the students will become confused rather than more knowledgeable. They will waste time trying to decipher what the teacher has said or be discouraged in their attempts to learn. Thus, at a more advanced level of learning, a preferred discourse between teacher and student is one that relies on such principles as directness in approach and clarity in thought and expression; it deliberately aims at conviction and complete certainty.[23]

Specifics of Child Education and Psychology: Ibn Sina (Avicenna, 980–1037)

Ibn Sina, an eminent Muslim physician, philosopher, natural scientist, and administrator, known in the West as Avicenna, was born near Bukhara in present-day Uzbekistan. He never left the eastern parts of the Islamic lands and spent his most productive years in Iran, in cities such as Isfahan and Hamadan. Although Persian was Ibn Sina's native language, he wrote his principal works in Arabic, the lingua franca of medieval Islamic civilization.

Ibn Sina envisaged a world resting on two pillars: (*a*) Greek philosophy and (*b*) the Qur'anic revelation and the virtues of Islam. In uniting philosophy with the study of nature, and in understanding the perfection of man as lying

---

[23] Al-Farabi, *Kitab al-Alfaz*, 86–93; see also Haddad, *Alfarabi's Theory of Communication*, 134–37.

in both knowledge and action, Ibn Sina creatively adopted key principles of ancient Greek philosophy. Hence, his general conception of learning profoundly reflects Aristotelian premises. Ibn Sina was a highly spiritual and ethical person, considering that, for him, teaching and learning should lead also to rooting the faith deeply in the soul of the individual. Yet, these particulars of his convictions do not undermine the fact that many of Ibn Sina's more specific discussions of education are medical or psychological in essence and approach.

Ibn Sina believed that the actual process of knowing begins with the five external senses: hearing, touch, smell, taste, and sight. These senses reached their pinnacle in humankind, thus distinguishing humans from animals. Furthermore, by the presence of the soul, humans have two intellectual faculties: the practical and the theoretical intellect, with the practical intellect governing bodily movements and the theoretical the higher order of reasoning and thought processes within the soul. Interestingly, Ibn Sina specifies that the theoretical intellect comprises four distinct processes that are characteristic only of humans. Listed from the lower to the higher, they are: (1) The "potential to acquire" knowledge (i.e., the *intellectus materialis* or "material intellect," *al-ʿaql al-hayulani*), which serves (2) the "ability to use" acquired knowledge and to actually think (i.e., the *intellectus in habitu* or "intellect being in a certain state or habit," *al-ʿaql bi-l-malaka*); it serves (3) the "ability to generate" intellectual activity in order to understand more complex concepts (i.e., the *intellectus in actu*, the "intellect in act" or "acting intellect," *al-ʿaql bi-l-fiʿl*), and, finally, (4) the "ability to internalize" knowledge of the intelligible world (i.e., the *intellectus adeptus* or *aquisitus*, "adoptive" or "acquired" intellect, *al-ʿaql al-mustafad*, i.e., "the governor," whom all other intellects serve). To have obtained this capacity and to be able to make adequate use of it means to have reached the ultimate stage of learning.[24] Although rather theoretical and complex in the way they are expressed, these ideas are highly relevant for the various practical sides of learning. They are significant especially with regard to the education of children and youth, including particularly activities that involve young children in sensory experiences, for these help to stimulate children to identify, compare, and classify items as they explore the world around them.

[24] This hierarchy of intellectual development is discussed in Ibn Sina's *The Book of Salvation* [*from Error*], *Kitab al-Najat: Min al-gharaq fi bahr al-dalalat*, ed. Muhammad Taqi Danishpazhuh (Tehran: Danishgah-i Tihran, 1364 [1985–86 CE]), esp. 333–43. See also F. Rahman, *Avicenna's Psychology: An English Translation of Kitab al-Najat, Book II, Chapter VI, with Historico-Philosophical Notes and Textual Improvements on the Cairo Edition* (London: Oxford University Press, 1952), esp. 33–38, and Rahman's comments, 87–95. The latter study was reprinted in Fuat Sezgin et al., eds., *Islamic Philosophy*, vol. 34, *Abu ʿAli ibn Sina (d. 428/1037)*, Text and Studies Collected and Reprinted (Frankfurt am Main: Institute for the History of Arabic-Islamic Science at the Johann Wolfgang Goethe University, 1999), 39–175. See also Stanton, *Higher Learning in Islam*, 86–87, although no sources are given there. For the relation of these terms to Aristotle and Alexander of Aphrodisias, see also O. N. H. Leaman, "Malaka," in *Encyclopaedia of Islam*, 6:220.

The fact that Ibn Sina had a special interest in educating the young is evident, for example, in his monumental *Canon of Medicine* (*al-Qanun fi l-Tibb*), a summa of all the medical knowledge of Ibn Sina's time, augmented by his own observations.[25] Here he deals with child education as part of his discussion of the four stages of life. Insights into certain physical, emotional, and intellectual aspects of child development form for him the starting point for exploring aspects of more general importance to a child's education in the period from infancy to adolescence.[26] He states:

> The great principle here is the inculcation of control of the emotions. One should take care that they [the children] do not give way to anger and fear, or be oppressed by despondency, or suffer from sleeplessness. They should therefore be allowed that which is pleasing and appetizing, and one should avoid giving them anything arousing disgust.
>
> There are two useful objects attained in this way. The first is that the mind grows from its very start by being accustomed to favorable emotions, and develops a fixed habit for good. The second is that the body benefits. For just as bad habits of thought affect the temperament of the body, so also a physical intemperance may be traced to habits of the mind which are contrary to the ideal. . . . Therefore, in safeguarding the emotions, the health of the mind and body are at the same time maintained.[27]

Ibn Sina affirms that consideration of the characteristics of the human intellect (as he sees them) is vitally important in a child's education. Moreover, he seems to suggest that the way a child develops has a direct effect on his learning. Here he draws particular attention to the centrality of stable emotional conditions, for these safeguard the child's physical and mental development. Along these lines, Ibn Sina recommends that children begin to attend elementary school when they are both physically strong and mentally mature enough to do so. This includes, as he says, the requirement that children be in possession of the necessary language skills and be able to

[25] A.-M. Goichon, "Ibn Sina," in *Encyclopaedia of Islam*, 3:941–47, esp. 942.

[26] According to Ibn Sina, the four periods are (1) youth, i.e., the period of growth (up to 30 years of age); (2) the prime of life, i.e., the period of study and comprehension (up to 35 or 40 years of age); (3) elderly life, i.e., the period of decline and senescence, when one's best vigor has passed, the intellectual power begins to decline, and one is becoming old (up to about 60 years); and (4) decrepit age, or senility (to the end of life). More specifically, the first period of life, youth, comprises five subdivisions: (1) infancy, i.e., the period before the limbs are fit for walking; (2) babyhood, i.e., the period of formation of the teeth; (3) childhood, i.e., when the body shows strength of movement and the teeth are fully out; (4) juvenile, i.e., the period up to the development of hair on the [boy's] face and pubes; and (5) adolescence, i.e., the period up to the limit of growth of the body (to the beginning of adult life). Compare al-Shaykh al-Ra'is Abu 'Ali Ibn Sina, *Al-Qanun fi l-tibb*, new ed., ed. Idwar al-Qashsh (Beirut: Mu'assasat 'Izz al-Din li-l-Tiba'a wa-l-Nashr, 1987), 1:25. See also O. Cameron Gruner, *A Treatise on "The Canon of Medicine" of Avicenna, Incorporating a Translation of the First Book* (London: Luzac, 1930), 68–69.

[27] Ibn Sina, *Al-Qanun*, 1:208–9; the passage is a slightly altered version of Gruner's translation; cf. Gruner, *A Treatise on "The Canon of Medicine" of Avicenna*, 379.

concentrate and understand; this is, as he notes, usually at the age of 6.[28] However, harmony between the physical and mental components of education continues to be a major prerequisite at all stages of learning. Thus, he advises instructors to pay close attention to the "natural" intellectual capabilities of pupils and choose topics to be taught that match the pupils' mental capacity and level of education. Teachers and educators need to ensure, especially at the beginning of formal education, that the way to learning is paved as far as possible. Any obstacles must be removed and learning made an interesting, enjoyable, and exciting experience for the pupils; this, Ibn Sina says, is the most effective method to encourage pupils to learn and progress in their education.

As for the curriculum at the beginning of elementary school, two points from Ibn Sina's *The Book of Regimen* (*Kitab al-Siyasa*) will be presented here.[29] First, priority is to be given to teaching (*a*) the Qur'an (this means, traditionally, to have the pupils begin to memorize it), (*b*) reading and writing, and (*c*) the basic principles of faith (*ma'alim al-din*). Remarkable in this context is that Ibn Sina points to an important pedagogical principle when he advises teachers to combine the teaching of reading and writing. He exemplifies this idea by indicating that the teacher should write letters (on the board) so that the pupils get familiar with them, and then ask the pupils to copy the letters until they know how to write them.[30] Moreover, Ibn Sina also seems to argue here, as was concluded by A. Shams al-Din, a widely published contemporary Muslim researcher of Ibn Sina's educational theory, that studying the Holy Scripture provides young learners with all the eloquence and explanation of things they need to have at an early stage of life. Moreover, the various philological and thematic issues that emerge from learning and studying the Qur'an stimulate thought and help increase the pupils' mental abilities. In addition, the Holy Scripture in general is a great source for teaching children ethics, exemplary traditions, morals, and good behavior. All this is beneficial for helping youth to become eventually fully integrated members of the community and to find their place in society.[31]

Second, Ibn Sina, like the majority of medieval Muslim thinkers, values poetry highly as a means of education. In child education, poetry is important for several reasons: (1) in poetry the language is balanced and the composite structure well thought out and organized, which strengthens children's memory, trains their minds, and prepares them to understand eventually more complicated concepts; (2) poetry makes the pupils familiar with eloquent

---

[28] 'Abd al-Amir Shams al-Din, *Al-Madhhab al-tarbawi 'inda Ibn Sina: Min khilal falsafatihi al-'amaliyya*, 1st ed. (Beirut: Dar al-Kitab al-'Alami, 1988), 127–28, 130; based on Ibn Sina's *al-Qanun*.

[29] Compare the chapter "On Man's Regimen of the Child" of the *Kitab al-Siyasa* [The book of regimen] attributed to Ibn Sina. The work is published in *Al-Turath al-tarbawi al-islami fi khams makhtutat*, ed. Hisham Nashshaba (Beirut: Dar al-'Ilm li-l-Malayin, 1988), 25–45, esp. 40–42.

[30] Ibn Sina, *Kitab al-Siyasa*, 40. See also Shams al-Din, *Al-Madhhab al-tarbawi 'inda Ibn Sina*, 131–32.

[31] Shams al-Din, *Al-Madhhab al-tarbawi 'inda Ibn Sina*, 130–31.

and aesthetic speech, which helps them to speak correctly, using proper diction, as well as increases their imagination and broadens their intellectual horizons; (3) poetry makes the pupils familiar with "the virtue of good manners and the praiseworthy nature of knowledge" (*fadl al-adab wa-madh al-ʿilm*); and (4) poetry recitation is a pleasant experience that makes learning interesting, lively, and enjoyable for both the reciter and the listener. However, Ibn Sina leaves no doubt that, at the beginning of learning, the teacher must choose short poems with an easy meter for the class and only gradually proceed to using longer, more complicated ones.[32]

As for the instruction of pupils at school, Ibn Sina stresses that children should share the class with pupils of the same age. He expressly favors—and who would not—that a child's fellow pupils be children who have been brought up well and are well mannered: spending time with well-behaved children stimulates a child's activity and encourages the child to learn and to advance. In addition, communication and debate among children benefits their minds and may help to dissolve complications.[33]

Finally, Ibn Sina recommends that the educators of children be virtuous people, of laudable character, and possessing the pedagogical abilities to deal with children: "A child's educator must be a rational and devout [*dhu din*] person, insightful in developing moral [principles], possessing high ethics, skillful in educating children, dignified, decent, distant from frivolity and inanity, neither profuse nor longwinded, and neither inflexible nor dull. He must be kind-hearted, intelligent, gentleman-like, refined and honorable."[34]

Guidance versus Correction, and Rules of Conduct for Students and Teachers: Al-Ghazali (1058–1111)

Ibn Sina's main critic, Abu Hamid al-Ghazali—perhaps the greatest theologian in Islam, a mystic and religious reformer—approaches the question of learning from a distinctly different perspective. Al-Ghazali was born in Tus near the city of Mashhad in Iran. He and his younger brother Ahmad (later a noted mystic in his own right) were left orphans at an early age. Al-Ghazali pursued most of his education and higher studies in Nishapur and Baghdad. In 1091, at the age of 33, he accepted the head teaching position at the newly founded Nizamiyya College (the most famous institution of higher learning in Baghdad and perhaps the entire Islamic world in the eleventh century). Until 1095, he served there as professor of canonical Islamic law, lecturing to several hundred students. At a later stage in his life, he returned to teaching, albeit in Nishapur and later in Tus, not in Baghdad. Thus, his educational ideas arguably reflect real teaching experience and the pedagogical expertise

---

[32] Ibn Sina, *Kitab al-Siyasa*, 40–41. See also Shams al-Din, *Al-Madhhab al-tarbawi ʿinda Ibn Sina*, 134–35.

[33] Ibn Sina, *Kitab al-Siyasa*, 41.

[34] Ibid.

of an eminent educator rather than, simply, mere common sense or the idealistic declarations of a pious scholar.

Al-Ghazali is generally noted for accepting Greek logic as a neutral instrument of learning and for recommending it for theologians. It is, however, in his mystical writings that we encounter two things of significance to education: the first is his incorporation of basically Aristotelian ethical values into an Islamic mode, presenting them as Sufi values; the second is his insistence that the path to mystical gnosis must begin with traditional Islamic belief.[35] Based on this, "his writings and example solidified the religious sciences as the main body of studies for those seeking higher education."[36]

Al-Ghazali has come to be seen as one of the great architects of classical Islam's educational philosophy and ethics. His understanding of education as guidance rather than correction of the young, for example, became a prime pedagogical principle that recurs in many medieval writings on Islamic education. His most elaborate and influential views on teaching and learning are found in his *The Revival of the Sciences of Religion (Ihya' 'ulum al-din)*,[37] a work that is considered to be "a complete guide for the devout Muslim to every aspect of the religious life, worship and devotional practices, conduct in daily life, the purification of the heart, and advance along the mystic way."[38] It reflects al-Ghazali's deep conviction that religious knowledge and education are a means for humans in this world to attain salvation in the world to come.

Al-Ghazali's theological-mystical approach toward learning is evident, for instance, in his conception of both the "heart" and the human being, with the former being intimately linked to the latter. For al-Ghazali, the heart is a "transcendental spiritual subtlety which is connected to the physical heart; this subtlety is the essence of man, which comprehends, learns, and knows."[39] Therefore, he considers the heart of the child as being in particular need of special care and attention. For him, the heart of a child is "a precious jewel, neutral, free of all impressions, susceptible to every impression and

---

[35] Günther, "Education," 643.

[36] Stanton, *Higher Learning in Islam*, 87. See also M. E. Marmura, "Al-Ghazali," in *The Cambridge Companion to Arabic Philosophy*, ed. Peter Adamson and Richard C. Taylor (Cambridge: Cambridge University Press, 2005), 137–54.

[37] Important for the study of educational theory in Islam are, furthermore, (*a*) al-Ghazali's earlier and almost rationalistic work *The Balance of Action (Mizan al-'amal)*, ed. Sulayman Dunya (Cairo: Dar al-Ma'arif, 1964); the French translation is by Hikmat Hachem, *Critère de l'action* (Paris: G.-P. Maisonneuve, 1945); (*b*) *O Disciple (Ayyuha l-walad)*, written in reply to a former student, and advocating, among other things, the idea that knowledge proves its value by the fruits it produces in life (cf. the English translation by George Henry Scherer [Beirut: Imprimerie Catholique, 1951], xx of the introduction); and (*c*) *The Students' Guide (Minhaj al-mut'allimin)*, published in *Al-Turath al-tarbawi al-islami*, ed. Hisham Nashshaba (Beirut: Dar al-'Ilm li-l-Malayin, 1988), 55–92, a treatise attributed to al-Ghazali.

[38] W. Montgomery Watt, "Al-Ghazali," in *Encyclopaedia of Islam*, 2:1038–41, esp. 1040.

[39] Leon Zolondek, *Book XX of al-Ghazali's Ihya' 'Ulum al-Din* (Leiden: Brill, 1963), 3–4. See also Julian Obermann, *Der philosophische und religiöse Subjektivismus Ghazalis: Ein Beitrag zum Problem der Religion* (Vienna: Braumüller, 1921), 313–14.

every inclination to which it is brought near. If one accustoms it to good, the child will grow into a happy state in this world and the next, and his parents and educators will have part of this reward. But if one accustoms it to evil and the child is left to himself like an animal, he will be unhappy and will go to perdition, and his educators and teachers will bear the responsibility."[40] This line of thought is continued by his advice that the heart needs to be educated, since "just as the body is not created perfect but its perfection is achieved by means of sustenance which makes it strong and great, so also the soul (heart) is created imperfect but is susceptible to perfection which it can only attain by education, good morals, and knowledge."[41]

Al-Ghazali makes it very clear that, for him, true knowledge is not simply a memorized accumulation of facts but rather "a light which floods the heart." Therefore, the first and foremost aim of learning is the study of the divine. Al-Ghazali thus exhorts the students to attain the gem, that is, the knowledge of the hereafter, for "the noblest of all disciplines is the one of knowing God. . . . Seek, therefore, nothing else and treasure nothing besides it."[42] Despite al-Ghazali's predilection for the "science of the hereafter," he does not scorn other branches of scholarship; he merely ranks them lower. In fact, he praises those who study them and compares them with "those who have undertaken to guard the outposts of Islam where they are encamped, or . . . the conquerors who are warring on behalf of God."[43]

Since all who "seek God through knowledge, no matter what kind" are embarking on a blessed journey, al-Ghazali provides assistance to both those beginning the journey and those who guide others on the mystical path of learning.[44] It is to this end that he devotes the first chapter of *The Revival* to "The Excellence of Knowledge, Teaching, and Learning" (*Fadl al-'ilm wa-l-ta'lim wa-l-ta'allum*), which is followed, in chapter 5, by a great catalog of detailed advice on the duties and proper behavior of both the students and the teachers, entitled "Rules of Conduct for the Student and Teacher" (*Adab al-muta'allim wa-l-mu'allim*).[45] Given the fame *The Revival* has received throughout the Muslim world since it appeared, it is safe to say that the pedagogical ideas and practical educational directions al-Ghazali formulates here have long found their way into mainstream Muslim society.

---

[40] Al-Ghazali, *Ihya' 'ulum al-din*, 15 vols. (Cairo: Mustafa al-Babi al-Halabi, 1356–1357/1937–1938), 8:130. These passages are slightly revised quotations of Zolondek's translation, 4; see also Arent J. Wensinck, *La pensée de Ghazzali* (Paris: Adrien-Maisonneuve, 1940), 44.

[41] Al-Ghazali, *Ihya' 'ulum al-din*, 8:110, Zolondek, trans., 5. See also Wensinck, *La pensée de Ghazzali* 45.

[42] Al-Ghazali, *Ihya' 'ulum al-din*, Faris, trans., 121, 130.

[43] Ibid., 129, 130.

[44] Ibid.

[45] It should be noted that in *The Revival* al-Ghazali revisits educational issues that he already discussed in *The Balance of Action* (see n. 37), an earlier work that he wrote before he became a mystic. Yet, apart from details, the concepts of learning are nearly identical in both of these works.

Al-Ghazali specifies the rules of conduct for students in 10 points:

1. The student must first purify his soul by ridding himself of bad habits and other unpleasant character flaws. Thus he prepares himself to become a worthy vessel for knowledge.
2. The student must remove himself as far as possible from his ties to the affairs of the world, because the ties to family and country pull him away from fully focusing on knowledge. As al-Ghazali notes, "Knowledge will surrender nothing to a person unless the person surrenders his all to it."[46]
3. The student must not set himself above his teacher and should accept whatever his teacher teaches him. He should embrace all advice proffered by his teacher and trust his guidance implicitly: "The pupil [is to] be to his teacher like the soft soil which has received heavy rains and completely absorbed them."[47]
4. The student must ignore the contradictory opinions of others in his chosen field and concentrate on mastering the "one and only praiseworthy way" given by his teacher. Only then may he consider other schools of thought. Additionally, he should ensure that the teacher he chooses is one who follows his own line of reasoning and does not continually voice the opinions of others, for this behavior is "more misleading than it is helpful."[48]
5. The serious student must ensure that the nature and scope of all branches of knowledge become familiar to him, because all types of knowledge are linked and related to each other. If time permits, all of them should be studied in detail; if not, then mastering the most important is imperative.
6. The student, however, must not attempt to study everything at once. Rather, he should order his study, beginning with the most important disciplines.
7. The student must not study a new branch of knowledge until the previous has been mastered, because each new bit of knowledge builds on the foundation of the previous one. Moreover, no science or branch of knowledge should be deemed useless because of the faults of its practitioners or because of the disagreements that may arise among them.
8. The student must know how to judge the noble nature of a science. This is a twofold judgment: one entails being able to appraise the fruit of the science and the other is to be able to assess the validity of its principles.

---

[46] Compare al-Ghazali, *Ihya' 'ulum al-din*, Faris, trans., 129.

[47] Ibid., 130.

[48] Ibid., 132.

9. The student's immediate purpose should be the attainment of inner virtue, and his ultimate goal should be to draw close to God and achieve spiritual perfection rather than to gain authority and to look impressive in front of his peers.

10. Finally, the student is to have a clear idea of the "relation of the different sciences to the goal [of learning]."[49] This will enable him to give correct weight to those matters that he encounters rather than to judge the less important to be the more important and vice versa.

In complement to the student's role, al-Ghazali identifies the following eight rules of conduct for teachers:

1. The teacher should be sympathetic to his students and "treat them as his own children."[50]

2. The teacher should follow the example of the Prophet Muhammad and teach for free. He should not seek praise or payment for his services but should teach solely "for the glory of God." In this way, he is like the "Lawgiver" (i.e., the Prophet Muhammad) and, thus, will draw nearer to God.[51]

3. The teacher is obliged to ensure that each of his students works at the correct level for himself. He is to do this by supplying them with the necessary information they require to succeed and not allowing them to attempt to move to the next, more difficult level until they have mastered the simpler one that precedes it. On a different note, he should also tell the student that the reason he is learning is to get closer to God and not for any worldly gain.

4. The teacher must persuade his students to give up bad habits by subtle suggestion and compassion rather than by doing it openly and reproachfully. Direct attempts to dissuade people from following a bad course often lead to their open defiance.

5. The teacher must not say anything derogatory about sciences other than those he is teaching but, rather, use his own subject to prepare his students for learning other branches of knowledge later on.

6. The teacher must ensure that the materials he provides for the students' study and tests are not too difficult for them; student success is important, for it ensures that the student continues to enjoy learning.

7. With regard to students who are having difficulties learning, as al-Ghazali states firmly, the teacher must ensure that "only things clear and suitable to their [limited understanding]" should be taught to

---

[49] Ibid., 138.
[50] Ibid., 145.
[51] Ibid., 146.

them.[52] Additionally, the details or specifics that are not common should not be presented to them so as not to confuse and discourage them.

8. Last but not least, the teacher must practice and live what he knows and teaches, and not allow his work or behavior to contradict his words.

Al-Ghazali's catalog of advice for students and teachers clearly marks a high point in the classical Islamic educational tradition. It allows us to picture this scholar as an academic educator who is fully aware of his responsibilities. He is someone who passionately cares for his students and attempts to help them actualize their best potential. Likewise, he is concerned with the state of the teaching profession. These observations help us to understand why al-Ghazali's educational ideas have lost nothing of their significance over the centuries and why they are attractive even to today's educators. It is therefore not surprising that his requirements for students and teachers have provided many generations of Muslims with guidance and inspiration, including later medieval scholars who also wrote on pedagogic and didactic issues. Nasir al-Din al-Tusi (d. 1274), a Shiite philosopher-vizier and scientist from Iran, for example, suggests that education is a process involving the teacher, the student, and the student's parent(s); he also says that the process of obtaining knowledge is in itself a pleasure and that it can lead to everlasting happiness. Likewise, al-ʿAlmawi (d. 1573), a scholar and preacher at the Great Umayyad Mosque in Damascus, Syria, strongly promotes the idea of books being indispensable tools for learning. Of course, both of these ideas are so commonplace today that we easily forget that at one time they were novel.[53]

Conclusion

Several points are evident from our study. First, early Muslim scholars writing on education were well aware of the vital importance that accessible and efficient education holds for societies developing as dynamically as those of Islamic civilization were from the ninth to the twelfth centuries. This is evident from their discussions of educational matters, which display an awareness of principal issues, an open-minded approach, and a preference for

---

[52] Ibid., 151.

[53] Two major works on education by Muslim scholars from later medieval times are available in English translation: Burhan al-Din al-Zarnuji (first half of the thirteenth century), a Hanafi scholar from Iran, provides in his *Instruction of the Student: The Method of Learning* detailed, pious advice on the study of theology. He emphasizes—as many scholars of his and later times do—the integrity and purity of the transmission of knowledge of that which has already been definitely established; see the translation by G. E. von Grunebaum and Theodora M. Abel (New York: King's Crown Press, 1947). Furthermore, there is *The Memoir of the Listener and the Speaker in the Training of Teacher and Student* by Ibn Jamaʿa (d. 1333), a Shafiʿi chief judge in Egypt and Syria; this work was translated by Noor Muhammad Ghifari in the series One Hundred Great Books of Islamic Civilisation, vol. 10, *Education and Pursuit of Knowledge* (Islamabad: Pakistan Hijra Council, 1991).

analytical reasoning. Moreover, these scholars appear to have been remarkably creative and original in developing pedagogical theories that could be applied to the culturally diverse contexts in which they lived. These findings are of note for the intellectual history of Islam. However, they are also of interest within the paradigms of modern liberal democracies, with their appreciation of logical reasoning, scientific response to individual and societal needs, and pluralism.

The second point is a development of the first. It concerns the central place medieval Muslim scholars grant the "ethics" and "aesthetics" of learning. As we have seen, they perceived the ethical conduct of education to be essential for success at all stages of learning. Thus, intellectual instruction was not limited to imparting knowledge of facts and data. Rather, as al-Ghazali informs us, the responsibilities of teachers extend to bestowing on their students enduring values and to educating them to desire the good. Interestingly, al-Jahiz, Ibn Sina, al-Ghazali, and others suggest as well that the framework of education, designed for the imparting and acquisition of knowledge and skills, be transformed into something more desirable, so that learning becomes both effective and enjoyable for all participants, and nobody is left behind.

Third, medieval Muslim theorists of education value highly passion for instruction and passionate desire for learning. As Ibn Sahnun maintains, modesty, patience, and a passion for working with children are indispensable qualifications for teachers; al-Jahiz depicts teachers as knowledgeable and hardworking people who lovingly care for their students; al-Farabi argues that instruction be a student-centered process, in which the teachers facilitate in the best possible way their students' comprehension and own educational voyage; and Ibn Sina recommends that teachers need not only to possess adequate pedagogical qualifications but also to be virtuous people and of laudable character. These are ideas of great appeal to the modern educator, since the ethical and emotional aspects of learning seem almost to be disappearing in our technologically defined, bureaucratic world. Similarly, today's educators would benefit from reemphasizing the idea that teaching is a caring profession.

Although every era is determined by its own distinct characteristics, tasks, and impulses, both culturally and pedagogically, the circumstances and issues of each age are part of the larger picture of humankind's development and need to be viewed in this way. In other words, we cannot expect to obtain solutions to the questions we have in education today by simply "deducing" them from the past or "retrieving" them from some universal system of thought. Yet, we can clearly deal with today's educational issues more successfully when we know their historical contexts and have an adequate understanding of them, since "today's issues in education are often rooted deeply in the historical grounds of the past," as Albert Reble correctly observed in the introduction to his *History of Pedagogy*.[54] Moreover, with sufficient awareness of what has come before us in the field of education, we will also be more confident in our ability to assess what is, in truth, progress in the field and, thus, to determine what truly needs to be done next in order "to see further."

In terms of their importance to the development of pedagogy, early Muslim thinkers writing on education share a pool of great ideas with figures in the Western educational tradition such as Master Eckehart (ca. 1260–1327), a Dominican theologian and writer and one of the greatest German speculative mystics, who, like al-Ghazali, says that the learner first needs to "let go" and "free himself" from things and people in order to make education possible and successful.[55] One may also think of the first specifically pedagogical treatises in medieval European intellectual history written by fifteenth-century Italian scholars, including Piero Paolo Vergerio (1370–1444), a physician and humanistic educator, who deals with the prerequisites and methods of moral, intellectual, and physical education. Like Ibn Sina, Vergerio stresses the need to adapt learning to the child's individual abilities and combine moral with intellectual instruction and with physical exercise at the earliest possible age.[56] Desiderius Erasmus (d. 1536), a theologian and humanist from Holland, in turn pleads with us to honor a student's individuality and establish a relationship between teacher and student that is based on mutual trust. In the same way as al-Jahiz, Erasmus advises us also to care for and respect the student.[57] Furthermore, Philipp Melanchthon (1497–1560), professor of Greek, theology, and rhetoric at Wittenberg University, Protestant reformer and "Teacher of Germany" (as he was called due to his far-reaching educational reform work), uses a rationalist approach toward learning that has much in common with al-Farabi's, including the idea of extending the curriculum at the more advanced level to fields such as literature, history, philosophy, and mathematics. Melanchthon also highlights eloquence as a basic prerequisite and tool of learning in a way that recalls al-Jahiz.[58] Similarly, Johann Amos Comenius (1592–1670), bishop, great Czech reformer, and "Father of Modern Education," emphasizes—much like his Muslim predecessors—the need for teaching all aspects of language, since good language skills are a basic prerequisite for intellectual improvement. Moreover, Comenius maintains as well that education should aim, in particular, at equipping young people with a profound knowledge of the Holy Scriptures and religious duties—ideas that are major concepts also in Islamic education,

---

[54] Albert Reble, *Geschichte der Pädagogik*, 21st ed. (Stuttgart: Klett-Cotta, 2004; 1st ed., 1951), 14–15.

[55] Winfried Böhm, *Geschichte der Pädagogik: Von Platon bis zur Gegenwart* (Munich: Beck, 2004), 41–42; H.-E. Tennorth, ed., *Klassiker der Pädagogik*, vol. 1, *Von Erasmus bis Helene Lange* (Munich: Beck, 2003), 88.

[56] Tennorth, *Von Erasmus bis Helene Lange*, 21–27.

[57] Böhm, *Geschichte der Pädagogik*, 45; Tennorth, *Von Erasmus bis Helene Lange*, 28–31.

[58] Böhm, *Geschichte der Pädagogik*, 51; Tennorth, *Von Erasmus bis Helene Lange*, 32–33.

expressly advocated by Ibn Sahnun, among others. It is no less important, however, that Comenius affirms as well that teachers should ensure a rapid, pleasant, and thorough education that follows in the footsteps of nature and, furthermore, that intellectual, spiritual, and emotional growth are all woven together—views discussed most insightfully, as we have seen, by al-Ghazali and several of his predecessors and successors in the rich tradition of Islamic educational theory.[59]

This article started out to provide insights into the developments of Islam's classical pedagogical tradition, attempting to show that medieval Muslim scholars have made serious contributions to humanity in various areas of education. It has become evident in the previous pages that the theoretical considerations, which medieval Muslim thinkers offer, are highly intellectual. Yet, they also display a desire for practical wisdom about learning and teaching, along with care for the ethical, moral, and emotional aspects of education. Finally, spiritual and religious components of knowledge acquisition and learning are of fundamental significance to them, with the Qur'anic revelation and the virtues of Islam placed at the very heart of Islamic education.

I believe that medieval Muslim educators understood well the intimate relationship between knowledge, theoretical and practical wisdom, logical reasoning, ethics and aesthetics of learning, loving and caring, and spirituality. If modernity is willing to learn from the past and, as the great American educational reformer and pragmatic philosopher John Dewey (1859–1952) put it, "conceive education as the process of forming fundamental dispositions, intellectual and emotional, toward nature and fellow-men," we can be confident that we can recreate that which we seem to have lost and so restore our picture of an education system that gives credence to human development as a whole.[60]

---

[59] Böhm, *Geschichte der Pädagogik*, 53–54; Tennorth, *Von Erasmus bis Helene Lange*, 45–59. Hermann Weimer, *Geschichte der Pädagogik*, 19., völlig neu bearb. Auflage von Juliane Jacobi, Sammlung Göschen 2080 (Berlin: de Gruyter, 1992), 81–86.

[60] Jim Garrison, *Dewey and Eros: Wisdom and Desire in the Art of Teaching* (New York: Teachers College, Columbia University, 1997), introduction, xx.

Islamic Education and Civil Society: Reflections on the *Pesantren* Tradition in Contemporary Indonesia

FLORIAN POHL

Since the events of September 11, 2001, Islamic institutions of learning have received much attention. Indonesia's *pesantren* (Islamic boarding schools) have been increasingly described as fostering radicalism and violent militancy, particularly in light of purported links between a few of the country's *pesantren* and some of the perpetrators of recent violence, such as the 2002 bombing in Kuta, Bali. On the whole, media coverage has been negative.[1] In its September 2003 issue, for example, the *Journal of Asian Affairs* alleged, "Like Pakistan's madrassa, there exists an entire education system, the 'pesantren', which is independent of the government and provides the Islamists fertile ground to train the children of the poor in the mould of radical Islam."[2] Notably, Pondok Pesantren Al-Mukmin in Ngruki, which is close to the Central Javanese city of Solo, has been mentioned repeatedly in the international press and was also implicated by an International Crisis Group (ICG) report as the center for a network of militant Muslims in Indonesia with suspected links to al-Qaeda.[3]

In light of these allegations, the question about the possible civility-enhancing role of Islamic education may seem counterintuitive. How does Islamic education deal with such issues as antiviolence, interfaith and inter-ethnic tolerance, pluralism, secular institutionalization, human rights, gender equity, democracy, and political and social justice? This article answers some of these questions based on an analysis of ethnographic data collected during fieldwork in 2004 and 2005. At its center are a case study of Pesantren Al-Muayyad Windan, Solo, and an evaluation of this institution's contribution to Indonesia's emerging democratic civil society. Al-Muayyad Windan was founded in 1996 as a *pesantren* for students (*pesantren mahasiswa*) with a special emphasis on community development (*pengembangan masyarakat*). The focus on one distinct institution out of the more than 14,000 *pesantren* in Indonesia provides a limited view. While any sample selection will have limitations, the educational reality at this *pesantren* deserves attention not because it is rep-

---

[1] See, e.g., Timothy Mapes, "Indonesian School Has Chilling Roster of Terrorist Alumni," *Wall Street Journal*, September 3, 2003; Jane Perlez, "Saudis Quietly Promote Strict Islam in Indonesia," *New York Times*, July 5, 2003; Andrew Marshall, "The Threat of Jaffar," *New York Times*, March 10, 2002; Daniel Kestenholz, "Saudisches Geld für indonesische Terroristen? Radikale Islamisten gewinnen Einfluss—Fungieren Religionsschulen als Geldwaschanlagen der Al Qaida?" *Die Welt*, July 15, 2003.

[2] S. S. Misra, "Islamic Terrorism in Indonesia," *ASIANaffairs*, September 2003, available at http://www.asianaffairs.com/sept2003/focus_islamic.htm (last accessed December 13, 2005).

[3] International Crisis Group, "Al-Qaeda in Southeast Asia: The Case of the 'Ngruki' Network in Indonesia," ICG Asia Briefing no. 20 (International Crisis Group, Jakarta/Brussels, August 8, 2002), available at http://www.crisisgroup.org.

resentative of the majority of *pesantren* in all aspects of its educational program. Rather, within the wide diversity of Indonesia's *pesantren* it occupies a prominent position that opens the debate on questions of the appropriate role of religion in education and public life.

The discussion here is placed within the broader debate about religion in the public sphere. This means revisiting the secularization thesis that influences perspectives on expressions of public religion as much as it is a shaping force on perspectives on Islamic education. If secularization, understood as the privatization and subsequent marginalization of religious beliefs and practices, is seen as the necessary precondition for the successful accommodation of the epistemological and social changes ushered in by modernity, Islamic education, with its assertion of Islam's central role in the curriculum, can then be configured as "antimodern." By implication, Muslim educational institutions appear unable either to accommodate modern scientific and technological change or to incorporate or support the pluralization and democratization of public life. Here I argue that traditional Islamic education can and does make significant contributions to the empowerment of democratic civil society and that Indonesia's long-established Islamic boarding schools in particular are not inimical to such "modern" concerns as women's empowerment and good interfaith relations in a plural society.

How Liberal Educationalists Shape the Perspective on Islamic Education

Particularly since the events of September 11, 2001, Islamic educational institutions have been stigmatized as "fundamentalist schools" and "universities of *jihad*," characterized as having much larger enrollments than they do, and suspected of fostering a medieval mind-set and violent militancy.[4] Similar assertions are not new to the public debate about Islamic education. For example, in Germany, Bassam Tibi labeled attempts to institutionalize the teaching of Islam in German public schools as "Trojanisches Pferd der radikalen Muslime" (the Trojan horse of radical Muslims).[5] In Britain, David Bell commented that Muslim schools were not communicating a British "common heritage," nor were they teaching citizenship.[6]

As outlined above, Indonesia's system of religious schools faces similar accusations. In light of these charges, it may not be surprising that the United States announced in late August 2004 that it would provide $157 million to Indonesia over a period of 5 years in order to enhance the quality of in-

---

[4] A recent World Bank Study on Pakistani religious schools finds that the existing estimates in reports and articles are based on significantly overstated enrollment numbers and do not sufficiently explain the motivation of schooling choices; see Tahir Andrabi, Jishnu Das, Asim Ijaz Khwaja, and Tristan Zajonce, "Religious School Enrollment in Pakistan: A Look at the Data," in this issue.

[5] Bassam Tibi, "Trojanisches Pferd der radikalen Muslime," *Focus*, May 31, 1999.

[6] Sean Coughlan, "Muslim Schools 'Deeply Upset,'" *BBC News*, January 18, 2005, available at http://news.bbc.co.uk/go/pr/fr/−/1/hi/education/4184319.stm (last accessed December 14, 2005).

struction in the country's religious schools, thereby hoping to curb the growth of Muslim radicalism throughout the archipelago.

The question of whether there is a verifiable connection between Islamic education in Indonesia's *pesantren* and Muslim radicalism, however, has received different answers.[7] Radicalism and violence aside, problems and challenges for the *pesantren* tradition have long been identified by both Western and Indonesian educationalists when reflecting on the schools' potentials to prepare students for life in Indonesia's modernizing society. Their education is considered substandard, underfunded, and staffed by teachers of low quality. By and large, the *pesantren* are deemed unfit to produce the type of graduate capable of making creative contributions to the process of modernization and social transformation on which the country has embarked. Modernization, indeed, is deemed "the root problem facing the pesantren."[8]

The challenges of educational reform and modernization facing Indonesia's *pesantren* coincide with difficulties confronted by Muslim educational institutions worldwide. Since the advent of colonial rule in many Muslim countries, indigenous systems of education have either collapsed or been marginalized. The complex legacy of indigenous reform, colonial rule, postindependence nationalism and socialism, and more recent expressions of Islamic revival further complicates attempts at educational reform. The resurgence of Islamic educational institutions in countries such as Pakistan and Iran, as well as the growth of Muslim schools in Western countries, has been viewed with concern as a move toward exclusivism and intolerance. Intellectual efforts to modernize Islamic education and to create a unified model of Islamic education have been viewed with similar suspicion.[9] Muslim schools are portrayed as unable to prepare children adequately for the needs of the modern world. They are thought unfit to help students take advantage of the scientific, technological, and economic progress that characterizes modern life and,

---

[7] See, e.g., Ronald Lukens-Bull's descriptions of the *pesantren* as forward-looking regarding the relationship between general and religious education and primarily focused on character development ("Teaching Morality: Javanese Islamic Education in a Globalizing Era," *Journal of Arab and Islamic Studies* 3 [2000]: 26–48). In contrast, the target of research such as that undertaken by the International Crisis Group (ICG) has been on a number of *pesantren*, such as Ngruki and the Hidayatullah network, with ties to militant Muslim organizations in Southeast Asia. See International Crisis Group, "Jemaah Islamiyah in South East Asia: Damaged but Still Dangerous," ICG Asia Report no. 63 (International Crisis Group, Jakarta/Brussels, August 26, 2003), available at http://www.crisisgroup.org.

[8] Nashihin Hasan, "Character and Function of Pesantren," in *The Impact of Pesantren in Education and Community Development in Indonesia*, ed. M. Oepen and W. Karcher, with assistance from R. Kingham (Berlin: Technical University Berlin, 1988), 83–90, 87.

[9] One of the most notable intellectual efforts to modernize Islamic education was by the First International Conference on Muslim Education in Mecca in 1977. Muslim educationists deliberated over how to lay the intellectual groundwork for an Islamic system of education that was based on fundamental Islamic values and beliefs yet that at the same would accommodate the expansion of knowledge, modern social and economic developments, and the professional needs of students in the contemporary world. See S. Muhammad al-Naquib al-Attas, *Aims and Objectives of Islamic Education* (Jeddah: Hodder & Stoughton, 1979).

instead, are deemed to deliver what is dangerously akin to indoctrination.[10] Of particular concern are questions of how an Islamic system of education would work in a pluralist and multicultural society. How would it deal with the internal diversity of the Muslim community? Whose interpretation of Islam would be considered binding within such a system? How would it address the rights and sentiments of religious minorities and women?

It is striking that, as J. Mark Halstead points out, there is a convergence of questions and arguments against Islamic education with criticism by liberal educationists of religious education in Western countries, particularly in opposition to church-related education.[11] In *Religious Schools v. Children's Rights*, for example, James Dwyer offers a critique of parochial education in which he attacks religious schools for indoctrinating students and violating their individual rights of personal, physical, and political liberty, as well as their freedoms of thought and expression.[12] Dwyer's arguably one-sided account of the effects of religious schooling is congruent with a longer history of criticism by liberal educationists who question the relevance and legitimacy of religious learning in the school systems of secular, democratic, and pluralistic societies. Religious schools are described as institutions that propagate specific religious beliefs and through their education seek to initiate students into a particular faith, instead of providing them with the critical faculties to scrutinize traditional beliefs and practices. Their instruction is compared to indoctrination and understood to be opposed to concepts of education based on the autonomy and freedom of the individual.[13] A related concern has been to criticize religious educational theory for a narrow and rigid claim to truth. The alleged dogmatism implied in such a concept of education is tagged as a cause for intolerance toward those of a different persuasion, religious or otherwise. If one wants to avoid the pitfalls and dangers of religious education, a liberal educationist such as Paul Heywood Hirst suggests, religious beliefs should remain in the private sphere of an individual's life and must not "determine public issues" such as education.[14] Again, religious education is understood to be an essentially private matter. If one were to follow liberal educationists' advice, religious education would remain a separate and personal responsibility, having no place in public education.

Over the past years such challenges have opened up anew the debate over the appropriate status and role of religion in education in majority

[10] For an outline of what he calls a "secularist critique" of Islamic education, see Bradley J. Cook, "Islamic versus Western Conceptions of Education: Reflections on Egypt," *International Review of Education* 45, nos. 3–4 (1999): 339–57.

[11] J. Mark Halstead, "Towards a Unified View of Islamic Education," *Islam and Christian-Muslim Relations* 6, no. 1 (June 1995): 25–44.

[12] James G. Dwyer, *Religious Schools v. Children's Rights* (Ithaca, NY: Cornell University Press, 1998).

[13] John White, *The Aims of Education Restated* (London: Routledge & Kegan Paul, 1982), 166.

[14] Paul Heywood Hirst, *Moral Education in a Secular Society* (London: University of London Press, 1974), 3.

Muslim and non-Muslim countries alike. The objections to doctrinal religious instruction have been taken seriously, and trends toward the inclusion of a diversity of religions and interreligious perspectives can be observed. Increasingly, educators have sought new ways of integrating religious and spiritual topics into the curricula of modern schools without privileging one religious tradition over others.[15] A general skepticism about religion's involvement in education however, remains in part because recent conversations about religion and education are located in the context of a broader debate about religion's role in the public sphere of modern, pluralist societies.

Religion in the Public Sphere: Revisiting the Secularization Thesis

In the current debate about religion in the public sphere, the secularization thesis is the master paradigm. To put it simply, the idea of secularization supposes that in industrialized, highly educated, professionally specialized, and technologically advanced societies, religion will inevitably and progressively decline. However, while the process of modernization has undoubtedly had many secularizing consequences around the world, it has also triggered a myriad of countertrends as evidenced by the movements of religious revival worldwide. Expressions of religious commitment in the United States aptly demonstrate that a secular constitution and the separation of religion and state do not necessarily lead to secularization on the level of individual conviction. Recent polls show religious nonbelief to be a distinctly minority position in the United States.[16] Complexities abound when one considers that in the countries of northern Europe with their well-funded state churches very few people practice the religion represented by these institutions.

The foregoing considerations hint at an intricately rich story about religion and modern public life, a story that more recently has given rise to a lively debate over the strength of the secularization thesis. Intertwined with other Enlightenment narratives of modernization, rationalization, and progress, the secularization thesis has its origins in the European historical experience. It postulated the separation of almost all aspects of life and thought from ecclesiastical control, although the word "secular" was not used to refer to these developments until the nineteenth century. In the European historical experience shaped by the wars of the sixteenth and seventeenth centuries, the idea of secularization was upheld against the dominations inscribed

---

[15] See W. Weiße, ed., *Interreligious and Intercultural Education: Methodologies, Conceptions and Pilot-Projects in South Africa, Namibia, Great Britain, the Netherlands and Germany* (Münster: Waxmann, 1996). For a work that seeks to reopen the debate about the appropriate role of religion in education in the United States, see Martin M. Marty, with Jonathan Moore, *Education, Religion and the Common Good* (San Francisco: Jossey-Bass, 2000).

[16] In January 2004, the BBC program *What the World Thinks of God* published the results of an opinion survey in 10 countries indicating that about 9 out of 10 Americans believed in God or a higher power (available at http://news.bbc.co.uk/1/hi/programmes/wtwtgod [last accessed December 10, 2005]).

in religion. The establishment of a secular public sphere was considered to assure the nonviolent accommodation of growing religious diversity while at the same time guaranteeing personal freedoms and the democratization of public life.

The privatization and decline of religious beliefs and practices were seen as necessary and beneficial. Karl Marx, Emile Durkheim, and Max Weber all predicted that social developments would drastically alter and diminish the importance of religion in modern times. Progressive secularization was seen as central to modernity, progress, and emancipation. While it has been acknowledged at times that secularization might not necessarily entail the decline and disappearance of religion, subjective and privatized forms of religious expression alone were considered compatible with modernity, and the loss of religion's traditional societal and public functions was postulated as a precondition for modernization.[17]

More recently, however, the alleged inevitability of progressive secularization has been challenged. Far from fading away and disappearing in the modern world, many areas of the globe have witnessed strong movements of religious revival. The recognition of the continuing vitality of religion around the world has disrupted the consensus about the universality and inevitability of the process of secularization and has prompted Peter Berger to declare "that the whole body of literature by historians and social scientists loosely labeled 'secularization theory' is essentially mistaken."[18]

Prompted by the growing strength of revivalist movements, the scholarly debate about the theory of progressive secularization started about four decades ago. The works of David Martin and Andrew Greeley called into question the idea of a steady erosion of religion with empirical data to the contrary. While some scholars such as David Martin called for abandoning the concept of secularization altogether, others sought to reevaluate the secularization narrative by questioning its universal validity and demanding that the concept be understood in relation to the historical context in which it originated.[19] These works have advanced the realization that the theory of progressive secularization fails to describe not only changes in many parts of the "developing" world but also seriously misreads the situation of religion in countries of the "developed" world.[20]

[17] The view that religion should occupy a marginal and inconsequential role from a societal point of view is articulated in Thomas Luckmann, *The Invisible Religion: The Problem of Religion in Modern Society* (New York: Macmillan, 1967).

[18] Peter L. Berger, "The Desecularization of the World: A Global Overview," in *The Desecularization of the World,* ed. Peter L. Berger (Grand Rapids, MI: Ethics and Public Policy Center and Eerdmans, 1999), 1–18, 2.

[19] See David Martin's collection of essays spanning the years 1965–69: *The Religious and the Secular: Studies in Secularization* (New York: Schocken, 1969); Janet R. Jakobsen and Ann Pellegrini, "World Secularisms and the Millenium: Introduction," *Social Text* 18, no. 3 (Fall 2000): 1–27.

[20] The public role of religion in the United States is the focus of Hugh Heclo and Wilfred M. McClay, eds., *Religion Returns to the Public Square: Faith and Policy in America* (Washington, DC: Woodrow Wilson Center, 2003).

Of particular significance to these critiques of the secularization thesis are questions about religion and "civil society," loosely understood as society organized outside of the state. One of the most influential studies in this field, which has reopened the debate about religion in the public sphere, is Jose Casanova's *Public Religions in the Modern World.* As Casanova demonstrates in his study of Catholic and Protestant movements in Spain, Poland, Brazil, and the United States, not every public expression of religion is conservative or exhibits exclusivist, oppressive, or dominating tendencies. Sometimes the rise of religious expression in the public sphere is central to progressive politics and compatible with democracy and political civility.[21] It is precisely in the public sphere of civil society that Casanova sees a space for religion to make desirable contributions by participating in an open discussion about public affairs.

Within Islamic studies there has also been a debate over issues of public religion and civil society. John Kelsay and Richard Bulliet, for example, both argue that historically "Islam" has functioned not to legitimate or justify state power but to set limits to despotism and to hold uncontrolled state power in check.[22] Others contend that Islam has an inherently civil character, compatible with modern notions of democracy and human rights.[23] And in Indonesia, there has been a lively debate over Islam's role in society, leading Robert Hefner to declare that Indonesia espouses a large and growing number of "civil pluralist Muslims."[24]

Civil Islam: Current Debate about Islam's Role in Indonesian Society

Islam represents a crucial element in the current sociopolitical discourse in Indonesia. Within a wider spectrum of varying degrees of commitment to Islamic law, pluralism, and democracy, the emergence of militant and exclusivist Muslim movements throughout the archipelago is a disconcerting development. The cases of extremist violence, however, provide but a truncated and one-sided picture of the involvement of Muslim voices in the Indonesian public sphere. The country also exhibits, as Hefner describes it, an emerging

---

[21] Jose Casanova, *Public Religions in the Modern World* (Chicago: University of Chicago Press, 1994).

[22] John Kelsay, "Civil Society and Government in Islam," in *Civil Society and Government,* Ethikon Series in Comparative Ethics, ed. Nancy Rosenblum and R. Post (Princeton, NJ: Princeton University Press, 2002), 284–316; Richard W. Bulliet, "Twenty Years of Islamic Politics," *Middle East Journal* 53 (Spring 1999): 189–200.

[23] See, e.g., Abdulaziz Sachedina, *The Islamic Roots of Democratic Pluralism* (Oxford: Oxford University Press, 2001).

[24] In Hefner's words, these are Muslims who "deny the necessity of a formally established Islamic state, emphasize that it is the spirit and not the letter of Islamic law (*shariah*) to which Muslims must attend, stress the need for programmes to elevate the status of women, and insist that the Muslim world's most urgent task is to develop moral tools to respond to the challenge of modern pluralism" (Robert W. Hefner, "Secularization and Citizenship in Muslim Indonesia," in *Religion, Modernity and Postmodernity,* ed. P. Heelas, with the assistance of D. Martin and P. Morris [Oxford: Blackwell, 1998], 148).

democratic and civil-pluralist tradition that seeks to uncover and build on the resources of the Islamic tradition for the accommodation of modern democratic and pluralist change.[25] Most notably, sociopolitical commitment and support for democracy as well as religious and cultural pluralism can be seen in the statements of the late Nurcholish Madjid, one of the leading Muslim Indonesian intellectuals of his time. Madjid actively promoted a culture of democratic pluralism and public civility from an Islamic point of view. Through his many statements and publications, he shaped the public discourse on issues such as pluralism and democracy. He argued, untiringly, that the Islamic principles of justice and human dignity are not only compatible with notions of democracy, human rights, and civil society but are, in fact, demanded by them.[26]

Certainly, the success of democratic structures in Indonesia depends on more than the ideas and statements of the country's leading intellectuals. Although the influence of community leaders on the political attitudes and dispositions of the population cannot be underestimated, formal political structures of government as well as organizational structures apart from the institutions of the state are equally important for creating viable democratic institutions. And over the past years in Indonesia civil society organizations have played a significant role in spreading ideas about pluralism and democracy. These include but are not limited to a growing number of Muslim nongovernmental organizations (NGOs) that promote democratic pluralism and civility, often from within a distinctly Islamic framework. Among the most prominent contemporary NGOs are the Indonesian Society for Pesantren and Community Development (Perhimpunan Pengembangan Pesantren dan Masyarakat [P3M]) and the Institute for Islamic and Social Studies (Lembaga Kajian Islam dan Sosial [LKiS]). The main goal of Jakarta-based P3M is to promote community development with a particular focus on pluralism and democracy. In its work P3M often utilizes the extensive network of Indonesia's *pesantren*, which are both agents for and targets of community development programs. A social research organization, LKiS seeks to rethink critically Islamic values and ideas in the light of contemporary social change. In the process, it has become one of the leading Indonesian publishers of social studies research. More recently, the Liberal Islam Network (Jaringan Islam Liberal) has emerged as a leading advocate for interreligious tolerance utilizing a variety of media to spread their creative and progressive ideas and to further public dialogue within an Islamic context.

This rich tapestry of organizational structures, apart from the state ap-

---

[25] See Robert W. Hefner, *Civil Islam: Muslims and Democratization in Indonesia* (Princeton, NJ: Princeton University Press, 2000).

[26] See, e.g., Nurcholish Madjid, "Potential Islamic Doctrinal Resources for the Establishment and Appreciation of the Modern Concept of Civil Society," in *Islam and Civil Society in Southeast Asia*, ed. Nakamura Mitsuo, Sharon Siddique, and Omar Farouk Bajunid (Singapore: Institute for Southeast Asian Studies, 2001), 149–63.

paratus, which promotes an open and inclusive political climate, further includes Indonesia's two largest Muslim mass-organizations, Nahdlatul Ulama and Muhammadiyah. These two organizations have an influence reaching far beyond their combined membership of more than 50 million Indonesians, making them key actors in the present debate over the role of Islam in society. Notwithstanding the differences in religious perspective between the traditionalist Nahdlatul Ulama and the modernist Muhammadiyah, over the past years the leaderships of both organizations have consistently affirmed their commitment to democratic reform and participation within the political process, spoken out against the establishment of an Islamic state, and promoted the establishment of a Muslim civil society dedicated to an inclusive and tolerant Islam.[27] Both Nahdlatul Ulama and Muhammadiyah have been able to rely on Indonesia's Islamic educational scene to mobilize support for their more moderate brand of Indonesian Islam, which they saw threatened by the recent acts of incivility. Muhammadiyah maintains its own private universities, with more than 30 campuses throughout the country, as well as a network of schools that employ a curriculum combining general and religious subjects sanctioned by the Department of Religious Affairs. While the number of universities affiliated with Nahdlatul Ulama is far smaller, the majority of Indonesia's *pesantren* that pervade the country have strong cultural affiliations with Nahdlatul Ulama.

The *Pesantren* in the Context of Indonesia's Islamic Education System

When Indonesia became independent in 1945, the firmly established Dutch colonial system was immediately nationalized and provided the basic foundation for the public system of education. Today, not unlike other former colonies, Indonesia exhibits a dualistic structure of sectors: state and private schooling. Parallel to the state system—a remnant of Dutch colonial schooling—we find a broad system of private, mostly religious schools, some of which provide formal education recognized by the state. On the secondary level of schooling, the public schools (*sekolah*) are paralleled by the mostly privately organized *madrasah* system, which was championed by Muhammadiyah and the modernist movement in the early twentieth century. Essentially a graded school organization modeled on the Western education system, the *madrasah* system employs a curriculum sanctioned by the Department of Religious Affairs consisting of 70 percent general and 30 percent religious subjects. It thus qualifies its graduates to continue their education in the public sector at the postsecondary level.

In contrast to the *madrasah*, which is a religious day school, the *pesantren*

---

[27] For statements by representatives belonging to the leadership of Nahdlatul Ulama and Muhammadiyah about the role of their organizations in promoting civil society, see Mitsuo, Siddique, and Bajunid, *Islam and Civil Society in Southeast Asia*.

operates as an Islamic boarding school. The *pesantren* are traditionally providers of private, nonformal (religious) education and do not issue state-recognized certificates for these educational activities. They range from local Koran schools, in which students are instructed in the system of Koran recitation, to religious colleges akin to those found in the Middle East. Some have only a few regular students, a single teacher, and perhaps some small agricultural fields, whereas others instruct upward of 3,000 students. Zamakhsyari Dhofier describes the following elements as constitutive of traditional *pesantren* life: the mosque (as its religious, social, and educational center), student dormitories (*pondok*), the students (*santri*), the *pesantren* leader (*kiai*), and the study of classical Islamic texts (*kitab kuning*).[28]

This dualism of state and private institutions persists on the level of higher education. It would be wrong, however, to assume that the distinction between private and state institutions corresponds with a division between religious and secular schools. Since the 1960s, instruction in religion has been mandatory for all institutions in the public schooling sector. The state maintains its own *madrasah* as well as numerous Islamic colleges and universities, such as the State Institutes for Islamic Studies (Institut Agama Islam Negeri), State Islamic Colleges (Sekolah Tinggi Agama Islam Negeri), and State Islamic Universities (Universitas Islam Negeri). The state system of Islamic higher education comprises almost 50 campuses nationwide and has been described as "bastion of tolerant, liberal, pluralistic Islam."[29] The largest Muslim country in the world, Indonesia displays not only a diverse variety of institutions of Islamic education but also boasts a dynamic publishing sector for Islamic educational literature.

Answers to questions of the nature and function of Islamic education and of the relationship between religious and general education are, of course, anything but homogenous. The vibrant public debate in Indonesia about Islamic education exhibits elements that are well ahead of the corresponding debate in other South and Southeast Asian countries.[30] It is within the context of this wider debate about Islamic education that developments within the *pesantren* tradition have to be understood.

---

[28] Zamakhsyari Dhofier, *The Pesantren Tradition: The Role of the Kyai in the Maintenance of Traditional Islam in Java* (Tempe, AZ: Program for Southeast Asian Studies, 1999), 23.

[29] Merle C. Ricklefs, "Islamizing Indonesia: Religion and Politics in Singapore's Giant Neighbour" (public lecture at the Asian Civilizations Museum, Singapore, September, 23, 2004), available at http://www.ari.nus.edu.sg/docs/PLS_Merle_Ricklefs_Paper.pdf (last accessed December 10, 2005).

[30] The vibrancy of the debate was underscored by a workshop on issues of Islamic education in which I participated in Solo in July 2005. The "Regional Workshop on the Strategy of Islamic Education in South and Southeast Asia" was jointly organized by the Ridep Institute and the German Friedrich Ebert Stiftung and brought together leading experts in Islamic education from the countries of Indonesia, Singapore, Malaysia, the Philippines, Thailand, Pakistan, India, Afghanistan, and Bangladesh.

The *Pesantren*: Status and Development

Even before *pesantren* received international attention in the aftermath of the Bali bombing in October 2002, Western scholars had studied various aspects of the *pesantren* tradition.[31] Clifford Geertz's *The Religion of Java* depicted the *pesantren* as rural Koranic schools that were isolated from the centers of the Muslim world in the Middle East and from their intellectual traditions and that reflected a somewhat less than orthodox version of Islam mired in animistic and Hindu-Buddhist beliefs and practices.[32] More recent studies such as Dhofier's have taken exception to Geertz's characterization of the *pesantren* as syncretistic and somewhat less than orthodox. Rather they are described as "deeply rooted in the study of classical Arabic texts" while at the same time participating "in the modern life through the reformation of [their] education."[33] The latter point signifies a related shift in scholarship on the *pesantren*. Previous scholarly work described the *pesantren* historically as political protest movements against the colonial regime.[34] Consequently, the *pesantren*'s oppositional role to the cultural impact of the colonial powers was highlighted, and integrative aspects were not mentioned. Over the past decades there have been more balanced descriptions of the Indonesian *pesantren* system in scholarly essays. These works stress a gradual change after independence from separatist to more cooperative institutions within Indonesian society through the development of more integrative functions.[35]

The complex legacies of indigenous reform, Dutch colonial rule, postindependence nationalism and socialism, and contemporary socioeconomic realities have forced many Muslim parents to give priority to strictly secular education. The resulting challenges to the status of the *pesantren* tradition partially coincide with developments in other parts of the non-Western world in which indigenous educational institutions have either collapsed or been marginalized. Today the *pesantren* are under pressure from the expanding domain of government schools to adopt current teaching techniques and to

---

[31] Despite the scholarly interest, little is known with certainty about the *pesantren* tradition's origins. The oldest existing *pesantren* in Indonesia today is Tegalsari in Ponorogo, East Java. It was established in the eighteenth century. On the grounds of historical evidence (or rather lack thereof) it may be assumed, as has been suggested by Martin van Bruinessen, that the *pesantren* as an institution of Islamic learning in the way we speak of it today does not go back much farther than the nineteenth century. For an instructive review of the historical evidence, see Martin van Bruinessen, "Pesantren and *Kitab Kuning*: Continuity and Change in a Tradition of Religious Learning," in *Texts from the Islands: Oral and Written Traditions of Indonesia and the Malay World*, ed. W. Marschall (Berne: University of Berne, 1994), 121–45.

[32] Clifford Geertz, *The Religion of Java* (Chicago: Collier-Macmillan, 1960), 125.

[33] Dhofier, *The Pesantren Tradition*, xii.

[34] See Sartono Kartodirdjo, *Protest Movements in Rural Java* (Singapore: Oxford University Press, 1973).

[35] In addition to the work by Dhofier (*The Pesantren Tradition*), see Alois Moosmüller, *Die Pesantren auf Java* (Frankfurt: Peter Lang, 1989); Manred Ziemek, *Pesantren: Traditionell islamische Bildung und sozialer Wandel in Indonesien* (Frankfurt: Verlag für interkulturelle Kommunikation, 1986); Ivan Hadar, *Bildung in Indonesien: Krise und Kontinuitaet* (Frankfurt: IKO, 1999).

include nonreligious subjects. Many *pesantren* responded favorably to the introduction of secular subjects, often through the institutional integration of formal schools of the *sekolah* or *madrasah* type that work according to the curriculum approved by the Department of Education or the Department of Religious Affairs, respectively. Still others, mostly smaller *pesantren*, modified their daily educational routines so as to allow their students to visit formal schools outside the *pesantren* during the day.

A particularly notable effort at reform was the establishment of Gontor Pondok Moderen at Gontor Ponorogo in East Java in 1926. Inspired by reforms at Al-Azhar University in Cairo, Syanggit in North Africa, and the Anglo-Muslim college of Aligarh and Santiniketan University in India, Gontor sought to modernize the methods of teaching and broaden the scope of subjects taught. Over the years Gontor expanded its educational program, which now includes training from elementary grades to the university level. Arabic and English are the languages of instruction, and Gontor's achievements with respect to foreign language study have been noted even outside of Indonesia. As the certificate offered by Gontor is recognized by Al-Azhar, the *pesantren* is known to send a significant number of students to Cairo.

Other examples of *pesantren* that have undergone and continue to undergo similar reforms to the ones at Gontor include Pondok Pesantren Modern Islam Assalaam Surakarta, Darun Najah, Darul Falah, and Tebuireng. In the wake of such changes, some of these *pesantren* have become very large educational institutions, and many are increasingly integrated in the state-controlled education system. The incorporation of the *pesantren* into the national system of education via the adoption of national curricula was pursued under Suharto's New Order regime. Government control was established by standardizing the *madrasah* curriculum and providing financial benefits for the *pesantren* that adopted them. The integration continued after the fall of the New Order in May 1998. With a law passed in 2003 concerning the national system of education, the Indonesian government acknowledged the *pesantren* as an official part of the national system of education.

What consequences the integration into the state system has for *pesantren* is a topic of debate within the tradition itself. Some are confident that the integration will result in a well-balanced education that provides both religious and general training and allows graduates to continue their studies in state institutions of higher education. Others point to less desirable effects, such as enhanced state control and interference in the *pesantren*'s educational routines.[36] Consequently, there remain numerous *pesantren* that have rejected

---

[36] See Wolfgang Karcher, "Pesantren and Government Schools—How Do They Fit Together?" in *The Impact of Pesantren in Education and Community Development in Indonesia*, ed. Manfred Oepen and Wolfgang Karcher, with assistance from Robert Kingham (Berlin: Technical University Berlin, 1988), 183–96.

state-recognized curricula and schools and opted to stay outside the national system.

An example of a particularly well-known, large *pesantren* is Pondok Pesantren Sidogiri in Pasuruan, East Java. It has a combined student body of more than 8,000 and displays various levels and types of religious schooling. The option to remain outside the national system of education enables the *pesantren* to base its educational activities on a solid religious curriculum and to teach more advanced religious texts than would be possible with the standard state-prescribed *madrasah* curriculum. While Sidogiri's graduates cannot enter the country's state system of higher education, there exist agreements with individual institutions, such as the Islamic State University of Malang, enabling the *santri* to pursue higher education. In addition to religious training, Sidogiri has earned a reputation for its efforts and achievements with respect to economic development. Particularly well known in this respect is the Koperasi Pondok Pesantren (Kopontren) Sidogiri. Founded in 1961, the cooperative includes various businesses, for example, a cafeteria, grocery and clothing stores, and a bank inside the *pesantren* complex, as well as in the surrounding community. Over the past few years, Sidogiri has started to produce, package, and sell drinking water in collaboration with an outside company. Almost 20,000 boxes of "Santri" drinking water are being distributed monthly, using a distribution and marketing network in Pasuran, Probolinggo, Surabaya, and Bali. The revenues from these business activities provide income for the operation of the *pesantren*, thereby contributing to the school's independence. In addition to financial considerations, the cooperative offers a learning experience for the students. It is run and managed by the *santri* and provides practical training and experience in business management.

The training in applied skills is indicative of a more general trend in *pesantren* education. Drawing on ideas of critical pedagogy as expressed in the writings of such thinkers as Paulo Freire and Ivan Illich, many activists promoted the *pesantren* as model institutions for community development in the 1970s, offering specialized training in agriculture, crafts, and business alongside traditional religious subjects. Pondok Pesantren Pabelan in Muntilan, Central Java, is a particularly celebrated example. The *pesantren* trains *santri* to assist the surrounding villages in their economic development. In addition to the general education, the *santri*, together with people from the wider community, receive agricultural and medical training as well as training in building construction. In their efforts at community development, many *pesantren* cooperated with the growing number of NGOs in this field. The mushrooming NGO activity in and around the *pesantren* tradition was one of the most remarkable features of the 1970s and 1980s. A number of these newly emerging NGOs were affiliated with and supported by Nahdlatul Ulama, for which development work had become a major focus in the 1980s.[37]

With the changing political climate in the 1990s, the emphasis of the *pesantren* activity started to shift from community development to support for democratic civil society. Some *pesantren* have begun to see their educational and social activities as intimately connected with raising a critical political awareness among a wide spectrum of society for issues such as human rights, pluralism, political and social justice, democracy, and interfaith tolerance. Using classical Islamic texts, these institutions have geared their educational activities toward the affirmation of thought and praxis on antiviolence, civility, justice, and pluralism. Here Muslim organizations are not only involved in the theoretical and intellectual dimensions of building a pluralist society in a Muslim majority country but also preparing students to live as Muslims in diversity by empowering them in very concrete ways to participate in this process of social transformation.

A Case Study: Pesantren Al-Muayyad Windan, Solo

Pesantren Al-Muayyad Windan, Solo, is the fifth and most recent branch of Pondok Pesantren Al-Muayyad Mangkuyudan Surakarta. It was founded in 1996 as a *pesantren* for students (*pesantren mahasiswa*) with a special emphasis on community development (*pengembangan masyarakat*). The emphasis on community development, as indicated above, is common in the *pesantren* tradition and is premised on the idea that *pesantren* serve the local community. The *pesantren* board secretary, Muhammad Ishom, explained that *pesantren* are community institutions; as such they exist in and for the community and are responsive to its needs.[38] In 2005, 49 students (*santri*), female and male, lived at Pesantren Al-Muayyad Windan, while simultaneously pursuing degrees at colleges and universities in and nearby the city of Solo.

The city of Solo provides a unique context in which Pesantren Al-Muayyad Windan carries out its educational activities. Solo has earned a reputation as a place of repeated outbreaks of communal violence, such as the riots in 1998 and 1999, which saw the destruction of a large number of Chinese-owned shops and residences. In the context of Solo, the emphasis of Pesantren Al-Muayyad Windan on community development translates into pronounced efforts at conflict resolution, peace building, reconciliation, and interfaith dialogue. More recently, the empowerment of women and issues of gender have become foci of the *pesantren*'s work, at times overlapping with its other activities.

As an Islamic educational institution, Pesantren Al-Muayyad Windan is,

---

[37] See Martin van Bruinessen, *NU: Tradisi, Relasi-Relasi Kuasa, Pencarian Wacana Baru* (Yogyakarta, Indonesia: LKiS, 1994).

[38] Muhammad Ishom, interview by author, Universitas Gadjah Mada, Yogyakarta, Indonesia, October 1, 2005.

first and foremost, a place of learning. The *pesantren*'s mission statement emphasizes intellectual aspects, character formation, and the acquisition of operative skills relevant for community development. The various formal and informal learning activities that occur in the *pesantren* are all considered part of its educational program. One characteristic of traditional *pesantren* education is the absence of a centrally controlled curriculum and rigid school organization. In the study of the classical texts (*kitab kuning*), *santri* basically have the freedom to study any topic whatsoever, thereby promoting a process of self-motivated learning. The various Islamic disciplines taught at Pesantren Al-Muayyad Windan include the study of the Koran and the Prophetic traditions (*hadith*), Koranic recitation (*tajwid*), Koranic exegesis (*tafsir*), Islamic jurisprudence (*fiqh*), principles and sources of Islamic law (*usul al-fiqh*), principles of religion (*usul al-din*), Islamic ethics (*akhlaq*), history (*tarikh*), and Arabic grammar (*nahwu*). More recently, English (*Bahasa Inggris*) has also become part of the general curriculum at Al-Muayyad Windan. While *santri* are generally free to choose their level of involvement in the learning process, there are minimal requirements, and testing occurs. For example, the memorization of *Juz Amma* (the thirtieth and final part of the Koran) is an obligation for all *santri*. So, too, is the study of *Tafsir al-Ibriz*. In the teaching of the classical texts, traditional instructional methods are used.[39] These traditional learning activities usually take place in the morning and at night. Under the leadership of the *kiai* at Pesantren Al-Muayyad Windan, Kiai Dian Nafi', classical texts are studied after the communal morning prayer (*solat subuh*) and following the evening prayer (*solat maghrib*), which the *santri* also perform collectively. This organization of the traditional learning activities frees the *santri* to pursue their studies at the colleges and universities in and around Solo during the daytime hours.

In addition to studying the classical texts of the *pesantren* tradition, Al-Muayyad Windan's *santri* participate in seminars, courses, training sessions, and informal learning groups to acquire skills as community organizers. At the end of their educational programs, *santri* are required to become involved on a practical level in fields such as reconciliation, interfaith dialogue, crisis intervention, women's empowerment, economic empowerment, journalism, environmental protection, conservation of energy, and organic farming. Much of this practical work is carried out in conjunction with NGOs, some of which were founded by *santri* of Al-Muayyad Windan. Over the past years an emphasis on peace building, conflict resolution, and interfaith dialogue has been prominent.

---

[39] The traditional teaching methods for reading and translating classical texts are known as *sorogan* and *bandongan*. For a detailed description of the classical methods of instruction, see Dhofier, *The Pesantren Tradition*, 30–31.

Community Development through Peace Building, Conflict Resolution, and Interfaith Dialogue

The active engagement of Pesantren Al-Muayyad Windan in peace building efforts has been influenced by the occurrence of several outbreaks of violence in the city of Solo after the end of the Suharto era. The realization that religious symbols are often involved in violent conflict necessitates what Kiai Dian Nafi' calls a "proactive" *pesantren* that can empower society in a systematic fashion. In its peace building efforts, Pesantren Al-Muayyad Windan thus stresses methodological approaches. Kiai Dian Nafi' argues: "We have to address issues of methodology otherwise we will be trapped in blind activism, which is inefficient."[40] In conscious and systematic efforts to improve the methodology of conflict resolution and peace building, Kiai Dian Nafi' has for more than 7 years been involved in various advanced training programs on mediation, conflict transformation, and crisis intervention domestically and internationally. One of his latest training projects on conflict resolution was conducted with the Mennonite Central Committee (MCC) at Eastern Mennonite University, Virginia, in May and June of 2005. Many *santri* at Pesantren Al-Muayyad Windan have acquired similar skills in comparable programs. The emphasis on methodologies of peace building does not assist the activities of Al-Muayyad Windan alone but is also understood as a service to the local community. Individuals and organizations from the local community in Solo are able to learn directly about methodologies for conflict resolution and reconciliation, request speakers from the *pesantren,* and connect with its extensive network of organizations in this field.

In their educational effort to prepare students to participate in transforming Indonesia's society, many *pesantren* cooperate with NGOs, thereby utilizing as well as reinforcing the creative endeavors occurring on this level of society. Some of the highly visible and widely known organizations with which Pesantren Al-Muayyad Windan collaborates include the aforementioned P3M and LKiS, Rahima (the Center for Education and Information on Islam and Women's Rights Issues), the Center for Pesantren and Democracy Studies, Interfidei (Institut Dialog Antar Iman), the Yogyakarta Interfaith Forum, and Percik (Institute for Social Research, Democracy, and Social Justice). The objectives of these NGOs include rethinking Islamic ideals to promote democracy, pluralism, gender justice, and interfaith dialogue. Various training programs have been conducted at Pesantren Al-Muayyad Windan in cooperation with the aforementioned organizations, as well as with others.

In addition to using the network of NGOs around the *pesantren* for training purposes, these and similar organizations also provide the *santri* at Pe-

---

[40] Kiai Dian Nafi', interview by author, Pesantren Al-Muayyad Windan, Solo, Indonesia, August 26, 2005.

santren Al-Muayyad Windan with opportunities to involve themselves on a practical level in community development. To facilitate this process *santri* have established the Windan Interfaith Community, through which they work in a variety of interfaith groups and other NGOs in and around the city of Solo. Two of the most prominent NGOs thus connected with Al-Muayyad Windan are the Institute of Human Services of Interfaith Community (Lembaga Bhakti Kemanusiaan Umat Beragama [LBK-UB]) and the Center for Regional Studies and Information (Pusat Telaah dan Informasi Regional [PATTIRO]). The former is located in Boyolali, a half-hour drive from Solo. It addresses issues of religious conflict and strives to promote harmony among the different religious groups in the region that have witnessed violent conflicts. The peace building officer at LBK-UB is a graduate of Al-Muayyad Windan. Through him the cooperation with the *pesantren* continues on various levels of involvement; LBK-UB receives *santri* from Al-Muayyad Windan who work for the organization acquiring practical skills in community organizing, training programs are organized jointly, and Kiai Dian Nafi' functions as an advisor to a number of programs pursued by LBK-UB. By contrast, PATTIRO's activities in Solo are focused less directly on peace building and more on community development by involving local populations, especially marginalized groups, in public policy issues and promoting decentralized, participatory politics. The organization's branch in Solo was initiated by Kiai Dian Nafi' and established by *santri* from Al-Muayyad Windan in 2001. Over the short time of its tenure, PATTIRO has had, among other things, noteworthy success in their campaign to organize Solo's community of *becak* (pedicab) drivers.

Community Development through Empowering Women

As evidenced in the previous examples, the projects of community development undertaken by Al-Muayyad Windan in cooperation with a wide network of NGOs are not limited to peace building, conflict resolution, or interfaith dialogue but involve other sectors of critical importance to local society. A similar collaboration between Al-Muayyad Windan and Rahima (Center for Education and Information on Islam and Women's Rights Issues) draws attention to another aspect central to Al-Muayyad Windan's self-understanding as a *pesantren* for community development: the empowerment of women inside and outside the *pesantren* community. The beginnings of Al-Muayyad Windan's initiatives for the empowerment of women are linked to the foundation of the Center for Women Studies of Al-Muayyad (Pusat Studi Perempuan [PSP]) in 1999. An interview partner explained that the idea of the center arose out of practical concerns of female *santri*, who are a minority, constituting less than one third of the total *santri* population at Al-Muayyad Windan.[41] Pusat

---

[41] Muslich, interview by author, Pesantren Al-Muayyad Windan, Solo, Indonesia, June 15, 2005.

Studi Perempuan promised a stronger institutional representation within the *pesantren*. While the discussion about PSP was thus initiated by female *santri*, both male and female informants at Al-Muayyad Windan emphasized that the decision for its establishment was embraced and jointly supported by the whole student body and administrative staff.

Pusat Studi Perempuan activities concentrated initially on discussions of gender issues (e.g., intellectual empowerment and alternative interpretations of classical texts) and on drafting internal policy regulations concerning life and work in the *pesantren*. Later these activities were expanded, often involving seminars and workshops, which drew a wider audience than Al-Muayyad Windan's female *santri* and focused on such issues as women's reproductive rights, women's dress, women in professional careers, domestic violence, and sex trafficking. Through these initiatives PSP widened its concern for the general empowerment of women to include the specific local community around Al-Muayyad Windan.

Similar to the work on peace building, the *pesantren* built cooperative programs with other organizations to support and expand its work. For example, in 2003 Al-Muayyad Windan began cooperating with the YIS Foundation (Yayasan Indonesia Sejahtera) in aiding women's economic empowerment, concentrating on economic assistance (*pendampingan ekonomi*) for local women to establish small businesses. Assistance and expertise during the planning stages for the businesses, as well as interest free loans, are available for only a marginal administrative fee.

Interestingly, a convergence between the two fields treated above can be observed in the work of the aforementioned LBK-UB. Starting from the realization that many interfaith activities show a disproportionately low number of female participants, LBK-UB sought to empower women through an initiative entitled "Strengthening Women's Participation in Interfaith Dialogue in Boyolali, Sukoharjo and Wonogiri Regency, Central Java." As with other projects organized by LBK-UB, Pesantren Al-Muayyad Windan is involved institutionally as a partner in the planning process and as host to some of the seminars that are part of the program.

An Analysis of Pesantren Al-Muayyad Windan

In its approach to religious education, Pesantren Al-Muayyad Windan fulfills a dual function as an institution of formal and informal learning. It espouses a broad learning concept in which educational activities empower *santri* to become agents of change in society. The internal diversity of the *santri* living and learning at Pesantren Al-Muayyad Windan, with their dissimilar backgrounds in traditional *pesantren* studies as well as in higher education outside the *pesantren* at the colleges and universities of Solo, helps creatively to advance ideas about community development. "In fact, this diversity creates dynamic groups at Windan," stated one of my interview partners when asked about the inspirations for the *pesantren*'s activities.[42] Moreover, the urban context in the city of Solo includes not only colleges and universities but also a wide network of NGOs. These organizations provide invaluable resources for the *pesantren*. Since many of the NGOs function on a national level, Al-Muayyad Windan is part of the larger network of "civil Islam" described above.

The prolific presence of NGOs around the *pesantren* has already been noted as a more general development within the *pesantren* tradition. Similarly, the perspective on the relationship between religious and general education at Al-Muayyad Windan is indicative of broader trends mentioned earlier. All *santri* at Al-Muayyad Windan are enrolled in an institution of higher learning outside the *pesantren*, with the education received in the *pesantren* supplementary to the learning in the institutions of the national education system. In my conversations with them, *santri* and staff at Al-Muayyad Windan signaled an awareness of the possible and at times very real dilemma for the *pesantren*, namely, that students may at times conceive of themselves first as college or university students and second as *santri* of Al-Muayyad Windan. Contributing to these developments are economic constraints and the perceived necessity of state-certified education in order to ensure employment opportunities in the public sector on completion of one's education. Nevertheless, *santri* enrollment in institutions of higher learning outside the *pesantren* is a precondition for admittance to Al-Muayyad Windan, in part because the diversity of perspectives and practical skills acquired outside the *pesantren* are viewed as integral to realizing the aims and objectives of community development. Kiai Dian Nafi' is careful to point out that internal uniformity in the *pesantren* is undesirable.[43] The fact that *santri* are engaged in diverse fields of learning within and outside of Al-Muayyad Windan is what makes the institution a rich learning environment and directly contributes to the task of community development where different skills are practically applied.

Notwithstanding its forward-looking perspective on balancing general and religious education, Pesantren Al-Muayyad Windan challenges the idea of a privatized and marginalized role of religious education. Religious learning is neither a private nor devotional process. The educational program at Al-Muayyad Windan assumes an eminently public role by gearing its efforts toward community development and by raising a critical awareness among its students and the wider society about issues such as religious pluralism and the empowerment of women. It thereby displays a civility-enhancing function in society because its educational programs indicate "respect for the rights of other citizens and thereby contribute to a public culture of participation premised on freedom of association, speech, and participation for everyone

---

[42] Kurniawan, interview by author, Pesantren Al-Muayyad Windan, Solo, Indonesia, June 18, 2005.

[43] Kiai Dian Nafi', interview by author, Pesantren Al-Muayyad Windan, Solo, Indonesia, August 26, 2005.

regardless of race, religion, ethnicity, gender, or class."[44] Contrary to the stereotype of *pesantren* as supporters of radicalism and violence, Al-Muayyad Windan displays a strong commitment to values of civility, which find expression in the areas of peace building, conflict resolution, interfaith dialogue, and the empowerment of women. The interaction between Al-Muayyad Windan and the various organizational networks in and around the *pesantren* scene displays a marked affirmation of pluralism, democracy, and individual freedoms.

Conclusion: An Exception That Proves the Rule?

Is Al-Muayyad Windan an exemption that proves a general rule about the *pesantren*'s incompatibility with modern life and the empowerment of democratic civil society? It is safe to say that Al-Muayyad Windan is one of the most ardent promoters of democracy and pluralism among Indonesia's *pesantren*. With its emphasis on conflict resolution and interfaith understanding it belongs to a small number of institutions that are considerably more activist and forward-looking in this respect than the majority of Indonesia's *pesantren*.

I do not deny the existence of Islamic educational institutions that promote a more exclusive interpretation of Islam—one that opposes the process of democratization and pluralization and thereby closes down the space in which a strong civil society can grow. Indeed, another *pesantren* in the Solo region mentioned earlier, Pesantren Al-Mukmin in Ngruki, reflects another approach to Muslim education and Muslim politics in Indonesia at present. The existence of an institution such as Pesantren Al-Mukmin, however, does not contradict the broader point about the ability of Islamic education to contribute to a culture of pluralism and public civility. Nor does the admittedly exceptional character of Al-Muayyad Windan indicate that, somehow, the majority of Indonesia's *pesantren* are antipluralist or exclusivist.

Thus, I do not seek to paint a picture of Al-Muayyad Windan as representative of the *pesantren* tradition as a whole. I simply want to point out that some *pesantren* are quite capable of promoting a public religious culture that is democratic and pluralist. In many ways, Al-Muayyad Windan is quite exceptional, and it is widely considered by other representatives of the Islamic educational scene as such. However, Al-Muayyad Windan carries out its educational programs in a context of Islamic institutions of learning that are overwhelmingly moderate and committed to the idea of a multireligious and

[44] Robert W. Hefner, "Introduction: Multiculturalism and Citizenship in Malaysia, Singapore, and Indonesia," in *The Politics of Multiculturalism: Pluralism and Citizenship in Malaysia, Singapore, and Indonesia*, ed. R. W. Hefner (Hawaii: University of Hawaii Press, 2001), 1–58, 10.

multiethnic Indonesia.[45] And along with other institutions, Al-Muayyad Windan is part of a larger organizational network that displays a distinct commitment to pluralist discourse and democratic change. A *pesantren* such as Al-Muayyad Windan thus demonstrates that traditional Islamic education can and does make significant contributions to the empowerment of democratic civil society. More specifically, it shows that the *pesantren* tradition is not inimical to such concerns as women's empowerment and good interfaith relations in a plural society.

In the broader context of the debate over religion's appropriate role in the public sphere of modern societies, we are reminded that not every public expression of traditional religion is conservative, dominating, or exclusive but that religion can be part of progressive politics and strengthen civil society. Conversely, it may be safe to say that equality and the successful accommodation of the structural conditions of modernity such as pluralism, democracy, and individual rights are not simply the result of religion's absence from public life. It would be a poverty of imagination to suggest that we must choose between either progressive secularization with a complete absence of religion from public life and conservative religion that seeks to fuse religion and state, thus eliminating the boundary between public and private spheres. Not only does such an opposition force us to ignore or deny the ways in which religion can be central to progressive politics but it also overlooks the ways in which secular organization can oppose such politics. An uncritical understanding of secularization ignores the fact that secular freedom carries its own dominations, as it has also been one of the means of eliminating possibilities for substantive differences. Secularization, when it functions as an antireligious ideology, brings about another set of inequalities between those who are religious and those who are secular. The oppressive results of this discourse can be seen at present in France and Germany in the legal bans of Islamic dress in public schools whereby specifically secular forms of inequalities are sanctioned institutionally. The strategies with which an Islamic institution of education such as Pesantren Al-Muayyad Windan prepares its students for life in a modern democratic society and promotes an open and tolerant attitude toward pluralism and gender justice provide a fresh outlook on the contentious question of religion's appropriate role in education. Such evidence holds the potential to challenge secular academics on the issue of religious alternatives in education and public life.

[45] A similar point is made in a recent study by the Jakarta-based research institute LP3ES, *Laporan Penelitian: The Role of Pesantren to Support Community Network and to Develop Peaceful Co-existence in Indonesia* (Jakarta: LP3ES, 2005).

Reclaiming an Ideal: The Islamization of Education in the Southern Philippines

JEFFREY AYALA MILLIGAN

Decentralization has been a common element of policy reform in education worldwide for decades. Such reforms are thought to promote the democratic empowerment of local families and teachers and thus to improve educational efficiency and accountability to local needs.[1] While decentralization has been widely touted as an essential response to educational problems by international development organizations, it has long been recognized that local conditions give rise to quite different approaches to decentralization, often with paradoxical consequences.[2]

For instance, this ongoing trend toward decentralization coincides, at the moment, with an increasing international concern over education in the Muslim world. The terrorist attacks on New York and Washington, DC, in 2001 focused the attention of Western governments and development agencies on the alleged radicalizing influence of unregulated Islamic schools in countries such as Pakistan as well as of government-approved schools in countries such as Saudi Arabia. Suddenly, the word *madrasa* appeared increasingly on the radar of international educational development discourse in ways that it had not heretofore.

One common feature of this renewed interest in Islamic education seems to be an assumption that the religious focus of many of these schools may be a significant factor in the growth of religious extremism; therefore, educational reforms that more carefully separate the sacred and secular and effectively promote the secular knowledge necessary for modern economic development are thought to be the appropriate antidote to radical Islamic education. However, exerting greater national/international secular authorities' control over the content and character of education in such contexts would seem to run counter to the ethos of decentralization.[3] But is the Islamization of schooling in certain local contexts a compelling argument against educational decentralization? In certain settings could the emergence of moderate, local Islamizing forces in education head off more radical al-

I would like to thank the U.S. Institute of Peace for its financial support of the research informing this article as well as Aida Hafiza Macada-ag, Mindanao State University, and Nagasura T. Madale, Cagayan Capitol University, for their invaluable support of fieldwork in the Philippines.

[1] M. Fernanda Astiz, Alexander W. Wiseman, and David P. Baker, "Slouching towards Decentralization: Consequences of Globalization for Curricular Controls in National Educational Systems," *Comparative Education Review* 46, no. 1 (February 2002): 66–88.

[2] E. Mark Hanson, "Editorial: Educational Decentralization around the Pacific Rim," *Journal of Educational Administration* 38, no. 5 (2000): 1–9.

[3] Jana Sackman Eaton, "The Russian Federation Islamic Republic of Daghastan: Curricular Decentralization, Social Cohesion, and Stability," *Peabody Journal of Education* 80, no. 1 (2005): 56–80.

ternatives? Such questions require more specific case studies to better understand the likely outcomes of decentralization policies in contexts of ethnic and religious conflict.[4]

The southern Philippines offer a useful case for exploring these questions in that political decentralization in general and educational decentralization in particular have long been topics of policy debate.[5] For decades before and after independence, centralization was thought to be necessary for creating and maintaining a national identity that could withstand the pressures of neocolonialism.[6] Centralization, however, has long proved problematic due to the extensive cultural and geographic diversity of the Philippines and the relative weakness of the Philippine state.[7] These inherent difficulties of centralization increased considerably as relations with the Muslim minority in the southern Philippines deteriorated in the early 1970s into an armed Islamic secessionist movement. In such a context, central authorities viewed decentralization and local autonomy as the only desirable alternative to a politically unacceptable independence for Muslim Mindanao. Muslim educational and community leaders, however, are using the devolution of policy-making authority to support *madaris*, introduce Islamic content and values into the curricula of public schools, and blur the lines that have heretofore separated public and Islamic education in Muslim Mindanao. These reforms, moreover, appear to reflect ongoing social trends toward an intensification of Islamic identity in the region. Thus, in Muslim Mindanao, decentralization has come to mean Islamization.

In what follows, I will attempt to describe three distinct but interrelated currents in this process of Islamization: the evolution of the "integrated" madrasah, the growth of the Jema'at al Tabligh as a form of nonformal Islamic education for adults, and the effort by the Department of Education in the Autonomous Region in Muslim Mindanao (ARMM) to Islamize public education through Project Madrasa Education (PME). I will analyze the conception of Islamic education common to all three developments as a reflection of local needs and aspirations and explore their possible consequences. Finally, I will argue that, rather than constituting an argument against decentralization, this case offers an argument for greater understanding of and openness to moderate Islamization as a potentially more effective bulwark against radicalizing Islamic education than government-enforced secularization.

[4] Christopher Bjork, "Local Responses to Decentralization Policy in Indonesia," *Comparative Education Review* 47, no. 2 (2003): 184–216.

[5] Alex Bello Brilliantes, "Decentralization in the Philippines: An Overview," *Philippine Journal of Public Administration* 31, no. 2 (April 1987): 131–47.

[6] See, e.g., Renato Constantino, *Neocolonial Identity and Counter Consciousness: Essays on Cultural Decolonization* (London: Merlin, 1978).

[7] Patricio N. Abinales, *Making Mindanao: Cotabato and Davao in the Formation of the Philippine Nation-State* (Manila: Ateneo de Manila University Press, 2000), 45–68.

Historical Context

The Philippines' almost 400 years of colonial domination by Spain and then the United States are well known.[8] Perhaps less well known is the even longer history of Islam in the country's southernmost islands.[9] The clash between these two cultural influences, first felt in the mid-sixteenth century, reverberates to this day along a social fault line traced in the dichotomization of Philippine society between the Christian majority and Muslim minority. This clash has repeatedly erupted into armed conflict over the past four centuries, most recently in the form of an armed Islamic secessionist move-ment that has waxed and waned since the early 1970s.[10] The intractability of the conflict has forced the Philippine government in the past decade to experiment with political autonomy for Muslim Mindanao even as ties be-tween local Muslim insurgents and international extremist groups like Jemaah Islamiya and al-Qaeda have earned the conflict in Mindanao a dubious dis-tinction as one of the fronts in the so-called war on terror.[11]

While the history of armed conflict has been, perhaps, the most prom-inent feature of relations between successive Philippine governments and the minority Muslim community, education and educational policy have been significant.[12] Although there is little direct, documentary evidence of its na-ture and extent, Islamic education in one form or another was introduced into the Philippines along with Islam itself as early as the fourteenth century. Accounts by American colonial officials early in the twentieth century de-scribed what they called *pandita* schools—a small group of boys studying Islam under the tutelage of a local learned Muslim—as a common feature of the educational landscape of Muslim Mindanao.[13] While catechism schools had long been a relatively common feature of Spanish-controlled areas of the Philippines, the Education Decree of 1863 initiated Spain's effort to establish public schools in the country.[14] Throughout most of the Spanish colonial period, however, these public schools also focused on the inculcation of

---

[8] See Renato Constantino, *The Philippines*, vol. 1, *A Past Revisited*, and vol. 2, *The Continuing Past* (Quezon City: Foundation for Nationalist Studies, 1975).

[9] See Cesar A. Majul, *Muslims in the Philippines* (Manila: University of the Philippines Press, 1999).

[10] See Marites Danguilan Vitug and Glenda M. Gloria, *Under the Crescent Moon: Rebellion in Mindanao* (Quezon City: Ateneo Center for Social Policy and Public Affairs/Institute for Popular Democracy, 2000).

[11] See Zachary Abuza, *Militant Islam in Southeast Asia: Crucible of Terror* (London: Lynne Rienner, 2003).

[12] See Jeffrey Ayala Milligan, *Islamic Identity, Postcoloniality, and Educational Policy: Schooling and Ethno-Religious Conflict in the Southern Philippines* (New York: Palgrave-Macmillan, 2005).

[13] Charles R. Cameron, "The Schools of Moroland," *Mindanao Herald*, February 3, 1909, 35–36.

[14] Karl Schwartz, "Filipino Education and Spanish Colonialism: Toward an Autonomous Perspec-tive," *Comparative Education Review* 15, no. 2 (June 1971): 202–18, 203.

Catholicism, and thus they did not attract enrollment by Muslims living in areas of Mindanao tenuously controlled by Spain.[15]

It was not until the American occupation and administration of Muslim Mindanao from roughly 1899 onward that the first systematic program of public education was established in the region. Its first superintendent, a Lebanese-born American physician named Najeeb Saleeby, identified the policy alternatives confronting the U.S. administration of Muslim Filipinos as a choice between force, a tactic tried for 300 years that "history has declared [a] failure and humanity has condemned," or gradual reformation "by patient instruction and good example."[16] Saleeby inaugurated a policy of deploying education as a tool in U.S. efforts to "civilize" Muslim Filipinos and foster their integration and subordination into a Philippine nation-state administered by Christian Filipino elites. As one American observer put it in 1920, "The day of the fighter was past. The day of the teacher had come."[17] For the next century successive colonial and postcolonial governments would concentrate on the introduction and expansion of public education with a uniform, state-mandated curriculum intended to bring Filipinos—Muslim and Christian—into a single vision of modernity and national identity conceptualized by a relatively small Manila-based elite positioned to determine educational (and other) policies for the entire country.

Thus Spanish and American colonization of the Philippines not only highlighted the Muslim-Christian dichotomy as a cultural and religious divide; it also led to the development of two parallel systems of education: one ostensibly secular but Christian-influenced and government-controlled and the other Islamic and largely outside government control. Though government education was firmly established early in the twentieth century, many Muslim Filipinos continued to regard it with deep suspicion as an effort to Christianize them. Many Muslim parents, therefore, refused to send their children to government schools. The government's response was to redouble efforts to foster Muslim integration through agencies such as the Bureau of Non-Christian Tribes, established when the Jones Law turned over direct administration of Muslim Mindanao to Christian Filipinos in 1920 and charged with the aim of achieving "the complete fusion of the Christian and non-Christian elements populating the . . . Archipelago."[18]

After the establishment of the Philippine Commonwealth in 1935, Pres-

[15] Queen Maria Cristina, "Royal Decree of Queen Regent Maria Cristina, 1892," in *Documentary Sources of Philippine History*, ed. Gregorio F. Zaide and Sonia M. Zaide, 12 vols. (Manila: National Bookstore, 1990), 8:158.

[16] Najeeb Saleeby, "The Moro Problem: An Academic Discussion of the History and Solution of the Problem of the Government of the Moros of the Philippine Islands" (originally published in 1913), *Dansalan Quarterly* 5, no. 1 (October 1983): 8–42, 42.

[17] O. Garfield Jones, "Our Mandate over Moroland," *Asia* 20 (July 1920): 609–15, 609.

[18] Camilo Osias, "Notes on Education" (unpublished report to the president of the Philippines, September 16, 1940).

ident Manuel Quezon declared "the so-called Moro Problem is a thing of the past" and issued, via executive order, a "Code of Civic and Ethical Principles" that supplemented educational goals contained in the new constitution, strengthening the educational system's focus on national integration.[19] Postindependence governments continued the policy of integration via education established by Najeeb Saleeby, passing Republic Act 1387 in 1955 for the establishment of a state university in Lanao del Sur, designed to foster the integration of Muslims, and Republic Act 1888 in 1957, establishing the Commission on National Integration (CNI). By providing scholarships to Muslim students, the CNI sought "to render real, complete and permanent the integration of all said cultural minorities into the body politic," a goal reflecting a continuation of the policies of the Bureau of Non-Christian Tribes established under the American regime almost 40 years before.[20]

Government education gradually won over more and more Muslim families as the century wore on. Though participation rates as late as the 1960s remained as low as 20 percent in some Muslim provinces, by the late 1990s they were comparable to those in majority Christian provinces, though cohort survival rates remained low.[21] At the same time, Islamic education grew in popularity as well, especially after World War II. By the 1950s large, formal Islamic schools such as Kamilol Islam Institute and Jamiatul Philippines Al-Islamia had been well established. Increasing ease and freedom of travel after World War II facilitated the growing influence of transnational *dawa'ah* (call for the renewal of faith) movements in Mindanao through Muslim missionaries from the Middle East as well as Filipino Muslims educated in Islamic centers of learning such as Cairo, Medina, Riyadh, and Tripoli. These religiously educated Muslims contributed to the growing network of *madaris* in the region throughout the 1950s and 1960s. After the outbreak of the armed secessionist movement in the early 1970s, the number of Islamic schools reportedly doubled to more than two thousand by the late 1980s.[22]

As tensions between Muslims and Christians escalated through the late 1960s and early 1970s, there emerged a growing recognition of the need to

---

[19] Manuel Quezon, "Presidential Address to the First National Assembly," in "Muslim but Filipino: The Integration of Muslim Filipinos, 1917–1946," by Ralph Benjamin Thomas (PhD diss., University of Pennsylvania, 1971), 263; Rolando Gripaldo, "Quezon's Philosophy of Philippine Education," *Technician* 3, no. 2 (December 1990): 40–47, 40. The Spanish word for the Moors—Moro—was used for centuries as a collective, generally pejorative, term for all Muslim Filipinos. Gradually, it has been embraced by many Muslim Filipinos as an expression of a distinct national identity encompassing all 13 of the Islamized ethnic communities of the southern Philippines.

[20] Antonio Isidro, *Muslim-Christian Integration at the Mindanao State University* (Marawi City: Mindanao State University Research Center, 1968), 376; Leothiny Clavel, *They Are Also Filipinos: Ten Years with the Cultural Minorities* (Manila: Bureau of Printing, 1969), 16–17, 84.

[21] Antonio Isidro and Mamitua Saber, eds., *Muslim Philippines* (Marawi City: Mindanao State University Research Center, 1968), 103–4; Mahad Mutilan, *Leading a New Beginning at DepEd ARMM* (Cotabato City: Department of Education, Autonomous Region in Muslim Mindanao, 2003), 117–21.

[22] Manaros Boransing, Frederico Magdalena, and Luis Lacar, *The Madrasah Institution in the Philippines: Historical and Cultural Perspectives* (Iligan City: Toyota Foundation, 1987), 17, 26, 59–62.

respond to Muslim demands for political autonomy and a relevant education in order to end the conflict. After the declaration of martial law, for instance, President Ferdinand Marcos issued a letter of instruction permitting the use of Arabic as a medium of instruction "in schools and areas where the use thereof permits," and the Tripoli Agreement, which brought major combat between the government and the Moro National Liberation Front (MNLF) to a temporary end in 1976, gave authorities of the envisioned autonomous government the right to set up schools consistent with Muslim values and interests.[23] Neither policy, however, was ever meaningfully implemented.

The language of multiculturalism in education continued to find its way into official agreements between the government and Muslim Filipino groups after the restoration of democracy under Corazon Aquino. A new constitution drafted in 1986 authorized the establishment of an autonomous region in Muslim Mindanao with authority over local educational and other policies and committed the state to "protect the rights of indigenous cultural communities to preserve and develop their cultures, traditions, and institutions."[24] These constitutional provisions were enacted in 1990 via Republic Act 6734, which created ARMM and authorized the new regional government to establish schools that "teach the rights and duties of citizenship, and the cultures of Muslims, Christians and tribal peoples in the region to develop, promote and enhance unity in diversity."[25] The authority of the ARMM government over education in its jurisdiction was reemphasized in the final peace agreement between the MNLF and the Philippine government in 1996. This agreement confirmed the regional government's authority to supervise *madaris* and to approve textbooks, establish curricula, and implement policies for public schools designed to "perpetuate . . . the Islamic values and orientations of the Bangsamoro [Filipino Muslim] people," provided such reforms included the core courses and minimum standards established for all Filipino children by the national Department of Education, Culture, and Sports.[26]

The educational history of Muslim Mindanao is therefore characterized by several centuries of separate Islamic and Christian education followed by almost a century of deliberate efforts to subordinate Muslims, under the rhetoric of integration, to Christian-dominated "secular" norms. Within the past decade this history has been followed by a rather belated recognition of distinct Muslim educational desires. The net effect is an extensive network

[23] Department of Education and Culture, *A Year of Progress under Martial Law* (Manila: Department of Education and Culture, 1973), 48; "Tripoli Agreement," in *Educational Visions for Muslim Mindanao*, ed. Salipada Saud Tamano (Cotabato City: Department of Education, Culture and Sports Autonomous Region in Muslim Mindanao, 1996), 220.

[24] Constitution of the Republic of the Philippines, Art. X, secs. 15 and 20, and Art. XIV, sec. 17.

[25] Republic Act no. 6734, Art. XV, sec. 2.2, cited in Tamano, *Educational Visions*, 223.

[26] "1996 GRP-MNLF Peace Agreement," pt. 1, sec. C, in *Peace Matters: A Philippine Peace Compendium*, ed. Miriam Coronel-Ferrer (Quezon City: University of the Philippines Center for Integrative and Development Studies, 1997), 280–82. The term *bangsamoro* was coined by the MNLF to convey the notion of Filipino Muslim (*moro*)–national identity (*bangsa*).

of nongovernmental Islamic schools that exists alongside the system of public schools heretofore administered by the Philippine government. Some of these *madaris* meet on weekends and are intended to offer an Islamic education to those students who attend public school during the week. Others are intended to offer an alternative to government education altogether.[27] Both endeavor to sustain an Islamic identity that has been largely ignored, if not openly disparaged, in the policies, textbooks, and curricula of public schools from at least the American colonial period to the present.[28]

Parallel systems of education, however, offer Muslim Filipinos a difficult choice. Government schools offer the curricula and training that might enable access to jobs and university education in the Philippine mainstream, but they are largely silent about, if not openly disparaging of, Muslim Filipinos' history, culture, and religion.[29] Some local Muslim educators criticize the centralized curricula of these schools as a *lutong makao* curriculum, a Chinese restaurant style of curriculum "cooked" in Manila and served to students throughout the country regardless of local tastes.[30] Islamic schools, on the other hand, offer the religious and cultural knowledge that is important to the students as Muslims, but few offer the curricula or the quality of instruction that would enable them to prepare for employment or university-level instruction in the wider society. As one Muslim educational official explained, "Muslims who study in the *madrasa* are virtual foreigners in their own country," and those who study only in the public school are "Muslim in name only, but they do not know their religion."[31]

Some Muslim families negotiate this dilemma by opting for an Islamic education. Others choose government education and its promised access to socioeconomic mobility. Many try to do both by sending their children to public schools during the week and Islamic schools on the weekend, a choice that commits children to school 7 days a week and forces them to negotiate as many as five different languages in order to receive an education that meets their needs as Philippine citizens and as Muslims. Not only does this strategy mean that there is "no time to be a normal child," but it also physically reinforces the separation of sacred and secular knowledge, a separation that is rejected in Islam.[32]

[27] Manaros Boransing (Undersecretary of Education for Muslim Affairs), interview by the author, Cotabato City, Philippines, July 7, 2004.

[28] D. Bula, "Muslims in the Philippine Public Elementary and Secondary Textbooks: A Content Analysis," *Dansalan Quarterly* 10, nos. 3–4 (April–July 1989): 122–202.

[29] Ibid. See also Basher Salic, "A Content Analysis of Instructional Materials in Philippine History: Towards Utilization of Muslim History in Social Studies I" (master's thesis, University of the Philippines, 1990).

[30] Malawi Panambulan, interview by the author, Marawi City, Philippines, June 22, 2000.

[31] Boransing, interview.

[32] Cabaybay Abubakar, interview by the author, Cotabato City, Philippines, July 8, 2004.

The Integrated *Madrasa*

The problem of securing an education for children who are both Muslim and Filipino has inspired the development of what are known locally as integrated *madaris,* essentially Islamic parochial schools.[33] These schools attempt to resolve the dilemma of choosing between an Islamic and a public education for Muslim Filipino children by combining key elements of the *madrasa* curriculum with the subjects required by the Department of Education in Manila. Where they have been successful in doing so and acquiring official government recognition, their graduates are able to sit for national examinations and earn admission to public and private universities.[34]

One of the better known of these new integrated *madaris* is the Ibn Siena Integrated School in the Islamic City of Marawi. The school was established in 1994 by two groups representing the dual educational systems existing in Muslim Mindanao: the Ranao Council, consisting of Western-educated academics at the nearby Mindanao State University, and the Markazoshabab Al Muslim Fil Filbin, an organization of local *ulama* and religious leaders in Lanao del Sur, products of the growing transnational ties between the Filipino Muslim community and the Muslim communities of the Middle East, North Africa, and South Asia. Ibn Siena was created in response to the perception of both groups that the public schools were failing to meet the needs of Muslim children. While some of these perceived failings were academic, the primary perceived shortcoming of the public schools was moral. In a social climate plagued by drug smuggling, kidnapping, and other crimes, as well as by armed insurgency, there is a widespread assumption that only Islam can offer an ethical system with the historical and cultural resonance in local communities to counter the short-term payoffs of such illegal activity. According to one former administrator, "You cannot just recruit educated people to go to the mountains."[35] The Values Education Program developed by the national Department of Education for the public schools is perceived as good but inadequate because it is not grounded in the ethical and epistemic values of the knowledge revealed in the Qur'an even though it is conveyed by Muslim teachers to Muslim students in Muslim communities.

The curriculum of Ibn Siena, therefore, includes study of the Qur'an, the *hadith,* and the *sunna* as well as Islamic history and values and the Arabic language. It also includes secular curricula required by the Philippine Department of Education, including English-language instruction. Its objective is to produce graduates who are "a Muslim engineer, a Muslim doctor, or a

---

[33] See Lolita Junio Damonsong-Rodriquez, *A Madrasah General Education Program for Muslim Mindanao* (Marawi City: Mindanao State University Office of the Vice Chancellor for Research and Extension, 1992).

[34] Despite moves toward decentralization, the national Department of Education still determines the core curriculum, and national examinations determine entrance to the top universities.

[35] Macmood Maguindanao, interview by the author, Marawi City, Philippines, March 22, 2001.

Muslim lawyer."[36] By this is meant professionals who have the knowledge and skills necessary for economic advancement and social status within Philippine society but who also possess the knowledge of Islam and commitment to their religion required of a "good Muslim." Ibn Siena wants to transform both the reality and the perception of Muslim Filipinos, who are often perceived by their fellow Filipinos as dangerous and backward and by their fellow Muslims as ignorant of Islam. Implicit in the goal is the assumption that the existing *madrasa* and public school systems have failed to achieve this, thereby contributing to a dire socioeconomic and political predicament that is perceived to be, at least partly, the result of a moral failure on the part of Muslims. The rapid growth of Ibn Siena suggests that many in Lanao del Sur share this analysis of Muslim Filipinos' social predicament and agree with the school's response to it. Incorporated in 1994, Ibn Siena opened its doors in 1995 with 153 students; the following year 800 students were enrolled; and by 2000 more than 2,000 students were enrolled in kindergarten through high school.[37]

The Shariff Kabungsuan College in Cotabato City represents another model of the integrated *madrasa*. As with Ibn Siena, the director's articulation of Shariff Kabungsuan's purpose is grounded in a moral discourse centering on Islam. "It is our moral obligation," she claims, "to educate our people," and "we feel that Muslim children are morally safe in an Islamic school."[38] And, as with Ibn Siena, this perceived "morally safe" haven is being created within a social context plagued by material poverty, crime, political instability, and violence. In contrast, the system of public education is viewed as not offering a comparable moral security because it separates mosque and state. The public education system, with some justification, is also perceived as corrupt, bureaucratic, inefficient, and staffed by overburdened teachers who, because they are asked to accomplish so much with so little, often retaliate by shirking their responsibilities.[39]

Shariff Kabungsuan, therefore, purports to offer both an ethical and epistemic alternative to public education. While it offers ostensibly secular subjects such as mathematics, science, social studies, and English, which are required for Department of Education recognition and for the academic mobility of its pupils, the moral significance of these subjects is rendered meaningful within the framework of knowledge revealed in the Qur'an, the

---

[36] Ali Macarambon, interview by the author, Marawi City, Philippines, March 22, 2001.

[37] Maguindanao, interview.

[38] While the Philippine constitution's language on church-state separation (Art. III, sec. 5) is balanced by its charge to public schools to foster "spiritual values" (Art. XIV, sec. 3.2) and the boundary between religion and public education is quite porous in practice, the perception that the doctrine of separation precludes inculcation of a religiously centered morality stems from the fact that the public school curricula are not centered on the revealed knowledge embodied in the Qur'an. Abubakar, interview.

[39] Yvonne T. Chua, *Robbed: An Investigation of Corruption in Philippine Education* (Quezon City: Philippine Center for Investigative Journalism, 1999); Abubakar, interview.

hadith, and the *sunna* of the Prophet Muhammad. This is the heart of the integrated *madrasa* and constitutes the crucial distinction between it and either government or other private schools. Because government schools are, ostensibly, secular, this revealed knowledge is ignored; therefore, the acquired knowledge represented in secular subjects either lacks a morally meaningful context or has a moral context that involves the Christian values held by the Manila-based educational bureaucrats who shape national curricula and policy. Both options are deeply problematic for many devout Muslim Filipinos. Shariff Kabungsuan attempts to ease this burden and resolve the dichotomization of revealed and acquired knowledge in the public schools by offering both curricula in the same school through teachers who are trained, to a significant extent, in Shariff Kabungsuan.

Ibn Siena and Shariff Kabungsuan are not the first or the only schools in Muslim Mindanao to attempt to offer both Islamic and secular curricula. Nor are they particularly unique theoretically or practically; they are, essentially, Islamic versions of the Catholic parochial schools that have long been a part of the educational landscape in the Philippines, albeit without the institutional structure and history of Catholic education. They offer evidence, however, of an ongoing sense of the inadequacy of government-sponsored "secular" education to meet the needs of Muslim children. Moreover, as entirely local initiatives, they can be read as alternatives that reflect the desires of local populations. As such, they suggest a growing desire for educational opportunities that will inculcate an appropriate mix of revealed and acquired knowledge, a truly Islamic education for the children of Muslim Mindanao that will enable them to be, first, good Muslims and, second, good citizens of the Philippine Republic.

Learning in the Path of Allah: The Jema'at al Tabligh as Nonformal Islamic Education for Adults

Schoolchildren are not the only ones in Muslim Mindanao who are viewed as needing a moral education based on Islam. There is also evidence of the Islamization of nonformal education for adults. One of the most striking of these developments is the introduction and growth of the Jema'at al Tabligh. The Tabligh movement originated in India in the 1920s in response to the problem of sustaining an orthodox Islamic identity in the midst of a larger, Hindu-dominated society. Since its inception it has grown into the largest transnational *dawa'ah* movement in the world, with adherents in dozens of countries.[40] Filipino adherents trace its origins to the practices of the Prophet Muhammad, arguing that Mawlana Ilyas simply revived the movement in India in the 1920s, a claim that points to the central goal of the movement:

---

[40] Muhammad Khalid Masud, *Travellers in Faith: Studies of the Tablighi Jama'at as a Transnational Islamic Movement for Faith Renewal* (Leiden: Koninklijke Brill NV, 2000), xxii.

to bring one's life and actions in conformity to the ideal embodied in the life of the Prophet, thereby becoming a better Muslim. As a movement devoted to self-development and to helping others develop within the framework of an Islamic ideal, Tabligh can be read as a form of nonformal Islamic education for adults. Some Filipino observers, in fact, refer to the movement as a "roving Islamic university."[41]

At the heart of the movement is a moral imperative—"to enjoin the good and prohibit the bad"—as both are conceived in Islam. In defining that ideal and judging one's conformity to it, participants look to the Qur'an and the example of the Prophet as both the revelation of that ideal and the most perfect embodiment of it. Calling Muslims to conformity with this ideal, therefore, is seen as a continuation of the work of the prophets from Adam to Muhammad, albeit leavened by a sense of humility that recognizes that "you cannot xerox the life and tradition of the Prophet."[42] One can only do the best one can to live up to the ideal. Such an effort, motivated by both the love of God and the fear of God, will lead, it is thought, to self-control and the avoidance of sin and thus to one's becoming, first, a good Muslim and, second, a better citizen.[43]

The accomplishment of this ideal requires sustained study of the Qur'an, the *hadith*, the *sunna*, and, where appropriate, authoritative commentators on these texts. It therefore places a premium on the development of literacy and careful analysis of authoritative texts, especially of the Qur'an, which is thought to contain all knowledge. According to Mawlana Faisal Abdullah, one of the Jema'at al Tabligh leaders in the Philippines, "We do not have the authority to interpret the Qur'an," but different people can have different levels of understanding, as in the following example: "If a small boy of four or five finds a mango seed in the road, he will throw it away. But a young man who finds it will plant it because he knows he might even become a millionaire from its fruit. That is the difference of knowledge between the child and the young man. How much more would an agriculturist know? And the scientist might know even more. Who knows? He might even be able to develop a medicine from that mango. It is the same with the Qur'an."[44] Perfect understanding comes only from God, but one can, through study, aspire to better and more complete understanding. Coming to that more complete understanding of the truth contained in the Qur'an requires a sustained, hermeneutical method of reading whereby a passage under study or an experience not explicitly addressed in the Qur'an is reconciled with more clearly understood passages or experiences explicitly addressed in the Qur'an in order to arrive at a measure of coherence between them. This

[41] Salic Abdul, interview by the author, Marawi City, Philippines, June 25, 2004.

[42] Mawlana Faisal Abdullah, interview by the author, Marawi City, Philippines, June 28, 2004.

[43] Aleem [pseud.], interview by the author, Marawi City, Philippines, July 12, 2004.

[44] Abdullah, interview.

learning takes place via reading and both formal and informal instruction in the mosque and during *khooroj*, regular travels in small groups described locally as "going out in the path of Allah."[45]

As with the Islamic education enacted in the integrated *madrasa*, there is a moral-epistemic ideal in Tabligh that is operationalized in an ethic of responsibility for others, in effect, a pedagogy. "The Prophet said," according to one participant, "we are responsible for 160 houses: forty in the east, forty in the west, forty in the south, and forty in the north."[46] That responsibility entails going out from the mosque into the local community to invite others to participate in the learning occurring there. Filipino participants see that responsibility as requiring, not a withdrawal from society in an effort to sustain spiritual purity, but rather an engagement with the surrounding society as Muslims first and citizens second. One Filipino Tabligh asserted, "We are not withdrawing. . . . We have been sent into this world by God to make the world better by following His commandments."[47] This does not necessarily mean, however, the conversion of non-Muslims. As the same individual said, "Why go to other communities when your community is burning?" Thus the work of Tabligh involves the explicit, though nonformal, education of others in the moral-epistemic ideal inherent in Islam.

As a form of religious pedagogy it fills a niche not served by more formal institutions of Islamic education in Muslim Mindanao. It is able to serve the needs of adults who aspire to greater knowledge of Islam but who cannot be accommodated in the age-grade organizational structure of formal schools. Its emphasis on one's moral responsibility to fellow Muslims reinforces a sense of community that transcends the barriers of class, ethnicity, and clan, which are perceived, with considerable justification, to be a primary source of the poverty and violence that plague much of Muslim Filipino society. Along with the continued popularity of the *madaris* and the growth of the integrated *madrasa*, the Jema'at al Tabligh reflects a widespread, fundamental belief that Islam—being better Muslims—is the only way out of the socio-economic distress in which they find themselves. This belief, unlike the abstract, alien goals of civilization during the U.S. occupation or Filipino identity in the postindependence period, represents an attempt to perfect a preexisting aspect of local identity—Islam. Therefore, it has a cultural resonance and power that such externally imposed ends do not and cannot have.

The attractiveness of this ideal is borne out by the growth of the movement in the Philippines. While there is no detailed census, the Jema'at al Tabligh has clearly grown significantly since its introduction to the region in the late 1970s and early 1980s. Local participants describe gatherings of 10,000–20,000 individuals, and the sight of individuals or small groups of Tabligh in their

[45] Ayoong Mala, interview by the author, Binidayan, Lanao del Sur, Philippines, July 6, 2004.
[46] Ibid.
[47] Salic Abdul, personal communication, June 25, 2004.

distinctive white dress is common throughout Muslim Mindanao. The movement has reached the point, moreover, where key figures in it are positioned
to take advantage of the process of educational decentralization to exercise,
along with other advocates of Islamization, a measure of influence on educational reforms in public education in Muslim Mindanao.

Project Madrasa Education and the Islamization of Public Education in Muslim Mindanao

Movement toward the decentralization of education—shaped and justified within a multiculturalist policy discourse—has created spaces for new
voices and perspectives on educational reform in Muslim Mindanao. The
most prominent of these voices at the moment seem to be the products of
the transnational Islamist movements that have increasingly influenced Muslim Mindanao since at least the 1970s. Their perceived superior knowledge
of Islam and often-lengthy sojourns in the wider Muslim world give them
status within the local Muslim community as individuals who embody, to a
greater degree than most, an ideal with profound cultural resonance: the
good Muslim. Thus, they are seen as especially well qualified to reshape local
education in the spaces opened up by decentralization and multiculturalism
in order to bring it into greater conformity with that ideal. Two particularly
prominent examples of this phenomenon are Mahad Mutilan, a highly respected Muslim scholar educated at Al Azhar University in Egypt and founder
of Ompia, an Islamically oriented political party, and Mawlana Faisal, one of
the Jema'at al Tabligh's most respected leaders.

While serving as vice-governor and secretary of the Department of Education in the ARMM, Mutilan launched PME, an effort simultaneously to infuse
aspects of the public school curriculum into the *madaris* and to Islamize public
education in the ARMM. He then appointed Mawlana Faisal to serve as director
of the project and assembled a team of Western-educated Muslims and local
ulama educated in the Middle East to design and implement PME.[48] Thus,
decentralization and the rhetoric of multiculturalism enabled, for perhaps the
first time in the educational history of the region, an attempt to merge three
distinct approaches to the education of Muslim Filipinos—public/secular education, *madrasa* education, and the Jema'at al Tabligh—into a more or less
unified, Islamized vision of education for Muslim Mindanao.

Mutilan's approach to educational reform in the ARMM is premised on
an analysis of the Mindanao problem that differs somewhat from that of
many other observers, most of whom have tended to emphasize poverty,
underdevelopment, cultural bias, and the colonial legacy as root causes of
the conflict. Mutilan, in contrast, argues that these are also problems in other
provinces of the Philippines and that the "main factor is religion," the long

[48] Mahad Mutilan, interview by the author, Marawi City, Philippines, July 5, 2004; Aida Hafiza
Macada-ag, interview by the author, Marawi City, Philippines, June 23, 2004.

colonial and postcolonial effort to subordinate, if not eradicate, Islam in the southern Philippines and Muslim Filipinos' struggle to retain Islam as the core of their religious and cultural identity.[49] The solution to the problem is to allow both sides to cultivate an identity that is attractive to them, as he explains in the following example: "Supposing you invite me to eat lunch, and you want me to enjoy eating with you in this. What are you going to do? You prepare me the food I like. And you eat your food that you like. Give me the one I like when I eat with you . . . enjoying together . . . on the same table. After eating we become all satisfied and stronger; we can work together for the preservation of our people."[50] Mutilan's explicitly multiculturalist metaphor is precisely the opposite of the centralized *lutong makao* curriculum that has dominated educational fare in Muslim Mindanao for more than a century. Mutilan asserts that the extension of the Arabic language and Islamic values will, perhaps paradoxically, mitigate Muslim Filipinos' suspicion of and hostility toward the Philippine government: "If that will be implemented religiously, the Muslims will feel that this is their government. This is not the same as previous governments. This is a government that is not only going to preserve and defend our culture and faith but even struggle for its flourishing and development. So this is our government. So they will behave and stop resisting."[51] The PME, therefore, has three broad objectives that encompass public education, *madrasa* education, and the idea of the integrated *madrasa*: to infuse Islamic values and Arabic-language instruction into the curricula of public schools in the ARMM, to integrate and standardize the curricula of *madaris* with the curricula of the public schools, and to establish one pilot integrated *madrasa* in each of the provinces of the ARMM.[52]

The first of these objectives builds upon two relatively uncontroversial and long-standing aspects of the current public school curriculum. Arabic-language instruction, for example, has been an option for those schools in Muslim Mindanao that wanted to offer it since 1973.[53] And a spiritually grounded values education program has long been part of the curriculum of Philippine public schools.[54] Ostensibly, therefore, PME simply seeks to ensure that Arabic instruction is more widely available than it has been heretofore and that the values education program in predominantly Muslim schools reflects the spiritual values of Muslim Filipinos. To achieve these goals, a group of *ulama* was assembled to collaborate with educators from the ARMM

[49] Ibid.

[50] Mutilan, interview.

[51] Ibid.

[52] Ibid.; Macada-ag, interview.

[53] Ahman Mohammad H. Hassoubah, *Teaching Arabic as a Second Language in the Southern Philippines* (Marawi City: Mindanao State University Research Center, 1983), 24–25.

[54] Department of Education, Culture, and Sports, *Values Education for the Filipino* (Manila: Department of Education, Culture, and Sports, 1997).

Department of Education to prepare curricula and textbooks in both Islamic values and Arabic for dissemination to public schools in the region.

Islamization of education, however, refers to more than the simple addition of content and language. It involves rather the acceptance of a "semantic structure" of concepts and values revealed in the Holy Qur'an and articulated in the language of Islam (Arabic) as a framework within which all other subjects—acquired knowledge—are rendered meaningful.[55] The *ulama* involved in PME, all of whom are graduates of Islamic universities in Saudi Arabia and Kuwait, clearly understand the relationship between revealed and acquired knowledge in Islam.[56] Their effort to Islamize public education in the ARMM therefore suggests a much more radical reorientation of education than the addition of another foreign language and the minor adjustment of the values education curriculum.

The second objective of PME represents an effort to "upgrade" *madrasa* education and bring it under some measure of control by the regional government. The vast majority of *madaris* in the Philippines are small institutions operated by a single proprietor or small groups of proprietors who have received an Islamic education either in the Philippines or abroad. As such, their curricula tend to reflect the training of their proprietors. Most do not offer the secular subjects such as mathematics, science, social science, or English offered to students in government-approved schools and required for advancement in the Philippine educational system. Where they do offer such subjects, the quality of instruction is so low that students are effectively barred from the government-approved system, which is perhaps the only means of access to the socioeconomic mainstream. The PME, therefore, is intended to standardize the religious curriculum of these independent *madaris* and infuse the government-approved, secular curriculum into their programs to facilitate their students' access to the mainstream of Philippine education and society. The *madaris* would retain, however, their identity as institutions that render acquired knowledge meaningful by interpreting it in the light of the revealed knowledge contained in the Qur'an.[57] Those *madaris* that choose to "integrate" in this fashion would then be eligible for government recognition and, potentially, access to limited government financial support.

The third and least well-articulated objective of the project involves the establishment of pilot integrated *madaris* in each of the provinces of the Autonomous Region. These institutions are intended to serve as laboratories in which curricula and methods can be developed and their effectiveness

[55] Syed Muhammad Naquib Al-Attas, *The Concept of Education in Islam: A Framework for an Islamic Philosophy of Education* (Kuala Lumpur: International Institute for Islamic Thought and Civilization, 1999), 2–20.

[56] Ulama [pseud.], interview by the author, July 12, 2004.

[57] Macada-ag, interview.

demonstrated prior to dissemination to participating *madaris*.[58] Interviews with PME staff left unclear how the pilot integrated *madaris* would differ from existing private integrated *madaris*, such as the Ibn Siena Integrated School in Marawi or Shariff Kabungsuan College in Cotabato City, other than the presence of ARMM Department of Education control over the pilot schools. As of the end of 2005, however, this aspect of PME seemed to have seen the least progress toward realization.

Ultimately, the objectives of PME are to make public schools in the Autonomous Region more attractive to Muslim families by better reflecting the religious and cultural values of local communities and to improve the education offered in the *madaris* by (*a*) standardizing the Islamic curriculum and (*b*) infusing government-required secular curricula. Doing this, it is hoped, will not only improve the education of Muslim Filipino children but also transform the relationship between the Muslim community and the Philippine government. In this effort the promoters of PME have the apparent support of the national Department of Education.[59] It is unclear, however, how much concrete support will be forthcoming or whether the ramifications of PME, if successfully implemented, are fully understood.

Soul Food? Islamic Education as Existential Sustenance in Muslim Mindanao

The most common metaphors deployed by Muslim Filipino educators to describe both the problems of public education and the promise of the Islamization of education in Muslim Mindanao revolve around food, sustenance, and growth. The government-approved curriculum was described as a *lutong makao* curriculum, a term that, while it refers loosely to Chinese cooking, is meant to convey the image of a menu settled and prepared elsewhere and merely served to captive diners, whether it suited their tastes or not.[60] Combined with the dilapidated facilities, lack of books, low graduation and college entrance rates, and other indices of educational poverty in the government schools of Muslim Mindanao, the metaphor paints a critical picture of educational malnutrition, of schools feeding students on a curricular diet many find unpalatable in quantities inadequate for their intellectual sustenance.

Metaphors of appropriate reform also revolve around images of food and sustenance. Mutilan's plea illustrates this as it argues rather explicitly for decentralization and local control: "You prepare me the food I like. And you eat your food that you like. . . . [Then] we can work together for the preservation of our people."[61] Mawlana Faisal Abdullah's parable of the mango

---

[58] Ibid.

[59] Boransing, interview.

[60] Panambulan, interview. This image is reinforced by their almost uniform description of their teaching as "spoon feeding."

[61] Mutilan, interview.

seed quoted above not only refers to the presumably unlimited growth of knowledge in Islam; its use of a ubiquitous item of household trash and roadside debris—a discarded mango seed—draws attention to the unlimited potential for intellectual growth in content as local and homely as the mango, an almost universally enjoyed item in the local diet.[62]

Such metaphors were particularly evident in descriptions of Shariff Kabungsuan College by its founder and director. The school is built on soil that was trucked in to fill a swampy site. Where they had the resources to place fill dirt they built school buildings and planted—interestingly —mango and other trees. Where they lacked the resources to displace the water they planted rice and made fishponds. The produce of these endeavors is given to supplement the meager income of teachers, who are themselves "grown" locally inasmuch as they are trained in the school itself to teach the integrated curriculum.[63] Taken together, these metaphors point to the perceived importance of local responses to local needs in local conditions—decentralization—and the perceived inefficiency of externally determined responses to imagined local needs in order to achieve others' purposes—excessive centralization.

Another theme common to the interviews conducted for this inquiry is the concern with morality and moral safety. While there was criticism of government failures, oppressive military policies, majority bias, and neo-colonial interference from the United States, much of the blame for the problems of crime, drug smuggling, kidnapping, violence, and terrorism in local communities was attributed to the moral failings of the people themselves.

> America is not our enemy. . . . Our enemy is Satan, who tries to take us from the right path. . . . [W]hat is happening to the Muslims is because of the deviation of the Muslim from the right path. . . . Lots of groups, they believe that what is happening now to the Muslims, for example, the attacking of Afghanistan by your [the United States] . . . they say, oh, imperialism, we will try to fight them. . . . For us, the Tablighi, what is happening to the Muslims is a form of punishment from God. . . . God has many soldiers: the fire, the volcano, the tidal wave, the rat, the earthquake. . . . So, the message of Tabligh is, if problems are there, check yourself.[64]

While not every respondent agreed with this individual's analysis of the problems that plague Filipino Muslim society, most recognized a significant degree of moral responsibility on the part of Muslim Filipinos for these problems. And the response was, rather uniformly, the need to struggle toward an ideal conception of the good, an ideal articulated in the "semantic structure" of Islam. The belief that "if Muslims will only be good Muslims then all of their

[62] Abdullah, interview.
[63] Abubakar, interview.
[64] Abdul, interview.

problems would be solved" was expressed repeatedly in interviews. And, significantly, this faith in faith reprises the key element in the food metaphors discussed above, for the concept of the Good Muslim idealizes the unlimited potential of a central feature of local identity in response to local needs and local aspirations.

These two themes—sustenance and morality—constitute an implicit critique of the education offered to Muslim Filipinos heretofore by successive colonial and postcolonial governments. Beyond the obvious and widely acknowledged absence of resources, the bureaucratic inefficiency and corruption, and the cultural biases of textbooks and curricula is the absence of a locally meaningful purposefulness that can offer existential and spiritual sustenance for Muslim schoolchildren. This suggests that, even if the material problems that plague Philippine education were miraculously solved, it would still fall short of Muslim Filipinos' needs if it remained silent—on constitutional grounds—regarding students' moral purpose as Muslims or substituted some alternative ideal—the majority's Christian ideals, say, or Filipino identity—in its place. These themes help to explain the phenomenon of Islamization happening at the moment in the spaces opened up by the decentralization of educational decision making in Muslim Mindanao.

Islamization of Education and/as Democratic Educational Reform?

The three streams of Islamization examined here—the concept of *madrasa* integration, the growth of the Jema'at al Tabligh, and the Islamization of public education in the ARMM—are in many respects merely the latest channels of a powerful current that has run through the history of Muslim Mindanao: the consolidation and spread of Islam. Despite centuries of pressure, Islam has been and remains a central element of cultural and religious identity in Mindanao and the Sulu Archipelago. These latest trends appear, in fact, to signal an intensification of that identity as Filipino Muslim educators use the space created by decentralization to strengthen the Islamic character of society in Muslim Mindanao and to project it into private and public, formal and nonformal education in the region. In short, in this particular sociohistorical context, the trend toward decentralization as a key element of democratic educational reform may be leading to the Islamization of education.

Such a development is likely to be viewed with some alarm by Western observers who assume that secularization is crucial to educational development, particularly in the current international political climate, where Islamization is often seen as synonymous with radicalization. But in the peculiar context of Muslim Mindanao—where both real and imagined threats to Muslims' religious identity have conspired with endemic poverty, cultural bias, and political manipulation to fuel Islamist insurgencies and thus create conditions hospitable to even more radical foreign elements—there may well be something to the locally common notion that many of their problems can be solved by being better Muslims. This is not just naive faith, but an assertion that the orienting ideals and the motive energy capable of resolving the problems of Muslim Mindanao are to be found in the spiritual, intellectual, and cultural resources of Muslim Filipinos themselves, not in the imported ideals of civilization, Filipino identity, or modernity enacted in the educational policies of successive colonial and postcolonial governments, however well-intentioned.

Islamization of education in Mindanao can be seen as an assertion of local ownership: "These are our schools." The director of one integrated *madrasa* pointed to this sense of ownership as one of the key reasons for her school's success and its lack as a key factor in the problems faced by government schools. Teachers and students in government schools were expected to implement curricula and achieve goals they had no hand in determining by a system that repeatedly failed to provide them with the books, classrooms, and other resources necessary to accomplish them. This leads, she argued, to a sense of futility and cynicism that contributes to widespread corruption, absenteeism, and other problems plaguing government schools.[65] In such circumstances there is little sense of accountability to a distant and ineffectual government, which not only fails to deliver on its promises but also, viewed in the context of conflict between the Moro Islamic Liberation Front and the Government of the Republic of the Philippines, often seems hostile to Muslim Filipino aspirations. The integrated *madrasa*, on the other hand, places Islam, the most highly respected and revered element of local identity, at the core of its educational mission. Thus accountability is to one's neighbors and one's God, not to a government still widely considered *gobirno a sarawang a tao*—"a government of foreign people."[66] This is, in a sense, a local variant on the basic argument for decentralization. In this context, therefore, decentralization is likely to lead to further Islamization.

The arguments for Islamization made by those involved in *madrasa* integration, Tabligh, and PME clearly represent an optimistic view of the trend. There are, however, significant dangers beyond the real, but perhaps excessive, Western fears of the danger of blurring mosque-state lines. For instance, what are the likely consequences of a failure to follow through on the goals of PME? There is a not inconsiderable likelihood that PME will not get too far past the drawing board; after all, the roofs and walls of schools across the Philippines are decorated with the fading slogans of past policy reforms launched with as much fanfare and good intentions as PME. Most foundered quickly on a chronic shortage of financial and material resources, bureaucratic inertia, corruption, and a host of other impediments to educational reform.

Private and nonformal trends toward an intensification of Islamic identity

---

[65] Abubakar, interview.

[66] Nagasura Madale, interview by the author, Marawi City, Philippines, June 23, 2004.

in Muslim Mindanao, such as those manifested in the integrated *madaris* and the Jema'at al Tabligh, are likely to move forward since they are largely a result of and reliant on local initiative, albeit often with the spiritual and material support of benefactors from the Middle East. This suggests the very real possibility of a widening gap between the desires of the community and the goals of the government schools that serve them, a result that would, to paraphrase former Vice-Governor Mutilan, suggest to Muslim Filipinos that this government indeed is the same as previous governments, that it is not their government, and that, as one teacher complained bitterly, "they don't give a damn about us."[67] Such a reinforcement of an already strong sense of alienation from the Philippine government could motivate even more Muslim Filipinos to entertain more radical solutions to their predicament.

There are, moreover, potential dangers in the success of efforts like PME to Islamize public education in Muslim Mindanao. Historically, for instance, the centralization of policy making and the unified curriculum, though clearly an artifact of colonialism, was nevertheless continued in the postcolonial period as an effort to create a common Filipino identity out of the geographic, cultural, and linguistic diversity of the Philippine archipelago.[68] The PME may succeed in making public education in Muslim Mindanao more consistent with local needs and aspirations, but it does not address education in the rest of the Philippines. Thus, while Muslim Filipinos' knowledge of and pride in their Islamic heritage are strengthened through their educational experience, the silence on these matters in the curriculum of the majority is likely to leave relatively intact the age-old biases that have fueled Muslim-Christian tensions for centuries, biases that have by no means disappeared from Philippine society.[69] The Islamization of education in Muslim Mindanao could reinforce Filipino Muslim bias against their Christian fellow citizens, while the lack of a multicultural education that promotes positive awareness of Islam in the rest of the country fails to address Filipino Christian biases against their Muslim fellow citizens. Again, the result could be a widening of the gap between the Christian majority and Muslim minority.

Another potential danger of the trend toward Islamization of education in Muslim Mindanao is the possibility that decentralization facilitates a kind of recentralization of educational policy and philosophy in a monolithic vision of Islamic education authorized and imposed by the ARMM Department of Education or by Islamic leaders abroad. Most of the officials of the ARMM Department of Education have come of age professionally in the centralized, top-down bureaucratic culture of the national Department of Education. Such habitual practices may be reinforced by the sense that the educational policies

---

[67] Mutilan, interview; Nuraida [pseud.], interview by the author, Siawadatu, Lanao del Sur, Philippines, November 13, 2000.

[68] Milligan, *Islamic Identity, Postcoloniality, and Educational Policy.*

[69] Solita Collas-Monsod, "Anti-Muslim Bias," *Philippine Daily Inquirer,* November 5, 2005, edit. sec.

and practices one is promoting are divinely, rather than merely politically, sanctioned. Moreover, the way an Islamized education is conceived may mitigate or exacerbate such tendencies. For instance, if fundamentalist interpretations of Islam, or even the apparently pacifist but nevertheless conservative Islam espoused by the Tabligh, dictate the character of education in Muslim Mindanao, then the consequences may be profound for, say, Muslim Filipino women or the indigenous communities and Christian Filipinos that constitute significant minorities in the ARMM. If the direction of Islamization takes a fundamentalist turn, Muslim women might lose some of the relative freedoms they currently enjoy, and minority groups could wind up occupying the role of marginalized outsider that so many Muslim Filipinos chafe under today.

At the moment, however, the potential for good or ill of these trends toward Islamization of education in the southern Philippines is hypothetical. Time will tell whether the effort to forge an approach to education more consistent with local values in the spaces created by decentralization is the beginning of real educational reform in Muslim Mindanao or simply one more in a long history of well-intentioned disappointments. It is not yet clear what the end result of this trend will be. What is clear, however, is that the century-long effort of colonial and postcolonial governments to assimilate Filipino Muslims into the mainstream of Philippine society—on terms defined by the Christian majority—has not worked. Muslim Filipinos have fought, literally and figuratively, to sustain and enhance their identity as Muslims. There is no reason to believe that that will change any time soon. Moderate Islamization, such as that envisioned in PME and the concept of the integrated *madrasa*, may succeed in convincing more Muslim Filipinos that, as the leaders of PME hope, "this is their government" and that "it is going to preserve and defend our culture and faith."[70] A system of public education that offers Muslim Filipinos the cultural and spiritual sustenance that they find palatable may succeed where the *lutong makao* curriculum of educational centralization has failed. There are, to be sure, risks in the Islamization of education in Mindanao. However, to assume the inevitability of the dangers and minimize the possibility of success would mean prejudging the results of a policy experiment, the hypothesis of which is the idea that, in this context, lowering the wall between mosque and state may be more effective than raising it. Given the similarities between the educational problems facing Muslim Mindanao and those facing other minority religious communities around the world, it is an experiment worth watching.

[70] Mutilan, interview.

124

"A Modern, Integral, and Open Understanding": Sunni Islam and Lebanese Identity in the Makassed Association

MANDY TERC

Lebanon's violent past and sectarian strife have made the country's name synonymous with violence and disunity. Yet the discourse of at least one Lebanese religious institution can complicate the simplistic narrative about a country of warring religious groups with no national sentiments. The writings produced by the Makassed Philanthropic Islamic Association of Beirut, a Sunni Islamic charitable organization that operates over 42 schools throughout Beirut and the rest of Lebanon, continually describe an identity that includes both religious and national components.[1] This article discusses how these Sunni schools express simultaneously their religious and national affiliations. Their presence in a diverse society such as Lebanon, with its large Muslim population, requires a reconsideration of the interplay between national affiliation and Islamic education. In addition, this article examines how the Makassed Association reconciles these two concepts by embracing a pluralistic vision of Lebanese society. To do this, the article looks at the association's publications both in the 1980s and today to understand how the association consistently articulated its Sunni-ness and Lebanese-ness as equally important and relevant parts of its identity.

Sectarian and/or National Identity

When scholars or journalists write about Lebanon—a country that recently engaged in a 15-year civil war—the continued existence of sectarianism and the confessional political system are often cited as proof that no sentiment of national belonging does or can exist.[2] Intellectuals reference the relationships between different Lebanese religious communities and foreign polities, for example, pointing to the links between the Shi'i community and

---

[1] In this article, I use the French transliteration of the association's shortened Arabic name (المقاصد, or "intentions") because that is the spelling and name the association uses in its English-language publications. The English transliteration is Maqasid. The association's full name in Arabic reads جمعية المقاصد الخيرية الاسلامية في بيروت.

[2] During the Lebanese civil war from 1975 to 1990, militias representing Lebanese sectarian communities and Palestinian factions battled in various sites over the country. The Syrian and Israeli armies also invaded, occupied parts of Lebanon, and engaged in a series of alliances with certain militias to fight against others. For a thorough journalistic account of the entire war, see Robert Fisk, *Pity the Nation: Lebanon at War* (New York: Oxford University Press, 2001). For a comprehensive explanation of the war's causes, see Farid El-Khazen, *The Breakdown of the State in Lebanon, 1967–1976* (New York: I. B. Tauris, 2000).

Iran or to the relationship between the Maronites and France.[3] The dominant assumption in the literature is that Lebanese national identity is the ugly stepsister to the numerous sectarian affiliations of the Lebanese.[4] This idea portrays the civil war as an inevitable struggle between "tenacious and obsolete units" unnaturally grouped together by foreign powers.[5] If a legitimate Lebanese identity does exist, the argument goes, it is always portrayed as embattled by sectarian politics or as less important than the real identities in Lebanon, the religious ones. According to Walid Khalidi, "Moslem sects by and large think of themselves as constituting an integral part of the worlds of Arabdom and Islam. Lebanon is meaningless to them in any other context. They tend to equate Lebanism with Arabism."[6]

However, I argue that the links between sectarian communities and other international interests do not appear to diminish the relevance and importance of "being Lebanese" to these communities' identities. By highlighting the continued presence of Lebanese national identity, I am not implying that Lebanese sectarian communities are disconnected from their coreligionists in other nations. My argument is not that Lebanese Sunnis are unaffected by or not interested in Sunnis in other countries. I am aware of the strong and important links between the Sunni community and Arab nationalist movements and Sunni religious movements and Islamic communities. As Elizabeth Thompson writes, in her meticulously researched account of paternal power structures in greater Syria during the French mandate period, the "Sunni nationalists' ideology of a unified Syria" was a powerful voice for joining Lebanon and Syria based on a shared religion.[7] In describing the deal making that enabled the creation of an independent Lebanon, Peter Sluglett and Marion Farouk Sluglett also portray the Lebanese Sunni community as emotionally and politically tied to the larger Sunni world: "The sense of an embattled community is of course not present, since the Sunnis especially have always been aware of their membership of a wider Sunni world beyond the borders of Lebanon. In fact, for most of the French Mandate, the Sunnis refused to accept the idea of Lebanon as a permanent entity,

---

[3] See Walid Khalidi, *Conflict and Violence in Lebanon: Confrontation in the Middle East* (Cambridge, MA: Center for International Affairs, Harvard University, 1979); and Farès Sassine, "A Lebanese Education," *Beirut Review* 6 (Fall 1993): 37–44.

[4] See Ussama Makdisi, "Reconstructing the Nation-State: The Modernity of Sectarianism in Lebanon," *Middle East Report* (July–September 1996): 23–26; Samir Khalaf, *Civil and Uncivil Violence in Lebanon: A History of the Internationalization of Communal Conflict* (New York: Columbia University Press, 2002); Kamal Salibi, *A House of Many Mansions: The History of Lebanon Reconsidered* (London: I. B. Tauris, 1988); and Sassine, "A Lebanese Education."

[5] Sassine, "A Lebanese Education," 43.

[6] Khalidi, *Conflict and Violence in Lebanon*, 146.

[7] Elizabeth Thompson, *Colonial Citizens: Republican Rights, Paternal Privilege, and Gender in French Syria and Lebanon* (New York: Columbia University Press, 2000), 82.

hoping that the country would eventually be re-absorbed into Syria."[8] The Slugletts report that it was only after political bargaining that the Sunni community finally acquiesced to sharing political power in an independent Lebanon, though the Lebanese Sunni community's connection to other Sunnis has not disappeared today.

Although many intellectuals insist that Muslims in Lebanon "imagine their community," to borrow from Benedict Anderson's seminal work, to be largely outside of their country, other theorists of the relationship between Islam and nationalism have found that the two concepts are often compatible.[9] John Esposito's work on the complex relationships between Islam and politics describes a "gradual transformation in which the sharp dichotomy between a pan-Islamic supranational ideal and modern nationalism have been softened."[10] He believes that ardent opposition in the Muslim world to the formation of nation-states had less to do with Islamic tenets and more to do with a political reaction to the painful legacy of colonialism in most of the Muslim world: "Though the Western concept of nationalism and the nation state adopted by Muslim political elites seem initially Islamically unacceptable, the seeds for an Islamic adaptation or Islamization of nationalism are present. Objections to modern nationalism were primarily a reaction to the continuation of Western imperialism through the displacement of Islamic institutions by Western, secular models."[11]

Another political scientist, Sami Zubaida, formulated a similar view of the relationship between Islam and nation-states in the contemporary Muslim world. He also argues that there is nothing inherent in Islamic theology that makes it impossible for practicing Muslims to live and function within a nation-state. Similar to Esposito, Zubaida views much of the resistance to nationalism in the Middle East as a rejection of forms of colonial domination, rather than a direct gripe with the nation as a form of political organization. However, Zubaida singles out Lebanon as a counterexample to the generally congenial relationship between Islamic populations and nation-states: "The challenges to the territorial state, pan-Arab or pan-Islamic, have come primarily from elaborate modern ideologies worked out by intellectuals, but who have in practice pursued their politics within the territorial state. The major exception to this rule is the Lebanon, whose war-torn polity has been a stage for forces and allegiances of other regional states and ideologies."[12] Zubaida is correct to observe that the civil war in Lebanon provided an opportunity for other players in the Middle East and beyond to get involved

---

[8] Peter Sluglett and Marion Farouk Sluglett, "Aspects of the Changing Nature of Lebanese Confessional Politics: Al-Murabutin, 1958–1979," in *Islamic Dilemmas: Reformers, Nationalists, and Industrialization*, ed. Ernest Gellner (New York: Mouton, 1985), 269.

[9] Benedict Anderson, *Imagined Communities* (London: Verso, 1983).

[10] John Esposito, *Islam and Politics* (Syracuse, NY: Syracuse University Press, 1987), 233.

[11] Ibid., 233.

[12] Sami Zubaida, *Islam, the People and the State* (London: I. B. Tauris, 1993), 170.

with Lebanon's affairs; some of those actors, notably Syria, remain involved in Lebanon's affairs some 15 years after the war officially ended. However, his statement implies that Lebanon as an entity has been reduced to a mere geographical reality in which foreign interests replace local affiliations in importance. Perhaps in 1993, when the country was just beginning to rebuild and its ability to coalesce was dubious, this statement seemed obvious to Zubaida.

However, I argue that, despite local and national dysfunctions too numerous and complicated to discuss in this article, today Lebanon still exists and even inspires its citizens to discuss a national identity. Rather than insist on a tension between Makassed's sectarian and national affiliations, I prefer to follow anthropologist Lucia Volk. In her study of Lebanese teens developing postwar identities, she noted that a strong sectarian identity strengthened the teens' Lebanese identities: "National affiliation did not necessarily run against the grain of sectarianism, as many students told me they felt proudly Shiite, Druze or Maronite for the first time upon returning to Lebanon. Being Lebanese meant belonging to one of these groups and therefore, national identity was an integral part of the other group affiliations."[13] Lebanon as a country is sectarian; thus being Lebanese means associating oneself with a sect. Sectarianism is an important dimension of being Lebanese, but its existence does not render the label "Lebanese" irrelevant or meaningless.

Moreover, when speaking of religious groups in Lebanon, we should not overlook their religious components and focus only on their political implications. I believe that religious identity in Lebanon is complex, spanning and connecting many different realms of an individual's life and experience. These include the political, social, economic, and, not insignificantly, religious. Lara Deeb, writing about public piety among Shi'i women in Beirut's southern suburbs, also reminds us that theorizing about a connection between religious and national identities should not mean reducing religion to a political tool. Coining a new phrase, "the betwixt and between of faith and identity," she refutes the idea that faith is always in the service of political or economic goals:[14] "I am working from the premise that faith is not a façade, not just a mystifying thing that we need to look past in order to understand what is 'really' going on. Instead faith is what is going on, it is a very real thing in and of itself, located in practices, discourse, inner and outer states, relationships and real effects on the world."[15] Many Lebanese—whether they consider themselves Shi'i (like the informants in Deeb's ethnography) or Sunni (like the Makassed Association) or any other religious

---

[13] Lucia Volk, "Missing the Nation: Lebanon's Post-war Generation in the Midst of Reconstruction" (PhD diss., Harvard University, 2001), 86.

[14] Lara Deeb, "An Enchanted Modern: Gender and Public Piety among Islamist Shi'i Muslims in Beirut: (PhD diss., Emory University, 2003), 14.

[15] Ibid., 13.

identity—have genuine and intense feelings of religious devotion, piety, and belief.

The Makassed Philanthropic Islamic Association of Beirut

Twenty-four prominent members of the Sunni community of Beirut founded the Makassed Philanthropic Islamic Association of Beirut in 1878 to offer a wide range of charitable services to the Sunni Muslims in Beirut and the rest of Lebanon. One of its most important and prominent original services was its educational directorate, which provided Sunni Muslims with an alternative to the Istanbul-oriented Ottoman schools and the Christian education offered at the various foreign schools. Makassed aimed to provide an education with a Muslim character that stressed rigorous preparation in math and the sciences and intense training in foreign languages.[16] In the 1920s, the association expanded its educational offerings beyond its original two schools by opening more than a dozen new schools. In 1922, Makassed established the Committee on Educating Muslim Children in Rural Areas, a body charged with overseeing and expanding Makassed's educational initiatives outside Beirut.[17] In 1930, the association opened Makassed General Hospital, now one of Lebanon's largest and most respected hospitals. Makassed created its own publishing house in 1982, which continues to print primarily its own publications and educational materials. Today, the association also includes among its many divisions the Center for Development and Environment, which promotes environmental protection, a women's league, a children's shelter, Higher Institutes of Nursing and Islamic Studies, an Institute of Teacher Training, and the Abdul Hadi Debs Vocational and Technical Center.[18]

Education was the original imperative of Makassed, and it remains the cornerstone of the association's activities and focus.[19] Today, the association's educational directorate runs 42 schools in Lebanon, including 38 elementary and middle schools. In Beirut they operate four elementary and middle schools and six high schools; the remaining schools are scattered throughout the north, Mount Lebanon, the south, and the Bekaa Valley. In total, the schools educate over 11,000 students annually. According to the Makassed Web site, students receive free education in most of the elementary schools. At the middle and high school levels, Makassed offers subsidized fees for families that cannot

---

[16] Issam Shbaro, *The Makassed Philanthropic Islamic Association of Beirut (1878–2000)* (Beirut: Thinking Lamp, 2000), 29.

[17] Ibid., 201.

[18] http://www.makassed.org.

[19] Michael Johnson observes that the mission of educating Sunni youth was inextricably connected to a desire to compete economically with the Christian community, since "the Makassed founding fathers seem to have linked economic success with educational opportunity." See Michael Johnson, *Class and Client in Beirut: The Sunni Muslim Community and the Lebanese State, 1840–1985* (London: Ithaca, 1986), 15.

afford the entire tuition and coordinates a school grant system in which underprivileged students receive full-tuition scholarships.[20]

Makassed and Lebanese Politics

From its inception, the Makassed Association has mixed religious practice and its Sunni faith with concrete social, political, and economic goals. Michael Johnson, a historian who has written extensively on various aspects of the Makassed Association, notes that religious leaders always served in leadership positions within the organization.[21] In fact, from 1918 to 1931, the mufti of Beirut was always the Makassed president, and, after that, the association continued to bestow the post of honorary president on the mufti.[22] Issam Shbaro, a former Makassed student and an active member of the association, published a history of Makassed in 2000. He explains why the Sunni community founded Makassed and then details its activities from its early days under Ottoman rule until the present day. Shbaro views the Sunni religious leadership as so important to Makassed that he divides his historical narrative into segments based on which sheikh was leading the association at the time. He sees the association's religious leadership and ideology as critical to shaping the essential Makassed emphasis on charity, social improvements, and education.[23]

The Makassed Association's impact on and influence over Lebanese society extends far beyond those who benefit from its services or receive education in its schools. Lebanese sociologist Samir Khalaf calls Makassed "the major charitable and welfare association in the [Sunni] community," and Johnson has published much research on Makassed's relationship to Sunni notables in Beirut.[24] Johnson's work on Makassed illustrates the inextricable interplay between religion and national politics described above. By highlighting how Sunni elites promoted both their political power and personal piety through participation in Makassed, Johnson helps to demonstrate how the Makassed Association's identity could be simultaneously strongly Sunni and Lebanese. He depicts Makassed as the organization through which urban Sunni elites promulgated a system of patronage, in which families of lesser status and wealth received employment and financial assistance in exchange

---

[20] http://www.makassed.org.

[21] Of course, this merging of religious leadership and political or civic institutions was not unique to Makassed, nor was it limited to the period before independence. Jakob Skovgaard-Petersen's article on Druze and Sunni religious leadership after the civil war aptly demonstrates how religious leaders in these communities continue to fill roles that are at once religious and political. See Jakob Skovgaard-Petersen, "Religious Heads or Civil Servants? Druze and Sunni Religious Leadership in Post-war Lebanon," *Mediterranean Politics* 1, no. 3 (Winter 1996): 337–52.

[22] Michael Johnson, "Factional Politics in Lebanon: The Case of the 'Islamic Society of Benevolent Intentions' (Al-Maqasid) in Beirut," *Middle Eastern Studies* 14, no. 1 (January 1978): 56–75, 58.

[23] See Shbaro, *The Makassed.*

[24] Samir Khalaf, "Ties That Bind: Sectarian Loyalties and the Restoration of Pluralism in Lebanon," *Beirut Review* 1 (Spring 1991): 32–59, 47; Johnson, *Class and Client.*

for their political loyalty to the elite families. He writes that "the Salams, in particular, were able to provide assistance because they controlled the Makassed Society and could distribute the educational services which were necessary to raise the status and improve the economic opportunities of poorer members of the family."[25]

In addition to enabling the elites to distribute tangible benefits to those loyal to them, the Makassed Association also provided an opportunity for Sunni elites to publicly display the religious, moral, and philanthropic qualities necessary to win adherence from other Sunnis. "Increasingly, notables performed their philanthropic role through organizations such as the Makassed Society. By becoming leading members or directors of this Society they were able to fulfill another 'requirement'—that of religious or communal identification."[26] In fact, Johnson provides compelling evidence that the Makassed Association was of utmost importance to intra-Sunni politics and even to the larger Lebanese political situation. In his article "Factional Politics in Lebanon," Johnson describes how a 1970 "conflict which developed over the election of the charity's Board of Directors not only split the Sunni community of Beirut, but also brought the Lebanese government close to resignation and even threatened to start a civil war."[27] While it was educating its youth throughout the country, the Makassed Association simultaneously afforded Sunni elites the opportunity to further their political and economic aspirations. This intertwining of charitable services and jockeying for Lebanese political power means that the entire Makassed Association, including its educational activities, directly affected all of Lebanon.

Despite Makassed's deep connection with the elite Sunni community in Beirut, the organization educates children from a wide variety of socioeconomic backgrounds in Lebanon, ranging from the children of the notables in Beirut to children from impoverished families in the countryside. This commitment to educating the poor and building schools in underresourced areas—combined with a policy of offering tuition assistance to financially disadvantaged students—ensures that the association's values and priorities cut across socioeconomic lines. Johnson reports that in 1971 60 percent of elementary school students and 40 percent of high school students received free tuition. An even larger number of students received financial assistance and did not pay the full tuition.[28] The association's Web site announces that this practice of financial support continues today.[29]

In a 1985 edition of its short-lived cultural magazine, *Makassed*, the as-

[25] Johnson, *Class and Client*, 91. The Salams were, and are, an influential and wealthy Sunni Beiruti family. For many years in the twentieth century, members of the family controlled Makassed's Board of Directors, often occupying the post of president.

[26] Ibid., 46.

[27] Johnson, "Factional Politics," 56.

[28] Ibid., 57.

[29] http://www.makassed.org.

sociation published an extensive interview with the director of rural schools, Adel Bahalwan. The article, "The Village Schools Are a Continuous Makassed Community Service," underscores the energy, resources, and interest that the association invests in its rural education program. Bahalwan's comments reveal that rural and poor students were not incidental to the Makassed system but were in fact an integral part of its mission. In his introduction to the interview, the author describes the rural education program as "arteries that transport the hot blood for the pulsating heart in Beirut."[30] Throughout the interview, Bahalwan emphasizes his desire to make the rural schools into examples of educational excellence. At the conclusion of the interview, he says that he intends "that the experience of the rural schools should expand to all parts of Lebanon, and that these schools be turned into exemplar schools in the fullest meaning of the word."[31]

Although Makassed began and continues its educational program as a Sunni endeavor, early in its history the organization adapted its policies to popular trends in Lebanese education. In Makassed's early years under Ottoman rule and then during the French mandate period, its schools taught math and science in French and sometimes in English, as did most of the schools around them. Although Makassed tried to differentiate its education from both the non-Arabic focus of the Ottomans and the non-Islamic focus of the foreign schools, its schools adopted teaching methods from the foreign schools at the beginning of the French mandate period in the 1920s. As Nakhlé Wehbé and Adnan El-Amine report, "They made the first step toward foreign culture by employing Christian teachers . . . but under their control. They began to have meetings with instructors from other establishments to deal with questions of 'teaching methods.'"[32] El-Amine, of the Lebanese University and president of the Lebanese Association for Educational Studies, hypothesizes that many of the policy changes were the result of competition for students as other Sunni schools attracted high enrollment.[33] Regardless of the practical or economic issues behind these policy changes, the Makassed Association adapted the discourse about its identity to its policy changes.

Religious and National Identity in Makassed Publications in the 1980s

This and the following section examine publications from the Makassed Association, mostly pertaining to education, that illustrate the convergence

---

[30] Said Taha, "The Village Schools Are a Continuous Makassed Community Service," *Makassed* 5, no. 47 (1986): 106. This is a translation. The original Arabic reads الشرايين التي تنقل الدم الحار لينبض في بيروت.

[31] Ibid., 111. This is a translation. The original Arabic reads
بأن تعم تجربة مدارس القرى كافة أنحاء لبنان و ان تتحول إلى مدارس نموذجية بكل معنى الكلمة.

[32] Nakhlé Wehbé and Adnan El-Amine, *Système d'enseignement et division sociale au Liban* (Paris: Editions Le Sycomore, 1980), 18 (my translation).

[33] Interview with Adnan El-Amine (president of the Lebanese Association for Educational Studies and professor of education at the Lebanese University), by author, Beirut, May 30, 2003.

of the religious and the national at Makassed.[34] This section focuses on documents from the mid-1980s, during the period of the most intense fighting in the civil war, when the Makassed discourse about identity focused on connections with the larger Arab world and pride in a long, illustrious heritage in the Arabic-speaking world. At this time, Makassed schools taught most of their subjects in Arabic. The next section discusses writings from the late 1990s and today, when Lebanon has been in the midst of massive rebuilding, both physical and intellectual, and when the discourse on identity has focused on modernity and technological advancement. Accordingly, the Makassed schools at this time teach many more classes in English or French. The reason for including documents from two distinct historical periods is to demonstrate that despite a change in what aspects of its identity have been highlighted, the Makassed discourse has always incorporated both religious and national aspects. Whether they have argued for an Arabic-focused curriculum or for incorporating English-language technologies into the school system, they have depicted these policies as the natural and proper decisions for fulfilling Makassed's role as a charity that is both Sunni and Lebanese.

Classical Arabic and the Lebanese Dialect

In the 1980s, Makassed played the role of cultural critic and arbiter by publishing a magazine, *Makassed*. Entirely in Arabic, the magazine attempted to cover a variety of aspects of Lebanese culture, from history and literature to medicine, travel, and the arts. It also published a section on language in the issues of its first volume in 1982. One of the articles from this section on language, titled "The Rooted-ness in Arabic of the Lebanese Dialect," deals explicitly with the role of Arabic in Lebanese society and the Lebanese dialect of Arabic.[35] Written by Ahmed Abu Saad, the article traces the historical uses of both colloquial (*'ammiyya*) and classical Arabic (*fusha*) and the relationship between the two linguistic forms.[36] Abu Saad considers whether classical Arabic's relationship with colloquial dialects is analogous to the situation of Latin and the Romance languages, in which the dialects of one now "dead" language became distinct languages. Abu Saad concludes that this is not the case. However, Abu Saad's primary focus is on the legitimacy of the Lebanese dialect—whether it is a valid form of the Arabic language and how that validity

[34] Munir Bashshur has written persuasively, from an academic perspective, of the educational system's function as a mirror to other societal factors. Education "has been subservient to other forces" and "gave them expression, articulated them, promoted them and planted them deep in the consciousness of its recipients." See Munir Bashshur, "The Role of Education: A Mirror of a Fractured National Image," in *Toward a Viable Lebanon*, ed. Halim Barakat (London: Croom Helm, 1988), 42–67, 42.

[35] Ahmed Abu Saad, "The Rooted-ness in Arabic of the Lebanese Dialect," *Makassed* 1, no. 3 (1982): 79–86, 79. This is a translation. The original Arabic reads الاصالة العربية في اللهجة اللبنانية.

[36] Abu Saad uses the Arabic words العامية and الفصحى, respectively. The author could be using *fusha* to indicate Modern Standard Arabic or Arabic from the classical age (both of which can be written forms of Arabic). He does not mean by it the language of the Qur'an, which he calls العربية القرآنية, or Qur'anic Arabic.

can be assessed and argued. The underlying assumption of this article is that language and identity are synonymous, for the individual and the collective.

Abu Saad gives a history of the political uses of *'ammiyya* Arabic in Egypt and Lebanon, reporting that the prolific use of Egyptian *'ammiyya* in official settings and efforts to institute a written *'ammiyya* began in the nineteenth century during the British colonial occupation. The British colonizers encouraged Egyptians to favor their colloquial Arabic over the widely understood *fusha*. At the same time, the British pushed the Egyptians to develop a specifically Egyptian identity, based on their Pharaonic past and disconnected from the rest of the Arab world. Abu Saad argues that this was a British strategy to facilitate the continuation of their colonial rule in Egypt. The reasoning was that an Egyptian people standing alone would be easier to dominate than an Egyptian people connected to and bolstered by millions of other Arabs. *Fusha* was the link between Egyptians and not only other Arabs but also "their heritage in religion, the sciences and literature."[37]

After his introduction of *'ammiyya* as the linguistic tool of imperialists, Abu Saad assesses the debate in Lebanon between advocates of *'ammiyya* and those of *fusha*. After laying out the historical roots of the Lebanese issue, he suggests using a fresh perspective to consider the issue. He examines the structure and pronunciation of Lebanese *'ammiyya* and finds that the Lebanese dialect preserves many of the expressions and idiosyncrasies of pronunciation found in *fusha* and older forms of spoken Arabic. Therefore, he concludes that Lebanese Arabic is exempt from questions about the legitimacy of *'ammiyya*, since the Lebanese *'ammiyya* is, in reality, merely a slight variation on *fusha*, the legitimate connection to Arab heritage and history.

Abu Saad's article clearly and unapologetically argues for the Arab and Muslim character of Lebanon and its spoken language, Lebanese *'ammiyya*. The Lebanese credentials for being considered Arab are so strong because even their language—unlike most other forms of spoken Arabic—preserves the authentic Arabic grammar, pronunciation, and vocabulary. It follows, then, that speaking Arabic as a Lebanese would be the best demonstration of an Arab and Muslim identity. In addition, the article posits ability in the Arabic language as the strongest connection between a rich Arab history in religion, literature, and science and Arab political strength in contemporary times. Without knowledge of the Arabic in which past generations wrote down their culture, the Lebanese of today do not have access to their strong and proud heritage. The article continually cites Islam as one of, if not the most, important components of that heritage.

---

[37] Abu Saad, "The Rooted-ness in Arabic," 79. This is a translation. The Arabic reads
تراثها في الدين و العلوم و الادب.

The "Mother Tongue" and Science

To explain an educational policy change that shifted classes previously taught in English or French into Arabic, the *Makassed* magazine published a lengthy interview with Director of Education Rafik Ido detailing the change of policy.[38] The article describes how the Makassed schools would translate mathematical concepts from French or English into Arabic and explains why teaching these subjects in Arabic is the most effective and appropriate way to educate Makassed middle school students. Like the other 1980s articles from the *Makassed* magazine, this article emphasizes the Arab and Muslim identity of both the Makassed organization and its pupils. It also stresses that the Arabic language is a connection to the rich heritage and history of Arab culture. The article's text and accompanying graphics expand this basic message. The article's author praises the eloquence and strength of the Arabic language, calling it "the most inclusive and richest of languages." In addition, the article uses the phrase "mother tongue" or "native language" to refer to the Arabic language.[39]

Throughout this discussion emphasizing an Arabic heritage and the need for language to serve as a connection to that heritage, Ido emphasizes Makassed's connection to and interest in the rest of Lebanon. At one point, he notes that part of the motivation to introduce Arabization at Makassed came from the observation that all Lebanese students had weak abilities in foreign languages, inhibiting their ability to learn scientific knowledge conveyed in those languages.[40] During the interview, the interviewer notes that the Lebanese government allows educational foundations to select their own language of instruction in middle and secondary schools. He then asks Ido why, if Makassed can select any language, the association decided on Arabic. One of Ido's responses invokes Makassed's sense of its Lebanese identity and its connection to Lebanon as a whole. He responds "that we are Lebanese, and the Constitution has established that Arabic language is the official language of the state and the language of education in general. It is our national duty

---

[38] During the debates of the 1960s and 1970s over whether to teach Lebanese students in Arabic or in foreign languages, groups on both sides of the debate cast the problem as one of identity and character. Although some of the debate did focus on the practical benefits of the languages (that students learned better in their natural language of Arabic or that French and English were more marketable in the global economy), most of the debate was argued in terms of defining Lebanese culture. Kassem Mansour, the director of a Beirut school, proposed that all schools Arabize because "Lebanon is simply of Arabic culture." See Michel Allard, "Arabisation," *Travaux et jours* 39 (April–June 1971): 5–22, 7 (my translation).

[39] Said Taha, "The Issue of Arabization in Makassed in a Discussion with Doctor Rafik Ido: The Success of Teaching in Arabic Surpasses the Success in Foreign Languages," *Makassed* 4, no. 34 (1985): 116–23. These are two possible translations for the phrase used in the article. The phrase used in the article is اللغة الأم, or, literally, "the mother language."

[40] Ibid., 118.

to use it in all our teaching subjects."[41] Although most of the article discusses the proud heritage of the Arabic language and its importance to a Muslim identity, this quote demonstrates how these interests are not in spite of—but rather because of—Makassed's Lebanese identity.

Religious and National Identity in Makassed Publications in the 1990s and Today

The Makassed Association's high-tech and visually appealing Web site offers many important insights into how the administration, at least, see religion and national identity as two symbiotic forces that shape their outlook and activities. For example, in explaining why the Makassed Association founded the Institute for Islamic Higher Learning in 1981, the Web site expresses the opinion that stronger religious affiliation and more religious knowledge will strengthen, rather than weaken, Lebanese society: "Lebanon was then in the throws of civil strife. . . . The Institute was, in a sense, the response of Makassed to the strife, which divided the people of Lebanon into warring fragments. It was to promote a better understanding of Islam . . . to overcome the obstacles which stand in the way of the development of a healthy civil society in Lebanon."[42] In its depiction of the aims of the institute, with a very Islamic structure and curriculum, the association still considers the institute's religious activities as significant national issues. Later in the description, the Web site indicates that Makassed envisions the institute as a "forum of thought and freedom of expression and a center for the Islamo-Christian dialogue and cultural exchange in general." This again signals that Makassed's Sunni identity and affiliation does not weaken its relationship to Lebanon and pull it toward the larger Sunni world. Rather, Makassed views its religious tenets as a way of contributing to a stronger, more unified Lebanon.

Today, the organization continues to center various aspects of identity on its religious and national affiliations. On the current English version of the Makassed Web site, the organization offers an overview of its educational programs. This section touts Makassed's advantages as an institution, citing "modern science and computer laboratories," "playgrounds, sports halls and theatres," and the receipt of first prize in an international peace competition. In the same paragraph announcing that Makassed "recently adopted foreign languages in teaching sciences and mathematics," the organization adds that it now offers coeducation in all but one of its schools.

Although the Web site describes Makassed's goals to "strengthen the

---

[41] Ibid., 121. This is a translation. The original Arabic reads

بأننا لبنانيون أقر الدستور اللغة العربية لغة الدولة الرسمية و لغة التعليم عامة ومن واجبنا الوطني التعاطي معها في مواد

التدريس كلها.

[42] http://www.makassed.org.

understanding of our Arab heritage" and to provide "a moderate Islamic education," this overview highlights what it calls the modernity of a Makassed education. Makassed's literature and its philosophy continually emphasize its Lebanese identity, its interest in the entirety of Lebanese society, its openness to educating students of other faiths, and the role its students play in symbolizing Lebanon as a whole. Currently, the first page of the English version of their Web site proudly proclaims that Makassed is "proud of its nationality." Furthermore, the paragraph praises nationality as an important virtue, writing that Makassed is "built on sublime values."[43] The mission statement for the entire Makassed organization further illustrates how much importance the Makassed organization places on its ability to remain relevant to the students living in an age of technology and modernity. Makassed "aims at developing the human being and enabling him to build a country and cope with modernization through knowledge and faith, in accordance with the principles of Islam."[44]

Another section of the Web site, "The Personality of the Makassed Student," reveals how the religious and national components of identity actually serve to strengthen each other in Makassed's professed beliefs: "The Makassed student is attached to his Lebanese citizenship that is not distinct from his Arab identity. He is also attached to Islam of which he has a modern, integral and open understanding. Tolerant towards other races, religious beliefs and political convictions, the Makassed student is self-confident, independent and creative in his thinking and able to cope with the scientific and technological changes."[45] This quotation neatly summarizes the most salient characteristics of the various facets of Makassed's self-described identity. First, it addresses the national component of the identity, which is clearly an Arab identity. Next, it notes the religious aspect of the identity. Finally, it offers an explanation of how the two can coexist easily and without struggle for the Makassed community. Since the Muslim aspect of the identity has an "open understanding," a member of the Makassed community can effectively deal with "other religious beliefs and political convictions." This is a clear reference to the diversity of Lebanon and explains how Makassed's Sunni Muslim affiliation can make the community better at being Lebanese.

Conclusion

The Makassed organization explicitly portrays itself, particularly its educational component, as a symbol of various issues of national concern. In 1982, during the height of the civil war and with the Israeli invasion of

---

[43] Ibid. The Arabic version, which roughly translates to Makassed's own English wording above, reads مبني على القيم السامية فخور بانتمائه الوطني.

[44] Ibid.

[45] Ibid.

Lebanon reaching Beirut, the *Makassed* magazine published an article commemorating and describing the return of its students to school for the 1982–83 school year. Full of dramatic language and sweeping descriptions of the heroic students committed to continuing their education, "The Schools of Makassed Shake off the Dust of War" is explicit in its vision of Makassed students as symbols of a Lebanese "vitality" and determination to succeed in spite of the violence and hardship befalling the country.[46] The author, Siham Khalousy, writes that "Makassed Society is an ideal symbol of Beiruti society. . . . The horror of the Israeli war exhausted it but did not kill the will to life in it."[47] This description of both Lebanese society and the civil war minimizes the contested nature of Lebanese identity and emphasizes the unity of all people, irrespective of religious identity, living in Beirut. By labeling the war as "Israeli" and casting a foreign invasion as the source of the troubles, Khalousy obscures the intense sectarian violence that was raging that summer. She can—without difficulty—portray the students of an institution associated with a specific sect as representative of the entire embattled country.

Lebanon is often cited as definitive proof that a Middle Eastern country cannot tolerate religious and ethnic plurality or that strong religious affiliations, particularly Islam, render any sentiment of national affiliation impossible. Scholars enumerate the many horrors perpetrated by sectarian groups during the civil war to contend that a Lebanese national identity has no salience to sectarian communities. It is true that Lebanon has struggled, often violently, to form a government and a national character that incorporates all of its religious communities. However, the reality is much more complicated and far less decisive, as evidence from the Makassed Association demonstrates.

One certainly cannot deny that the country divided itself on sectarian lines for much of the war. Yet the Makassed Association, a sectarian Sunni Muslim charity, saw itself as Sunni and Lebanese both during and after the war. It never questioned its identity as Lebanese, never suggested that its Sunni identity meant it had a greater affinity to other countries, and always expressed great interest in Lebanon in its entirety. It sees itself as both Sunni Muslim and Lebanese; the two attributes work together to strengthen each other. As an Islamic educational institution, it embraced its affiliation to a pluralistic society. It did not simply react to ideas of pluralism around it but instead took a leading role in articulating a national identity that could ac-

---

[46] Siham Khalousy, "The Schools of Makassed Shake off the Dust of War," *Makassed* 8 (1982): 113–19, 113. This is a translation. The original Arabic reads مدارس المقاصد تنفض عنها غبار الحرب. The Arabic word used for "vitality" is حيوية, a noun derived from حياة, the word for "life."

[47] Ibid., 114. This is a translation. The original Arabic reads
و المجتمع المقاصدي هو رمز مثالي للمجتمع البيروتي . . . أنهكته فظاعة الحرب الإسرائيلية و لكنها لم تقتل إرادة الحياة فيه.

commodate both national allegiance and Islamic learning. The Makassed Association defies the myth of reactionary Islamic educational institutions and thus requires scholars not only to readjust their answers but also to revise their questions about Islamic education.

Religious School Enrollment in Pakistan: A Look at the Data

TAHIR ANDRABI, JISHNU DAS, ASIM IJAZ KHWAJA, AND TRISTAN ZAJONC

Introduction

In recent years, policy makers have expressed growing concern about Pakistan's religious schools, which are commonly known as madrasas.[1] These concerns have been fueled considerably by reports and articles in the popular press contending that madrasa enrollment is high and increasing. The "rise" is generally attributed to either an increasing preference for religious schooling among families or a lack of other viable schooling options for the household.[2] Yet while these theories have widespread currency, none of the reports and articles that we have reviewed have based their analysis on publicly available data sources or established statistical methodologies. Given the importance that is placed on the subject by policy makers in Pakistan and internationally, it is troubling that these theories remain unconfirmed.

Getting the madrasa enrollment numbers right has serious policy implications beyond the debate on national security. How madrasa enrollment (its size and growth rate) compares to enrollment in public and private schools matters greatly for the design of educational reform and for the

This study would not have been possible without the enthusiasm and continuous support we received from Tara Vishwanath. Charles Griffin first encouraged us to look at the data. We thank Veena Das, Shaila Andrabi, Sehr Jalal, Ritva Reinikka, and Carolina Sanchez for their encouragement and Hedy Sladovich for her excellent editorial suggestions. The manuscript has also benefited from comments by Ismail Radwan, Naveeda Khan, Shahzad Sharjeel, and Shanta Devarajan. The research department of the World Bank provided funding for this study through the Knowledge for Change trust fund. The findings, interpretations, and conclusions expressed in this article are those of the authors and do not necessarily represent the views of the World Bank, its executive directors, or the governments they represent.

[1] See, e.g., George W. Bush, "President Bush Welcomes President Musharraf to Camp David," Office of the Press Secretary, White House, Washington, DC, June 24, 2003 (available at http://www.whitehouse.gov/news/releases/2003/06/20030624-3.html); Pervez Musharraf, "Remarks by Pakistani President Pervez Musharraf," Carnegie Endowment for International Peace, Washington, DC, February 12, 2002 (available at http://www.carnegieendowment.org/events/index.cfm?fa=eventDetail&id=458&&proj=znpp,zsa); Colin Powell, testimony, "House Appropriations Subcommittee on Foreign Operations, Export Financing, and Related Programs Holds Hearing on FY2005 Appropriations," FDCH Transcripts, March 10, 2004; Hillary Rodham Clinton, "Addressing the National Security Challenges of Our Times: Fighting Terror and the Spread of Weapons of Mass Destruction," speech presented at a Brookings leadership forum, Brookings Institution, Washington, DC, February 2004 (available at http://www.brookings.edu/comm/op-ed/20040225clinton.htm); and National Commission on Terrorist Attacks upon the United States, *The 9/11 Commission Report: Final Report of the National Commission on Terrorist Attacks upon the United States* (New York: Norton, 2004), also available at http://www.9-11commission.gov/report/index.htm.

[2] Shahid Javed Burki, "Basic Education in Pakistan and Afghanistan: The Current Crisis and Beyond," transcript of presentation at the Brookings Forum on Universal Education, December 2001 (available at http://www.brookings.edu/comm/transcripts/20011217.htm); Peter W. Singer, "Pakistan's Madrassahs: Ensuring a System of Education Not Jihad," Brookings Analysis Paper no. 14 (Brookings Institution, Washington, DC, November 2001); International Crisis Group, "Pakistan: Madrassahs, Extremism and the Military," ICG Asia Report no. 36 (International Crisis Group, Islamabad/Brussels, July 2002), available at http://www.crisisgroup.org/home/index.cfm?id=1627&l=1.

allocation of scarce budgetary resources.[3] If madrasa actual and relative enrollments are much smaller than has frequently been reported, then the larger educational policy concern may be about improving access to quality education in the public and mainstream private sectors.

This article uses established data sources, as well as data collected by the authors themselves for a broader study on education enrollment in Pakistan, to examine the size and importance of the religious education sector in Pakistan. Methodologically, this study analyzes madrasa enrollment in a school-choice framework that is well known to empirical economists dealing with issues of poverty and school quality in developing countries. This approach allows us to evaluate various popularly proposed theories of how madrasas fit into the overall educational decision of households.

Our findings on the enrollment numbers differ by an order of magnitude from those reported by and in the media. According to our analysis, the madrasa sector is small compared to educational options such as public and private schooling, accounting for less than 1 percent of overall enrollment in the country. Even in the districts that border Afghanistan, where madrasa enrollment is the highest in the country, it is less than 7.5 percent of all enrolled children. Furthermore, we find no evidence of a dramatic increase in madrasa enrollment in recent years. The share of madrasas in total enrollment declined before 1975, and it has increased slowly since then. Since 2001, total enrollment in madrasas has remained constant in some districts, while it has increased in others. When we look at school choice, explanations for madrasa enrollment based on household attributes such as religiosity appear inadequate. Even among the less than 1 percent of families who have one or more children enrolled in a madrasa, more than 75 percent send other of their children to private and public schools.

What Do Reports and the Popular Press Say?

We looked at three different types of articles and reports: articles in mainstream American and international newspapers; reports and articles by American and international scholars affiliated with international think tanks, institutes, and the government (including *The 9/11 Commission Report*); and studies by Pakistani scholars working in Pakistan and abroad. Reported madrasa enrollment figures in newspapers varied widely, from 500,000 to 1.7 million children. Most newspapers did not benchmark their reported estimates with the percentage of children enrolled in schools. When reported, the proportions of enrollees in madrasas also varied dramatically—from 10

---

[3] For a discussion of the U.S. aid package for education reform to Pakistan, see K. Alan Kronstadt, *Education Reform in Pakistan*, CRS Report for Congress (Order Code RS22009, December 23, 2004), available at http://www.fas.org/man/crs/RS22009.pdf.

percent of all Pakistani students to 33 percent.[4] Importantly, the sources for all of these reports and articles were either newspaper accounts of police estimates or interviews with policy makers. We have yet to find a single article that tries to validate these numbers using established data sources.

The 9/11 Commission Report adopted the same methodology of using interviews and reporting numbers based on secondary sources, as the following illustrates: "Pakistan's endemic poverty, widespread corruption, and often ineffective government create opportunities for Islamist recruitment. Poor education is a particular concern. Millions of families, especially those with little money, send their children to religious schools, or madrassahs. Many of these schools are the only opportunity available for an education, but some have been used as incubators for violent extremism. According to a Karachi's police commander, there are 859 madrassahs teaching more than 200,000 youngsters in his city alone."[5] This report provides only a footnote quoting an interview with a police commander and does not attempt to validate the numbers provided. Moreover, even the secondary sources referred to in the report did not base their estimates on published data sources.[6]

The views from the academic world have been more nuanced, and many have provided valuable descriptions of the madrasa and the general Islamic learning environment.[7] Nevertheless, when talking about madrasa numbers, the academic accounts also cite secondary sources without providing any serious verification. Jessica Stern refers to the estimated 40,000–50,000 madrasas, and Peter W. Singer claims that "there are as many as 45,000 such schools within Pakistan" without identifying any verifiable source.[8] In the research of Mohammad Qasim Zaman and Tariq Rahman, the number of madrasa students and establishments is sourced from newspaper articles in Pakistan.[9] The newspaper articles, in turn, quote a police press release, where

---

[4] See Zahid Hussain and Daniel McGrory, "British Businessmen 'Are Funding Schools That Breed Terror,'" *The Times* (London), August 10, 2002, for the 10 percent figure. C. Kraul, in "Dollars to Help Pupils in Pakistan," *Los Angeles Times*, April 14, 2003, cites the aforementioned International Crisis Group, "Pakistan: Madrassahs, Extremism and the Military," for the 33 percent number. Table A1 in app. A provides a list of articles on the madrasa that appeared in major international newspapers in the time frame of December 2000 to June 2004.

[5] National Commission on Terrorist Attacks upon the United States, *The 9/11 Commission Report*, sec. 12.2, 367.

[6] Ibid.

[7] See Mohammad Qasim Zaman, *The Ulama in Contemporary Islam: Custodians of Change* (Princeton, NJ: Princeton University Press, 2002); Tariq Rahman, "The Madrassa and the State of Pakistan: Religion, Poverty and the Potential for Violence in Pakistan," *Himal Southasian*, online journal published and distributed by the Southasia Trust, Lalitpur, Nepal (February 2004), available at http://www.himalmag.com/2004/february/essay.htm; Jessica Stern, "Pakistan's Jihad Culture," *Foreign Affairs* 79, no. 6 (2000): 115–26.

[8] Stern, "Pakistan's Jihad Culture," 119; Singer, "Pakistan's Madrassahs," 2.

[9] Zaman, *Ulama in Contemporary Islam*, 126, table 1, cites Asif Shazad, "Over 250,000 Students in Punjab Seminaries," *The Dawn*, January 22, 2002, available at http://www.dawn.com/2002/01/22/nat44.htm. Rahman, in "The Madrassa and the State of Pakistan," cites "KARACHI: 11,000 Foreigners in Sindh Madaris," *The Dawn*, January 16, 2003, available at http://www.dawn.com/2003/01/16/local6.htm.

again the raw data are not available for verification. Similarly, Ahmed Rashid, in his best-selling book on the Taliban, states that "in 1988 there were 8,000 madrassas and 25,000 unregistered ones, educating over half a million students." He cites as source an unspecified intelligence report presented to the cabinet in 1992.[10] Finally, the newspaper articles and reports also attempted to explain the reasons behind the popularity of madrasas. The final column in table A1 (in app. A) describes the main reasons advanced in the newspaper articles. Of these, one of the most popular cause and effect arguments is the "failed state" advanced by Singer: "The reason for the madrassas' new centrality stems from the weakening of the Pakistani state . . . the madrassas became immensely popular by targeting the lower class and refugee populations, whom the Pakistani state has failed to provide proper access to education."[11] This kind of coverage has fostered two conclusions: (1) madrasa enrollment rates are high and increasing, and (2) the popularity of madrasas should be understood as a response by the poor to the government's inability to provide public education and social welfare. Where is the evidence?

The Data on Madrasa Enrollment

We examine three important questions related to madrasa enrollment: the number and fraction of children (both school aged and enrolled) attending madrasas; the geographical variation in madrasa enrollment across Pakistan; and enrollment trends over time, with particular attention to two benchmarks—the Soviet invasion of Afghanistan (and the rise of the jihad movement against them in 1979) and the events of September 11, 2001.

Defining Madrasa Enrollment

We define madrasas as schools that teach a religious curriculum instead of one prescribed by the Pakistan Federal Ministry of Education. Any school that teaches the government-prescribed curriculum but that adds elements of religious teaching is considered to be a mainstream private or public school, not a madrasa.[12]

---

[10] Ahmed Rashid, *Taliban: Militant Islam, Oil and Fundamentalism in Central Asia* (New Haven, CT: Yale University Press, 2000), 89.

[11] Singer, "Pakistan's Madrassahs," 2.

[12] We follow the principle of "additionality" of the Pakistan Ministry of Education in this definition. Most private schools that wish to teach computer programming or any other subject that is not part of the government curriculum will be counted as a general educational institution (and not a vocational institute), as long as they teach these subjects in addition to the prescribed curriculum. One type of school that could be mistakenly counted as a madrasa is a mosque school. These are schools housed in mosques that teach the normal state curriculum using regular education department teachers. These were started in the sixth 5-year plan (1983–88) under the Junejo government as a cost-effective way to use mosques; however, the program was not picked up later and is now gradually dying out. There are 8,000 or so mosque schools in Punjab. The Academy of Educational Planning and Management in Islamabad houses a comprehensive data series on Pakistan education; this is available at http://www.aepam.edu.pk/Education.htm.

143

Counting the number of children going to madrasas presents additional issues. First, defining whether a child is actually going to school is not an easy task in a low-income setting, where dropping out, as well as having sporadic attendance due, for instance, to family labor requirements, are common. Numerous debates in the literature discuss the advantages (and limitations) of using enrollment figures from school registers versus actual attendance as alternate measures.[13] Our measure of enrollment tries to get close to the respondent's meaningful attendance as a measure of enrollment.

Breaking down enrollment by the type of school that the child attends is potentially a harder task if people use multiple types of education facilities simultaneously. Our definition of madrasa enrollment focuses on the principal school that the child attends. A child who is enrolled in a public school and attends a tuition center in the evening for additional private tuition counts as being enrolled in a public school. Similarly, a child going to a public or private school in the morning and going to a madrasa for Qur'anic education part time, say, in the evening, is not counted as part of the madrasa enrollment.

One cautionary note regarding our definition is that it focuses on current enrollment. Children in Pakistan can and do move in and out of madrasas. Current enrollment by type of school, using an analogy from public health, provides a "prevalence" rather than an "incidence" rate. That is, if children use both types of schools in different years, asking what type of school a child is enrolled in provides an accurate picture of current enrollment patterns but does not tell us what percentage of children were "ever enrolled" in public or private schools. This is an alternate exercise, one that requires longitudinal data.

Data Sources

We use three different types of household-based data to verify our estimates and determine how sensitive they are to changes in definition and the year of the survey. Two sources are nationally representative but date from 2001 or before; the third is data from a census of households carried out by us, the current authors, in 2003 as part of a project on educational choice. The first source is the "long" form of the 1998 Population Census, a large sample-based survey with information on enrollment. This survey is representative at the level of the district and the region (rural or urban) and provides comprehensive coverage of the entire country.[14] We use these data to examine enrollment

---

[13] See Paul Glewwe and Michael Kremer, "Schools, Teachers, and Education Outcomes in Developing Countries," in *Handbook of the Economics of Education,* ed. E. Hanushek and F. Welch (New York: Elsevier-North Holland, 2006), chap. 16.

[14] Government of Pakistan, Statistics Division, Population Census of Pakistan, 1998; Federal Bureau of Statistics, Census of Private Educational Institutes in Pakistan, 2000. The 1998 Population Census, conducted by the Population Census Organization, was complemented with the Census of Private Educational Institutes of Pakistan, which was carried out by the Federal Bureau of Statistics in 2000 to

patterns across districts. The second type of data, based on household surveys, covers different rounds of the Pakistan Integrated Household Survey (PIHS), carried out in 1991, 1998, and 2001.[15] While the data are not as extensive as those of the census, they do contain detailed household information on schooling and income, and the data set has been used extensively by researchers both in Pakistan and the United States. Finally, we use data on schooling choice among households (referred to as the project on Learning and Educational Achievement in Punjab Schools, or LEAPS), which was conducted in August of 2003 by an independent team of academics. LEAPS is a complete census of all households in the selected villages in three districts in the province of Punjab.[16] Consequently, it yields sufficient madrasa enrollment to examine correlations with household attributes in a meaningful manner (this data source provides information on four times as many children as the PIHS). (Table B1 in app. B shows how these different data sources are used in the article.)

Each source asks about madrasa enrollment in a slightly different but comparable way. The 1998 Population Census asks about the field of education ("What is [NAME'S] field of education?") with options that include (among others) general education, engineering, medicine, or religious education. This question is also asked of all literate adults irrespective of their current enrollment status, allowing for comparisons in the stock of religious education over time. The PIHS rounds ask, "What type of school is [NAME] currently attending?" with options that include government school, private school, or *deeni-madrassa* (religious schooling). Finally, the LEAPS census directly asks, "Is the child enrolled in a madrassa or an Islamic education school?"

How Many?

According to the 1998 Population Census, 159,225 students (all ages) were enrolled in madrasas; this represents 0.31 percent of all children between the ages of 5 and 19 (table 1, row 1). Since the total gross enrollment rate (defined as total enrollment divided by the number of "eligible" children—in this case, children between the ages 5–19) is 45 percent, madrasa enrollment as a fraction of total enrollment increases to 0.7 percent. The numbers from the PIHS are very similar—with between 151,000 and 178,000 children enrolled in madrasas across the 1991, 1998, and 2001 rounds, ac-

provide statistics on private vs. public enrollment. See Federal Bureau of Statistics reports (various years). Information on both surveys and the reports is available at http://www.statpak.gov.pk.

[15] The Pakistan Integrated Household Survey (PIHS) is the equivalent of the widely used Living Standard Measurement Surveys that is implemented in various countries. Extensive notes on the 1991 PIHS are available at http://www.worldbank.org/lsms.

[16] This census was conducted in three districts of Punjab; villages were chosen randomly based on the criterion that each village must have at least one private school. Typically, this means that the villages lie somewhere between fully urban and fully rural populations and are not representative of the districts in which they lie.

TABLE 1
COUNTRYWIDE MADRASA ENROLLMENT: DIFFERENT SOURCES

Data Source	Madrasa Enrollment	Madrasa as % of Enrolled
Census of Population, 1998:		
Male	111,085	.82
Female	48,140	.53
Total	159,225	.70
PIHS 1991	151,546	.78
		(.16)
PIHS 1998	178,436	.74
		(.089)
PIHS 2001	176,061	.7
		(.093)

NOTE.—Survey standard errors are in parentheses where applicable. The Population Census covers all of Pakistan except the federally administered tribal area (FATA). Included are Punjab, Balochistan, North-West Frontier Provinces (NWFP), and Sindh, plus the federal capital Islamabad and the federally administered Northern Areas and Azad Jammu and Kashmir (AJK). The 1998 Population Census estimates are based on the census "long form," which was administered on a sample basis to a large number of households. These data are representative at the district level for both rural and urban regions. The next three rows show estimates from the Pakistan Integrated Household Survey (PIHS), which is a household survey; it is representative only at the provincial level for the four main provinces—Punjab, Sindh, Balochistan, and NWFP—which account for 97% of the country's population.

counting for less than 1 percent of all enrollment (around 0.7 percent of all enrollments in the 1991, 1998, and 2001 rounds). Despite the different definitions used and the problem of accurately estimating a low probability event in the PIHS (these surveys typically identify fewer than 100 children enrolled in madrasas), the numbers are well within the standard error bounds, and they are within 0.1 percentage points of each other—that is, there is less than 1/1,000th of a difference between the percentages of enrolled children going to madrasas for the different sources.

These numbers can be benchmarked to enrollment in regular schools. Public schools run by the government enrolled between 16 and 17 million children in 1998; private schools enrolled almost one-third as many, at 6 million in 2000.[17] As a percentage of children between the ages of 5 and 19, government schools accounted for 33 percent, private schools for another 12 percent. Again, since roughly one-half of all children between the ages of 5 and 19 are enrolled in school, as a percentage of enrollments, these numbers approximately double to 73 percent and 26 percent.[18] This com-

[17] Population Census of Pakistan, 1998; Federal Bureau of Statistics, Census of Private Educational Institutes in Pakistan, 2000.

[18] Boys are more likely to be enrolled in madrasas compared to girls. The census reports that there are only 43 females enrolled in madrasas for every 100 males. This imbalance is significantly greater than the 68 enrolled females for every 100 enrolled males in overall education. For both boys and girls, madrasa enrollment starts off at the same age cohort between 5 and 9 years, but girls' enrollment drops off sharply while boys' enrollment jumps for children between 10 and 14 years old and then tapers off for the cohort in their mid-twenties. That there are fewer females in madrasas is not surprising, but the similar number of girls as boys in the youngest age category is somewhat unexpected. Interestingly, for children between ages 5 and 9, the enrollment sex ratio is slightly higher in madrasa than in general education (76.9 vs. 75.6 percent) but drops off at a much faster rate in the madrasa as children become older. The usual disclaimers about the numbers being too small to draw finer comparisons still apply.

parison suggests that there are 38 times as many children in private schools and 104 times as many in government schools as compared to those in madrasas.[19]

Since the data were collected prior to 2001, geopolitical changes after September 11 could have led to increased madrasa enrollment. In addition, the household-based survey faces the usual problems of accurately estimating a low-probability event—although enrollment is less than 1 percent in these surveys, the sampling error is large.[20] Finally, while the 1998 Population Census does not face the problem of small samples, it is not that recent, and some may have reservations regarding the quality of government data.[21]

The LEAPS census of schooling choice, conducted in 2003, provides a rough check on these numbers (see app. C for details). Estimates from the LEAPS census show that, as a percentage of enrolled children, the numbers in two of the three districts are slightly higher than those of the 1998 Population Census. In the third district's data (that for Rahim Yar Khan), there is a large difference, with the census reporting that 1 percent of all school-going children attended madrasas and the LEAPS showing that the fraction is closer to 3.7 percent (table 2). There are three potential explanations for this difference. First, the LEAPS data are not representative of the district and could be off the mark for districts with wide variation in madrasa enrollment across rural and urban samples. Second, the experience of the last 5 years could have varied dramatically across districts—in some, the enrollment fractions did not change, and in others it increased substantially. Third, the data could point to systematic problems with the census estimates from certain districts or to statistical problems that arise when we try to estimate low-probability events.

[19] We could also compare these numbers to enrollment across countries. See Eli Berman and Ara Stepanyan, "How Many Radical Islamists? Indirect Evidence from Five Countries" (unpublished manuscript, University of California, San Diego, February 2004, available at http://www.econ.ucsd.edu/~elib/funfert .pdf). They compare a number of countries, including Pakistan (albeit based only on the Pakistan Integrated Household Survey). The comparison is fraught with difficulties, since they sometimes use stocks and sometimes use flows and the data are sometimes at the household level and at other times at the individual level. Nevertheless, using their numbers, as a percentage of total enrollment, madrasa enrollment in Pakistan is roughly equivalent to that in Bangladesh and Côte d'Ivoire and much less than that in India (two states only) or Indonesia. Interestingly, madrasa enrollment in Pakistan corresponds closely to census estimates of home rather than religious schooling in the United States—the former ranges from 1 to 2 percent, while the latter is closer to 8 percent; see Kurt Bauman, "Home Schooling in the United States: Trends and Characteristics," Working Paper Series no. 53 (Population Division, U.S. Census Bureau, Washington, DC, August 2001), available at http://www.census.gov/population/www/documentation/twps0053.html; National Center for Education Statistics, "Private School Universe Survey, 1999–2000," *National Center for Education Statistics Analysis Report* (Washington, DC: NCES, August 2001), available at http://www.nces .ed.gov/pubsearch/pubsinfo.asp?pubid=2001330.

[20] For a description of similar problems in estimating home schooling in the United States, see Bauman, "Home Schooling in the United States."

[21] In our own analysis, we found the quality of the data generated by the Federal Bureau of Statistics in Pakistan to be consistently high. We used the 2000 Federal Bureau of Statistics Census of Private Schools (PEIP) to guide our fieldwork and feasibility study for LEAPS and found that it tallied with the situation in the field quite well, even in remote villages.

TABLE 2
ENROLLED CHILDREN IN THREE DISTRICTS (%)

School Type	Data Source	Attock	Faisalabad	Rahim Yar Khan
Government	LEAPS	67.73	71.96	71.38
Private	LEAPS	31.56	27.33	24.92
Madrasa	LEAPS	.71	.70	3.70
Madrasa	Census of Population, 1998	.50	.49	1.03

SOURCE.—Learning and Educational Achievement in Punjab Schools (LEAPS) Census; 1998 Population Census.
NOTE.—LEAPS reports school type for enrolled children ages 5–15. The Population Census reports field of education for children ages 5–14. The sample of LEAPS villages was randomly drawn from a list frame of rural villages with at least one private school and thus are not representative of the district as a whole.

Explaining the Differences

If we take for granted that the existing data sources are dated, then reality is better represented by the more recent LEAPS census data. In this case, total enrollment in madrasas, using a population-weighted average across the three districts, would be 1.7 times that in the 1998 government census. Adding in a (generous) 5 percent enrollment growth rate for every year, this puts the total number of children enrolled in madrasas at 410,000. This estimate is still conservative if a significant proportion of those enrolled in madrasas are not linked to any household and therefore are not picked up in household-based surveys. This could happen if a substantial fraction of children in madrasas are orphans.[22] While there are no countrywide estimates, a study by the Institute of Policy Studies in Islamabad found that 15 percent of all children enrolled in a sample of madrasas were orphans. In the worst-case scenario (where all orphans are enrolled only in madrasas), our numbers would have to be inflated by 15 percent to arrive at actual enrollment.[23] Thus, to arrive at a liberal estimate, we can add in a further 15 percent for orphans to take the total up to (approximately) 475,000, which is still below the lowest estimate in the existing literature. What explains this difference?

Police surveys in Punjab and Sindh quoted in the literature estimate that there were 253,125 students enrolled in madrasas in Punjab in 2002 and 264,169 in Sindh in 2003.[24] Our equivalent number from 1998 for the Punjab is 96,125. For Sindh, the number is 10 times greater than that in the census, with Karachi accounting for all the difference. As we try to unearth further the details of the police numbers, there are two observations. First, there is no information available on the methodology of the police surveys. Our interviews with police personnel suggest a lack of documentation, certainly when compared to those of established statistical surveys. We have no way of

[22] The percentage of enrolled children going to a madrasa will only be affected if the share of orphans going to madrasas is higher than the share of orphans going to regular schools.

[23] Institute of Policy Studies (IPS) Task Force, *Pakistan Religious Educational Institutions: An Overview* (Islamabad: IPS, 2002).

[24] Shahzad, "Over 250,000 Students in Punjab Seminaries"; "KARACHI: 11,000 Foreigners in Sindh Madaris."

knowing whether these numbers are from enrollment records in the madrasas or children attending on a given day or whether they are based on a census of establishments or a sample. Second, the police surveys are establishment-based surveys that include all students who attend madrasas (full-time students and children attending part time for Qur'anic literacy classes), whereas the household-based surveys like the census and the PIHS question include only those who attend madrasas full time. Anecdotal evidence suggests that small stints in a madrasa, either for Qur'anic literacy or for a short time after primary school, are fairly common.[25] From virtually any policy perspective, including evening Qur'an classes in enrollment figures seems misguided. Regrettably, until now, almost all enrollment numbers cited have been based on establishment surveys that do just that.

Particularly surprising is the vast discrepancy in madrasa enrollment as a fraction of enrolled students. Prior to this article, the predominant estimate came from the aforementioned International Crisis Group (ICG) report, which estimated that a third of all enrolled Pakistani children attend madrasas. Our estimates, by comparison, are less than 1 percent. Upon investigating the discrepancy, we found that the ICG's estimate was the result of a misreading of the total enrollment numbers in Pakistan, which resulted in their estimate being inflated by a factor of 10. After a draft of this article was shared with the ICG, the organization retracted its estimate. Unfortunately, during the 2 years that it remained uncorrected, the estimate itself was widely propagated in a number of major newspapers. The immediate validation and propagation of this number without any attempt to fact-check is perhaps more troubling than the original error. For example, even if the number enrolled in madrasas were 1.5 million, the highest estimate in reports and articles, this would still imply that 6 percent of all children in the educational system are enrolled in madrasas.

Variation across Districts and Time

Using the published data sources, we can also look at how madrasa enrollment varies across different districts—the difference between Attock and Rahim Yar Khan in the LEAPS data suggests that enrollment variation may be substantial—and we can look at how such enrollment has changed over time. Both of these exercises yield similar conclusions, pointing to the importance of the border region with Afghanistan and the impact of the Afghan-Soviet war years on time trends in madrasa enrollment.

---

[25] Ali presents some indirect evidence that the distinction between part-time and full-time students is important. He finds the number of resident and nonresident students in madrasas to be roughly equal. His study, however, is subject to some of the same criticisms of establishment-based surveys and is limited only to Islamabad and one other *tehsil* (equivalent to a county) out of a total of more than 300 in Pakistan. See Saleem H. Ali, "Islamic Education and Conflict: Understanding the Madrassahs of Pakistan" (paper presented at the U.S. Institute of Peace, Washington, DC, June 24, 2005), available at http://www.uvm.edu/ ˜envprog/madrassah/resources.html.

Variation across Districts

Pakistan is divided administratively into four provinces with 102 districts—Punjab, Balochistan, North-West Frontier Provinces (NWFP), and Sindh—plus the federal capital Islamabad, the Federally Administered Tribal Areas (FATA), the Federally Administered Northern Areas, and Azad Jammu and Kashmir (AJK). The four provinces, together with Islamabad, account for more than 97 percent of the population. Geographically, parts of Balochistan, the NWFP, and the FATA border Afghanistan. Sindh and Balochistan are sparsely populated provinces, with the exception of Karachi in Sindh, which is the single biggest metropolis in the country, with a population approaching 10 million. We use data from the 1998 Population Census as well as the 2000 census of private schooling to estimate the madrasa, private, and government school enrollment in each district (except for those in the province of FATA).

The geographical dispersion of madrasa enrollment depends on how we define madrasa prevalence. There are three alternatives. We could present a geographical breakdown of the total number of children enrolled in madrasas. This number is related to the total population of the district, and it may thus reflect only the size of the district relative to others. Another option is to use the equivalent of the gross enrollment ratio, defined as the total enrollment divided by the number of "eligible" children—in this case, children between the ages of 5 and 19. This statistic provides an estimate of the "penetration" of madrasas, but it does not take into account the overall enrollment decision of the family. Thus, a district with two children enrolled in madrasas and 20 children enrolled in private or public schools, out of a total of 100 children, will have exactly the same gross enrollment ratio as a district with two children enrolled in madrasas and 98 children enrolled in regular schools. To the extent that we want to distinguish between these two districts, a third statistic, the ratio of children enrolled in madrasas to total enrollment (the madrasa fraction of enrollment) can also be used. The picture changes dramatically depending on whether we use the raw numbers or the ratio of children enrolled in madrasas to total enrollment. However, since enrollment in madrasas is highly correlated with total enrollment, there is little difference in the pattern of madrasa enrollment whether we use the gross enrollment ratio or the fraction of enrolled children in madrasas.

The number of children enrolled in madrasas for every district in the country is closely linked to population size—the three most populated districts account for one-quarter of the enrollment, with the bulk of enrollment in large urban metropolises. Madrasa enrollment is also higher in the *Saraiki-*language belt districts of southern Punjab (e.g., Rahim Yar Khan) compared to the rest of the country. Note, however, that the fact that the number of children enrolled in madrasas is higher in more populated districts indicates nothing more than the size of the district. When one normalizes this number by dividing it by the total enrollment figure, we can see more clearly the very high madrasa fraction along (and only along) the western border with Afghanistan. This is the Pashtun belt—the *Pashto*-speaking population most directly influenced by events in Afghanistan. (See figs. D1 and D2 in app. D.)

Pishin (the district bordering the Kandahar region of Afghanistan) is the only *Pashto*-speaking district in the top 15 when we use the total number of children enrolled in madrasas, but when we deflate this number by total enrollment (or the number of eligible children), all of the top-10 districts are in the *Pashto*-speaking belt. If we use 2 percent of total enrollment as a cutoff for "extreme" madrasa enrollment, all 14 districts that can be classified as such are either in Balochistan or the North-West Frontier Province. Leaving aside the Pashtun belt and Karachi, madrasa enrollment in the rest of the country is spread very thinly across all districts. That is, rather than districts with high enrollment and districts with low enrollment, a very small number of children in every district are enrolled in madrasas. Seventeen districts fall in the 1–2 percent range, with the remainder reporting showing a madrasa fraction of enrollment between 0.02 and 1 percent of total enrollment.

Thus, there are two distinct geographical patterns of madrasa enrollment in the country. Enrollment is systematically higher among districts that border Afghanistan (still with just over 4 percent of enrolled children in madrasas in all of them except Pishin). Apart from these districts, enrollment is thinly spread among all districts in the country. Perhaps this pattern also reflects variation in the types of madrasas in these different areas—clearly, differences (if any) between madrasas in the Pashtun belt and the rest of the country is a potential area for research.

Variation across Time

The PIHS data show that the growth in madrasa enrollment during the 1990s was the same as that in enrollment in all schools (approximately 16 percent). In fact, madrasa enrollment as a fraction of total enrollment decreased marginally, although the differences are well within the margin of error.

Over a longer time horizon, we also compare the stock of individuals who stated a religious "field of education" on the census long form.[26] The stock of individuals reporting religious education as their "field" displays a distinct U-shaped pattern (fig. 1). People born between 1944 and 1948 were more likely to have religious education than those born between 1949 and 1953. This pattern continues until the cohort born between 1959 and 1963, then stabilizes for the next two cohorts and finally starts increasing. Those born between 1974 and 1978 were more likely to report religious education

---

[26] This cohort-based analysis assumes that changes in madrasa enrollment will be picked up 10–14 years after the birth of the relevant cohort. That is, a sudden increase in 1980 would correspond to an increase in the stock of individuals reporting religious education for the cohort born between 1966 and 1970.

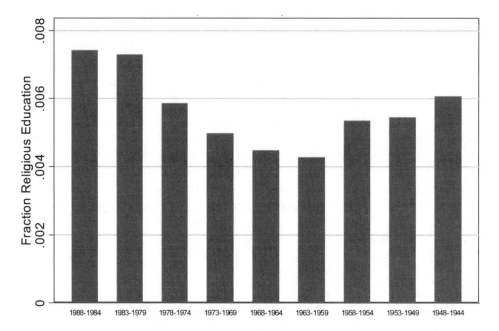

Fig. 1.—Literacy source by year of birth. Source: 1998 Population Census. Field of education is taken from the long form of the 1998 Population Census and is asked conditional on the interviewee being literate. Every bar shows the proportion of literate individuals in each birth cohort who reported that they received a "religious education." The first birth cohort is individuals born between 1984 and 1988, who were therefore between the ages of 10 and 14 at the time of the survey. The last bar is for individuals born between 1944 and 1948, who were between 56 and 60 at the time of the survey. The numbers only reflect people alive at the time of the 1998 census.

as their field than those before. This increase continues until the last cohort we have completed educational history data for, those born between 1979 and 1983.

Interestingly, the downward trend halts for the age cohort that comes of school-going age in the years surrounding the rise of the Zia-ul-Haq military government and the ensuing religion-based resistance to the Soviet invasion of Afghanistan starting in 1979. Further, the largest jump is in the cohort born in 1979–83. This cohort would be 10 years of age in the period 1989–93—coinciding with the withdrawal of the Soviet Union and the rise of the Taliban.

Variation across Households

This section looks at the variation in madrasa enrollment at the level of the household. This study was not designed to, and cannot, present definitive statements regarding the choice of madrasas among households as a schooling choice. Therefore, we do not attempt to go beyond simple tabulations and associations. Nevertheless, the exercise adds some value to our understanding of madrasa enrollment.[27]

[27] Differences in madrasa enrollment could be driven by differences across villages rather than by

Previous studies on this important question, such as that by Eli Berman and Ara Stepanyan, have been hampered by small sample sizes (there are 100 children who attend madrasas in the PIHS data) and lack of household-level data (the census only provides district-level aggregates).[28] In contrast, the LEAPS census has schooling choice data on 150,000 children at the household level; even with 1 percent enrollment, this gives us 1,500 children enrolled in madrasas, a number that is sufficiently large to draw meaningful conclusions.

We first ask a simple question: If we look at households that have a child enrolled in a madrasa, what type(s) of schools do other children in the household attend? We look at households that had at least two enrolled children and classify them as (*a*) "all madrasa," if all the children attend a madrasa; (*b*) "madrasa/public," if at least one child goes to the madrasa and one to a public school; (*c*) "madrasa/private," if one attends the madrasa and the other attends private school; and (*d*) "madrasa/public/private," if the households had three or more enrolled children using all three options simultaneously. Finally, we repeated this exercise in households with at least one child going to public school and with one child going to private school.

The results are startling (fig. 2). Among households with at least one child enrolled in a madrasa (call them "madrasa households"), only 23.5 percent can be classified as "all madrasa" households. The majority of "madrasa households" (just under 50 percent) use both madrasas and public schools, and another 28 percent use either madrasas and private schools or all three simultaneously. Among households with at least one child enrolled in private school, 48.5 percent enroll all their children in private schools and another 49.6 percent use the private/public option simultaneously. If the choice of a madrasa or a private school provides information about the ideology of the household, the data suggest that the choice of a private school is more ideologically driven than the choice of a madrasa. That is, almost half of households choosing private schools for at least one of their children select private schools for all of their school-age children, while less than one-quarter of households sending a child to a madrasa send all of their children to madrasas.

The fact that most variation in madrasa enrollment is within rather than between households implies that any predictions about who will send their child to a madrasa based on household attributes will be fairly poor. The comparison done by Berman and Stepanyan looked at differences between

---

differences across households, i.e., in some villages all of the children go to madrasas, while in others none of the children attend. Most of the variation in madrasa enrollment (in the set of enrolled children) is within rather than between villages. For example, the difference in enrollment ratios in a village at the ninetieth percentile of madrasa enrollment and one at the tenth percentile is only 3.4 percent. This also holds at the more disaggregated settlement level (some villages have more than one settlement), although less strongly, with more variation stemming from within than between settlements.

[28] Berman and Stepanyan, "How Many Radical Islamists?"

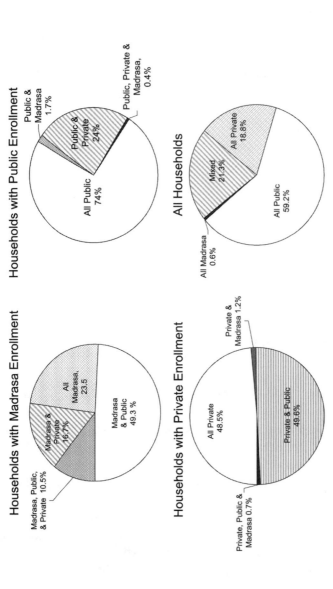

FIG. 2.—Household enrollment choices. Source: LEAPS Population Census, 2003. This pie graph shows enrollment choices among households with at least two enrolled children that have one or more children attending a madrasa (top left), a government school (top right), a private school (bottom left), and any school (bottom right). By construction, households with private, government, and madrasa enrollment (madrasa/public/private) must have at least three enrolled children. Thus, among households with at least one child in a madrasa, close to 50 percent have another child who is enrolled in a government school. The last pie graph (All Households) shows how prevalent every type of household is; e.g., only 0.6 percent of all households have all children enrolled in madrasas.

TABLE 3
CHARACTERISTICS OF MADRASA AND NON-MADRASA HOUSEHOLDS

Household Type	Household Head Illiterate	Monthly Expenditure under Rs7,500	No Land	Settlement Has Private School
Non-madrasa household	.4469	.9598	.6171	.7196
	(.0024)	(.0009)	(.0023)	(.0021)
Madrasa household	.5159	.9645	.6047	.4852
	(.0153)	(.0056)	(.0149)	(.0152)

SOURCE.—Learning and Educational Achievement in Punjab Schools (LEAPS) Census.
NOTE.—Standard errors are reported in parentheses. Households are classified as "madrasa households" if one or more children are currently enrolled in a madrasa. "Non-madrasa households" households have at least one child enrolled in a government or private school. Monthly expenditure under Rs7,500 accounts for 97% of households. There is no difference in means between household types when a more even expenditure categorization is used.

"madrasa households" and "non-madrasa" households.[29] A similar comparison in the LEAPS data (table 3) shows an association between lower-income households and madrasa enrollment and households with less educated heads and madrasa enrollment, but the magnitude of these associations is small. The heads of "madrasa households" are illiterate in 7 percent more cases and slightly poorer (0.5 percent more likely to earn less than Rs7,500 per month).[30] The largest difference between household types is their proximity to a private school—among households with a child in a madrasa, 49 percent live in settlements with a private school; this number is 72 percent for households with no children in madrasas.

Variations Related to Public and/or Private School Availability

Although the last finding could be seen as supporting the theory that madrasas have emerged as the only viable alternative to poor government schooling, a closer look shows that the prevalence of private schools substantially complicates matters. We look at the fraction of children enrolled and the market shares of schools offering public, private, and madrasa education under three different scenarios. One scenario is when both private and public schools are present in the settlement, the second is when either a private or a public school exists (nonexclusively), and the third is when neither is available in the settlement in which the household is located.[31] Three interesting findings emerge (see fig. 3): (1) In settlements with both

[29] Ibid.

[30] The significant difference between madrasa and non-madrasa households in terms of income arises only when we use Rs7,500 as the monthly income cutoff to distinguish poor and nonpoor households; alternative cutoffs of Rs2,500 or Rs5,000 show no significant differences between poor and nonpoor households. Importantly, 97 percent of all households earn below Rs7,500.

[31] Recall that the LEAPS sample was taken from a list of villages that had at least one private school. To look at schooling choices under these three scenarios, we divided villages into settlements and plotted enrollment shares in each type of settlement. These settlements are often far from each other and thus act more as self-contained units than the administrative definition of a village. In the LEAPS data, there are 112 villages but 253 settlements, generating considerable variation for this exercise. These findings are robust in a multivariate regression context.

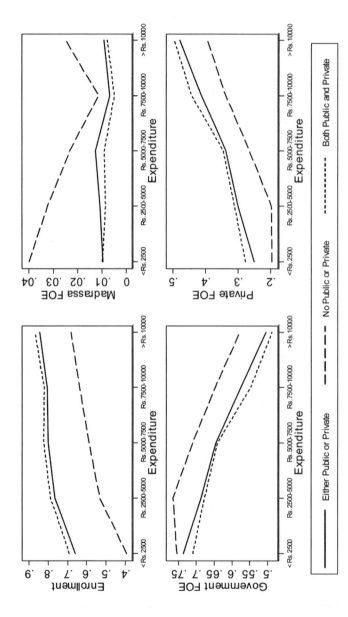

Fig. 3.—Enrollment by presence of school and expenditure. Source: LEAPS Population Census, 2003. This figure shows the fraction of children enrolled (top left) and the share of each sector in that enrollment. The top-right figure shows the share of madrasas, the bottom-left figure shows the share of government, and the bottom-right figures shows the share of the private sector. In each figure, we show the appropriate fraction for three types of settlements—those with both a private and a public school, those with either a private or public school (including settlements with both), and those with neither a private nor a public school. These settlements were constructed using a mapping exercise in every village, and for the 125 villages in our sample, we have 253 settlements. We plot the shares against the self-reported monthly expenditures of the household. More than 95 percent of all households fall below the Rs.7,500–Rs.10,000 cutoff.

private and public schools, the share of private schools increases with income. Nevertheless, even among the poor, more than 30 percent of all families send their children to private schools. Madrasas account for less than 1 percent of all enrollments, and this share is no higher among the poor compared to the rich. (2) In settlements with either a private or a public school, the same patterns are observed with regard to income and, again, madrasa shares are no different among the rich and the poor. (3) In settlements with no public or private schools, the enrollment patterns are very different. The largest differences arise in the choice of enrollment, rather than schooling choice conditional on enrollment. In settlements without a public or a private school, families are more likely to exit from the educational system altogether rather than enroll their child in a madrasa. The drop in enrollment is dramatic, falling from 70 percent to 40 percent among the poor and from 87 percent to 68 percent among the rich. The market share of the different types of schools also changes. Government schools and madrasas increase their share, while the private schools share drops. However, the increase in the market share of government schools is insufficient to overcome the drop in enrollment, so that total number of children in government schools still declines; the opposite is true for madrasas. These settlements are also the only ones where there is a clear relationship between income and madrasa enrollment—among the poorest, 4 percent of all enrolled children are in madrasas, and among the rich this decreases to 2.5 percent.

These numbers suggest that the schooling decision for an average Pakistani household in a rural region consists of an enrollment decision (Should I send my child to school?) followed by a private/public decision, with a madrasa as a possibility. When there are no nearby schools, households exit from the educational system altogether, although there is evidence of an increase in the market share of madrasas among the poor in these settlements. When both private and public schools are available, richer households exit to the private system, but there is no difference in madrasa shares with household income. It is possible that when richer households use the private sector, resources are freed up for use in public schools, leading to an overall increase in enrollment.[32]

The key issue then becomes the placement of public and private schools. Tahir Andrabi, Jishnu Das, and Asim I. Khwaja show that private schools overwhelmingly locate in villages where there are preexisting public schools.[33]

---

[32] For robustness, we also conducted a multivariate analysis of madrasa enrollment using household head education, household wealth, household land holding, availability of outside schooling options in the settlement, child gender, and child age. The above findings remain unchanged. The range of schooling options in the settlement matter, and it is only when no outside schools are present that madrasa enrollment shows sensitivity to income. These regression analysis results are not reported here as they do not add anything to what is provided in fig. 3.

[33] Tahir Andrabi, Jishnu Das, and Asim I. Khwaja, "Students Today, Teachers Tomorrow? The Rise of Affordable Private Schools" (unpublished manuscript, World Bank, Washington, DC, November 2005), available from the authors.

This may not be an insurmountable barrier as 2,500 new private schools were set up between 1994 and 1995. Just 3 years later in 1998, 6,000 new schools were set up, and in 1999 this increased to 8,000. Half of the growth in private schools occurred in rural villages. If current trends continue, and our data collected in 2004 suggests that it will, the number of villages in Punjab province (which has half of the country's population) with a private school will approach 50 percent by the end of the decade.

These schools are not particularly expensive to attend. The median annual tuition fee in rural Punjab is Rs650 (just under $1 per month). Using household expenditure data from the PIHS, this represents 1.7 percent of average household expenditure, so that a family with four children would spend less than 7 percent of total expenditure if all four children attended private schools.[34] By comparison, the ratio of private school fees to household income in high-income countries is high—for instance, the average annual fees in a private school in the United States of $2,200 corresponds to 9 percent of median per capita income.[35] The analog in Punjab is closer to 2.5 percent, suggesting a fourfold difference in the tuition to income ratio across the two economies.

Conclusion and Caveats

Analysis of published data sources and the LEAPS survey show that existing estimates in the literature of madrasa enrollment are highly exaggerated. Our most liberal estimate, which doubles the census/PIHS numbers and adds in a further 15 percent for orphans, is still below the lowest estimate in newspaper articles and policy reports. This imbalance is accentuated when we look at the fraction of children enrolled in madrasas, either as a percentage of school-aged children or enrolled children. This fraction has been overstated by a factor of 10 in the *Los Angeles Times* (April 14, 2003) and by a factor of 33 in the report by the International Crisis Group.[36] Moreover, there is currently no evidence of a dramatic explosion of enrollment in madrasas in the 1990s. Beliefs about the prevalence of madrasa enrollment in Pakistan are an example of conventional wisdom, in the classic Galbraithian sense—these numbers have been accepted simply because they have been found acceptable.[37]

As noted above, one hypothesis for the presumed dramatic rise of madrasa enrollment relates to the effects of the Afghan-Soviet war. In this regard, madrasas declined in popularity for cohorts born between 1947 and

[34] Tahir Andrabi, Jishnu Das, and Asim I. Khwaja, "Private Schools: Limitations and Possibilities?" (unpublished manuscript, World Bank, Washington, DC, October 2005), available from the authors.

[35] National Center for Education Statistics, *Private School Universe Survey, 1999–2000: National Center for Education Statistics Analysis Report* (Washington, DC: National Center for Education Statistics, 2001), available online at http://www.nces.ed.gov/pubsearch/pubsinfo.asp?pubid=2001330.

[36] Kraul, "Dollars to Help Pupils in Pakistan"; International Crisis Group, "Pakistan: Madrassahs, Extremism and the Military."

[37] John Kenneth Galbraith, *The Affluent State* (New York: Houghton Mifflin, 1958).

1974 and increased thereafter. The biggest jump is for the cohort born between 1979 and 1983; this corresponds to those children who would have started attending school around the rise of the religion-based resistance to the Soviet invasion of Afghanistan. The notion that the madrasa movement coincided with resistance to the Soviet invasion of Afghanistan is supported by the data from the 1998 Population Census. The increase in the stock of religiously educated individuals starts with the cohort that came of age in 1979 (the year of the Soviet invasion of Afghanistan), and the largest increase is for the cohort coterminus with the rise of the Taliban. Combined with the fact that the largest enrollment percentage in Pakistan is in the Pashtun belt bordering Afghanistan, this suggests that events in neighboring Afghanistan influence madrasa enrollment.

Moreover, there is a wide geographical dispersion in the prevalence of madrasa education in Pakistan, with madrasas being most popular in the Pashtun belt and with the top-10 districts in terms of the fraction of enrolled children in madrasas all bordering Afghanistan (where they still account for less than 2 percent of all school-aged children). Time trends also support a strong Afghan-Soviet war influence. Nevertheless, it appears that this "Afghan" influence is related more to geographical proximity than to preferences for religious schooling among Afghan immigrants or something intrinsic about Pashtun sensibility. The differentiation of the Pashtun and non-Pashtun districts does not extend to Pashtun and non-Pashtun households in the LEAPS data. We find no evidence that Pashtun households are more likely to send their children to madrasas compared to the rest of the sample, suggesting that geopolitical factors and geographical proximity to Afghanistan matter more than cultural preferences.[38]

At the level of the household, most variation in madrasa enrollment is within rather than between families. Among households with at least one child enrolled in a madrasa, 75 percent send their other children to a public school or a private school or both. Historians of religious education choices will find this reassuring—during the eighteenth and nineteenth centuries, most European countries followed a similar pattern, with one child sent to the church and the others sent for a secular education (or provided with no schooling at all).

Furthermore, there is no evidence for religiosity- or household-preference-based models of madrasa enrollment. The radical religiosity argument suggests that children are more likely to be sent to madrasas when the family favors a radical brand of Islam. If true, what are we to make of the fact that more than 75 percent of all households with a child in a madrasa also send

[38] The data from the LEAPS census asked about ethnic and caste identity, and households that classified themselves as "Pathan" or "Afghani" were used to represent Pashtun households. In line with the usual residential patterns of individuals with Pashtun backgrounds, most of these households are in the district Attock, located in the north of Punjab.

a child to a public or private school? In a multivariate context, we checked whether households identified as "radically Islamic" were more likely to send their child to a madrasa.[39] Again, we found no difference between these households and others—the probability of choosing a madrasa increased by 0.40 percent, but the increase was statistically insignificant and small.

Are poorer families more likely to send at least one child to a madrasa? Many interviews reported in the press suggest that madrasas provide free food, clothing, and stipends to the poor, implying a significantly higher madrasa enrollment among poorer segments of the population. At an aggregate level, there is little difference between poor and rich households in the choice of religious schooling. However, this masks an important difference between two different types of settlements. In settlements where other schooling options exist, less than 1 percent of all enrolled children go to madrasas and this fraction is the same for all income groups, while in settlements where there are no other schooling options, the fraction of children going to madrasas increases and is higher among the poor compared to the rich (although it stays below 4 percent for all income groups).[40] Nevertheless, the biggest difference between these two types of settlements is not the increase in the use of madrasas but the dramatic decline in overall enrollment. Thus, although the share of madrasas increases, this is offset by a sharp reduction in the size of the overall enrollment pie.

It is likely that the number of settlements without public or private schooling options will be reduced considerably during the next decade, primarily due to an ongoing dramatic explosion in the growth of private schools. In 1983 there were approximately 3,300 private primary and secondary schools in the four biggest provinces.[41] In 2000 the same four provinces had 32,000 private schools, an almost 10-fold increase in less than 2 decades.[42] The growth in low-cost rural private schools is particularly dramatic, a point that has been

[39] In a largely Islamic country, it is difficult to find good measures of religiosity. No data on religiosity were collected as part of the census, and a more recent and detailed household survey that includes information on time use elicits little variation—everyone reports high mosque attendance and regular prayers. An alternative, suggested by David Evans at Harvard University, which we pursue here, is to use recent developments in the use of "names." Research by Fryer and Leavitt demonstrates the increasing use of names to define race identity in the United States. We postulate that households that named (at least) one child "Osama" (also spelled Usamah, Usamma, or Usama) are more likely to favor a radical brand of Islam. The use of the name Osama was minimal until 1998 and then peaks in 1998 and 2001, following disruptive events. Of course, the naming of the child may reflect name recognition rather than ideology, and this must be kept in mind. To the extent that naming a child "Osama" is a good indicator of radical religiosity, we find no evidence of this effect in the data. See Ronald G. Fryer Jr. and Steven Levitt, "The Causes and Consequences of Distinctively Black Names," *Quarterly Journal of Economics* 119, no. 3 (2004): 767–805.

[40] Once again, this finding still holds in a multivariate analysis (not reported) of madrasa enrollment using household head education, wealth, land holding, availability of outside schooling options in the settlement, child gender, and child age.

[41] Emmanuel Jimenez and Jee-Pang Tan, "Decentralized and Private Education: the Case of Pakistan," *Comparative Education* 23, no. 2 (1987): 173–90.

[42] Das et al., "Private Schools."

left out of the current debate on education in Pakistan. For the average child (even a relatively poor one), the most popular alternative to government schooling is a private school, not a madrasa.

This article does not address a number of important questions. Both case studies and personal visits suggest that madrasas vary in their character and in the education that they impart; they range from being neighborhood evening religious education schools to facilities that incorporate a more extreme radical militant view. None of the data sources distinguish the different types of madrasas. All types of madrasas are included in our enrollment estimates. Furthermore, we are unable to provide an in-depth view of madrasa goers. Stern and various press reports provide a case-based approach with detailed studies of select madrasas.[43] These case studies describe the mindset of madrasa students, teachers, and religious leaders and provide psychological portraits of such individuals.

The results presented here will speak differently to people with different concerns. One concern is to obtain a better understanding of how madrasas are incorporated into the educational decisions of households. This article discusses madrasa enrollment in a framework that is well known to empirical economists, one that deals with issues of poverty and school quality in developing countries. Phrased in terms of household choice (should I send my child to public school, private school, or a madrasa?), the inclusion of madrasas as a schooling alternative has a negligible effect on household decisions. Consequently, for those interested in individual decision making, our results suggest that madrasas do not form an important part of the decision making of the average (or even the ninety-eighth percentile) of Pakistani households.

A second concern relates to global security issues and, under this view, absolute numbers matter. While we do not have data on whether madrasas promote extremist views and do recognize that this is likely to differ across different types of madrasas, we can conclude that current estimates of madrasa enrollment—both absolutely and in percentage terms—are significantly overstated. Moreover, existing theories fail to adequately explain madrasa enrollment and largely ignore intrahousehold considerations that appear to be important.

If, despite the small numbers, a proactive policy toward madrasas is necessary, more sophisticated theories, as well as additional up-to-date and publicly available and verifiable data, are needed. Achieving this, however, is not an easy task. Given the spatial and temporal patterns of overall madrasa enrollment we found, as well as the very small percentage of children enrolled in madrasas, the only reliable way to capture such enrollment and the correlates of madrasa use is with very large scale surveys, perhaps even censuses,

[43] Stern, "Pakistan's Jihad Culture"; Pamela Constable, "Growing Islamic Activism Challenges Pakistan; Religious Groups Offer Social Services That Help Spread Beliefs," *Washington Post*, September 20, 2001.

in a representative sample of villages throughout the country. This is a costly affair. Whether the money would be better spent for increasing school quality in Pakistan requires careful thought.

Appendix A

TABLE A1
ARTICLES ON MADRASAS IN PAKISTAN IN MAJOR NEWSPAPERS, DECEMBER 2000–JUNE 2004

Source	Date	Type of Study	Numbers	Reasons for Madrasa Enrollment
Los Angeles Times	December 28, 2000	Case study	8,000 madrasas	Afghan war against the Soviet Union
Financial Times	March 6, 2001	Interview with President Musharraf	10,000 madrasas, 1 million students	Welfare service to the poor
Los Angeles Times	August 12, 2001	General article	None	Welfare service to the poor
Los Angeles Times	September 19, 2001	Case study	18,000 in Peshawar	Religious indoctrination
Washington Post	September 20, 2001	Case study	None	Religious indoctrination
Boston Globe	October 4, 2001	Case study	11,000 madrasas, 1 million students	Afghan war against the Soviet Union; fills gap in public education
Financial Times	October 17, 2001	Discussion of meeting between Colin Powell and President Musharraf	10,000 madrasas	Religious indoctrination
Philadelphia Inquirer	November 9, 2001	General article	7,000–8,000 madrasas, 700,000 students	None
Financial Times	November 17, 2001	General article and interviews	4,000 Deobandi madrasas	Religious indoctrination
Philadelphia Inquirer	November 25, 2001	General article and interviews	8,000 registered madrasas, 25,000 unregistered madrasas	Afghan war against the Soviet Union; Pashtun tribal belt issues; religious indoctrination
Boston Globe	November 29, 2001	General article	None	Fills gap in public education; religious indoctrination
Los Angeles Times	December 10, 2001	General article and interviews	10,000 madrasas that dominate education throughout rural Pakistan	Religious indoctrination
Philadelphia Inquirer	December 16, 2001	Interviews in Pishin district	None	Religious indoctrination
Chicago Tribune	December 23, 2001	General article and interviews	None	Fills gap in public education
Chicago Tribune	December 23, 2001	General article and interviews	None	Welfare service to the poor; fills gap in public education
Boston Globe	December 25, 2001	General article and interviews	"Tens of thousands" of madrasas, 1 million children	Welfare service to the poor
Los Angeles Times	January 3, 2002	General article and interviews	5,000 madrasas	Religious indoctrination; Afghan war against the Soviet Union
Los Angeles Times	January 4, 2002	General article and interviews	None	None
Philadelphia Inquirer	January 5, 2002	News item on government	6,000 madrasas	None
Chicago Tribune	January 13, 2002	News item on government	None	None
Boston Globe	January 14, 2002	News item and interview	None	Religious indoctrination
Chicago Tribune	January 18, 2002	Case study	None	Religious indoctrination
Los Angeles Times	January 19, 2002	News item	None	Afghan war against the Soviet Union; religious indoctrination

TABLE A1 (Continued)

Source	Date	Type of Study	Numbers	Reasons for Madrasa Enrollment
Philadelphia Inquirer	January 23, 2002	News item	"Thousands" of madrasas	Afghan war against the Soviet Union; religious indoctrination
Chicago Tribune	January 24, 2002	Case study	None	Religious indoctrination
Washington Post	March 14, 2002	General article	500,000 plus children	Fills gap in public education; religious indoctrination; welfare service to the poor
Boston Globe	March 18, 2002	General article	Thousands of madrasas	None
Los Angeles Times	March 23, 2002	Case study	3,700 (NWFP only)	Fills gap in public education; religious indoctrination
Washington Post	April 28, 2002	General article and case study	7,000 madrasas	Afghan war against Soviet Union
Los Angeles Times	June 29, 2002	General article	1.5 million students	Afghan war against the Soviet Union; fills gap in public education; welfare service to the poor
Chicago Tribune	June 30, 2002	General article	8,000–10,000 madrasas	Afghan war against the Soviet Union; fills gap in public education; welfare service to the poor
Washington Post	July 14, 2002	General article and interviews	10,000 madrasas, 1.5 million students	Afghan war against the Soviet Union; Kashmir dispute; fills gap in public education; welfare service to the poor
The Times (London)	August 10, 2002	Report	1.5 million students from poor rural families	Religious indoctrination
Los Angeles Times	October 12, 2002	Report	8,000–10,000 madrasas with 1.5 million students	None
Los Angeles Times	February 2, 2003	Interview with Foreign Minister Mian Khursheed Mehmood Kasuri		Welfare service to the poor; fills gap in public education
Financial Times	February 8, 2003	General article and interviews	40,000–50,000 madrasas	None
Los Angeles Times	April 14, 2003	Report	10,000 madrasas; educate 10% of all Pakistani students	Fills gap in public education; welfare service to the poor
Financial Times	August 19, 2003	Expert comment	None	Afghan war against the Soviet Union; Pashtun tribal belt issues
Washington Post	September 2, 2003	Report	None	Pashtun tribal belt issues
Los Angeles Times	March 5, 2004	Report on politics regarding Musharraf	None	None
Washington Post	June 13, 2004	General article and interviews	10,000 madrasas	Religious indoctrination; Welfare service to the poor
Philadelphia Inquirer	June 15, 2004	General article and interviews	8,000 madrasas	Afghan war against the Soviet Union

Appendix B
Data Sources and Notes

The first data source is the 1998 Population Census, where the question asked of the respondent on the long form is the type of schooling attended. One of the coded response options is "*deeni taleem,*" exactly translated as "religious education." The long form is administered only to a sample of households in the census, so the response is an estimate of the population number. However, the numbers are representative at the district rural/urban level. These census numbers are used for delimiting electoral constituencies and also as a sampling frame for most government and international surveys. We have used the census document for designing village-level sampling and have found it to be generally consistent with our own fieldwork. We also exploit other district-level data in the census document, such as the extent of public utilities like electrification and piped water as well as the quality of the housing stock (as a proxy for wealth) to correlate with religious enrollment.

The second data source is the Pakistan Integrated Household Survey series, where we use data from 1991, 1998, and 2000. This data set is widely used internationally to examine poverty and related matters. (The data on religious schooling have been used by Berman and Stepanyan in their 2004 study as well.) In the surveys for all three years, the question asks about "type of school" and "Islamic/religious" is a coded response option.

The third source is a specially conducted household educational census conducted by our research team in 125 villages in three districts of Punjab in 2003. This is an extremely rich data source that allows us to extensively look at school choice in rural Punjab at the household level as well as within the household. Here again, we classify a school as a madrasa if it provides religious education and does not teach the state prescribed curriculum, and we classify a child as "enrolled in a madrasa" if he or she is attending a madrasa full time. The sampling for these data was based on an ongoing study of educational choices in Pakistan. We picked villages randomly from the three districts conditional on their having a private school. Typically, this meant that the villages in our sample are (*a*) bigger and (*b*) richer than the average village in the district.

The fourth data source is the census of private educational institutions conducted by the Federal Bureau of Statistics in March 2000. This is a complete enumeration of all the mainstream private schools in the country. It does not include any madrasas. We use this data set to provide information on mainstream private schools. Summary information on each of these data sets is provided in table B1.

TABLE B1
DATA SOURCE DOCUMENTATION

Data Set	Year	Advantages	Disadvantages	Used for
Pakistan Integrated Household Survey (PIHS)	1991, 1998, 2001	Representative for four provinces that account for 97% of the population.	Very low numbers for children enrolled in madrasas. The low numbers make it hard to study associations at the level of the household.	Representative numbers for madrasa enrollment in the four provinces over time.
Federal Bureau of Statistics Census of Private Schools (PEIP)	2000	Data set on private schools, collected at the school level by the Federal Bureau of Statistics. Provides wealth of information on private schools, their location, and their enrollment.	No household level information and no information on madrasas. Age of enrolled children not available.	Size of private school enrollment. Often combined with 1998 Population Census in our analysis.
Population Census, long form	1998	Countrywide coverage at the level of the district and region (rural/urban) excluding FATA.	Information is aggregated at the level of the district.	Numbers on countrywide enrollment and geographical dispersion of madrasa enrollment in the country. Associations at the level of the district.
Learning and Educational Achievement in Punjab Schools (LEAPS) Census	2003	Very recent data collected by the authors. Large number of children surveyed allows for flexibility in studying association between household attributes and schooling choice.	Very limited coverage—only three districts in Punjab. Limited household level information. Villages not representative of districts or country.	Presenting some recent numbers on madrasa enrollment. Associations at the level of the household.

Appendix C
Madrasa Estimates from LEAPS Data under Different Assumptions

Table C1 shows what happens under alternate assumptions regarding the definition of madrasa. The table presents three different estimates, the lowest of which we call the "conservative" estimate and the highest of which we call the "liberal" estimate. Typically, allowing for more liberal estimates doubles the percentage of children enrolled in madrasas. For this article, we use the moderate estimate as the relevant number.

However, this doubling highlights an important problem. Since madrasa enrollment is very small as a percentage of the total, estimating the number precisely requires very large samples and a precise definition of what we mean. Despite interviews covering over 150,000 children, we captured only 1,500 children enrolled in madrasas. Small changes in the definition cause small absolute changes in the percentages but could dramatically change the overall number. Likewise, for extremely low probability answers, errors in data entry even at a 1 percent rate can substantially affect the result.

TABLE C1
LEAPS MADRASA ENROLLMENT ESTIMATES

Estimate Definition	Madrasa as Fraction of Enrolled
Attock:	
Conservative	.0033
Moderate	.0070
Liberal	.0108
Faisalabad:	
Conservative	.0033
Moderate	.0069
Liberal	.0116
Rahim Yar Khan:	
Conservative	.0213
Moderate	.0367
Liberal	.0583
Total:	
Conservative	.0081
Moderate	.0148
Liberal	.0236

SOURCE.—LEAPS, 2003.

NOTE.—Madrasa enrollment can be determined from several variables in the LEAPS data set. Given data-entry and field errors, different estimates of madrasa enrollment can be obtained. Throughout this article, we use the moderate estimate. The conservative and liberal estimates should be viewed only as extreme lower and upper bounds.

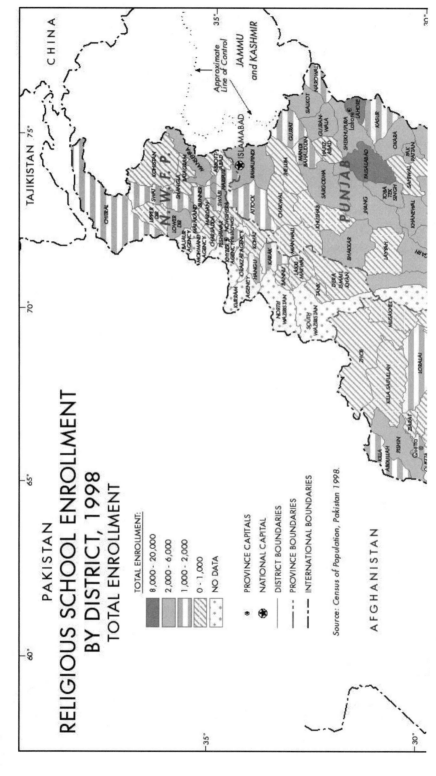

PAKISTAN
RELIGIOUS SCHOOL ENROLLMENT
BY DISTRICT, 1998
TOTAL ENROLLMENT

TOTAL ENROLLMENT:

8,000 - 20,000
2,000 - 6,000
1,000 - 2,000
0 - 1,000
NO DATA

PROVINCE CAPITALS
NATIONAL CAPITAL
DISTRICT BOUNDARIES
PROVINCE BOUNDARIES
INTERNATIONAL BOUNDARIES

Source: Census of Population, Pakistan 1998.

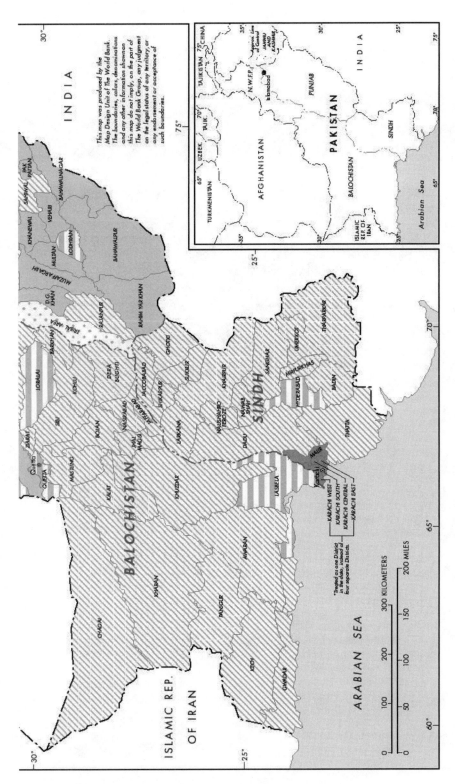

FIG. D1.—Number of children enrolled in religious schools, Pakistan, 1998. Source: The data for the districts are based on the long form of the 1998 Population Census. The long form is administered to a sample of households in the census and is representative at the district/rural-urban level. We classify a child as enrolled in religious school if he or she reports her "main field of education" as "religious education."

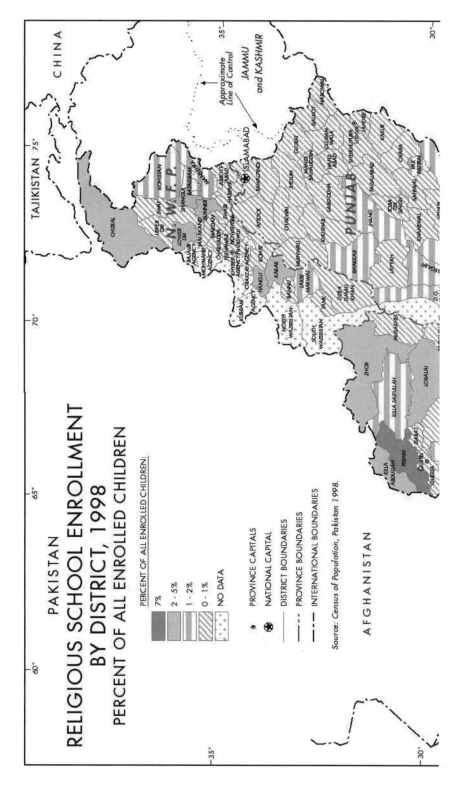

PAKISTAN
RELIGIOUS SCHOOL ENROLLMENT
BY DISTRICT, 1998
PERCENT OF ALL ENROLLED CHILDREN

PERCENT OF ALL ENROLLED CHILDREN:

7%

2 - 5%

1 - 2%

0 - 1%

NO DATA

⊛ PROVINCE CAPITALS

⊛ NATIONAL CAPITAL

———— DISTRICT BOUNDARIES

—··— PROVINCE BOUNDARIES

—···— INTERNATIONAL BOUNDARIES

Source: Census of Population, Pakistan 1998.

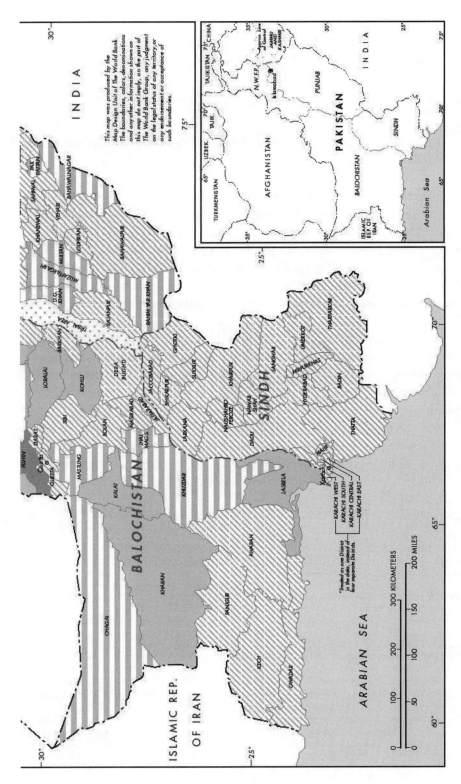

Fig. D2.—Percentage of children enrolled in religious schools, Pakistan, 1998. Source: 1998 Population Census. The percent of all enrolled children in religious schools is defined as the total number of children enrolled in religious schools divided by the total number of children enrolled in any school.

Memorization and Learning in Islamic Schools

HELEN N. BOYLE

Introduction

In the late 1990s, literature on Islamic schools focused on the characteristics and impact of the education received in relatively contemporary Qur'anic schools, much of it from Morocco.[1] There was also a whole body of historical research on Islamic education, mainly focused on institutions of higher education rather than on elementary education, again, with Morocco well represented.[2] Madrasas, *kuttabs* (preschools), Qur'anic schools—Islamic schools all—existed long before the Soviet invasion of Afghanistan and the resulting, very explicit politicization of religious education that began to occur in Pakistan and Afghanistan in the 1980s and certainly long before hijacked airplanes were crashed into the World Trade Center towers in New York and the Pentagon in Washington, DC, in the United States on September 11, 2001. However, after those critical events, issues related to Islamic schools grew from a relatively academic area of study within the fields of education, Islamic studies, and Middle Eastern studies to encompass a more heated public debate, both in the West and in Islamic countries, on the role of these schools in the growth of terrorists groups calling themselves Islamic.

In recent years, the purpose and methods of Islamic schools have received increased scrutiny from non-Muslim and Muslim leaders as well as the Western media, often leading to negative publicity, criticisms, and statements of official concern. For example, statements criticizing madrasas come from top

---

[1] See Azmi Bin Omar, "In Quest of an Islamic Ideal of Education: A Study of the Role of the Traditional Pondok Institution in Malaysia" (doctoral dissertation, Temple University, Philadelphia, 1993); Peter Easton and Mark Peach, *The Practical Applications of Koranic Learning in West Africa*, Nonformal Education Working Group Research Studies Series 8 (London: Association for the Development of Education in Africa, International Working Group on Nonformal Education, 1997); Jarmo Houtsonen, "Traditional Qur'anic Education in a Southern Moroccan Village," *International Journal of Middle East Studies* 26, no. 33 (1994): 489–500; Susan Pollak, *Qur'anic Schooling: Setting, Context, and Process*, Project on Human Potential ED 254 455 (Cambridge, MA: Harvard University, Graduate School of Education, 1983); Jennifer E. Spratt and Daniel Wagner, *The Making of a "Fqih": The Transformation of Traditional Islamic Teachers in Modern Times*, research report ED 254 471 (Cambridge, MA: Harvard University, Graduate School of Education, 1984); Daniel A. Wagner, "In Support of Primary Schooling in Developing Countries: A New Look at Traditional Indigenous Schools," PHREE Background Paper Series PHREE/89/23 (World Bank, Washington, DC, 1989), and "Rediscovering Rote: Some Cognitive and Pedagogical Preliminaries," in *Human Assessment and Cultural Factors*, ed. S. Irvine and J. W. Berry (New York: Plenum, 1983), 179–90; Daniel A. Wagner, and Jennifer E. Spratt, "Cognitive Consequences of Contrasting Pedagogies; The Effects of Qur'anic Preschooling in Morocco," *Child Development* 58 (1987): 1207–19.

[2] See Mohammed Abu-Talib, "Le didactique du Coran," *La grande encyclopédie du Maroc* (Cremona: GEP, 1987), 2:166–72; Dale F. Eickelman, "Traditional Islamic Learning and Ideas of the Person in the Twentieth Century," in *Middle Eastern Lives: The Practice of Biography and Self-Narrative*, ed. M. Kramer (Syracuse, NY: Syracuse University Press, 1991), 35–59, and *Knowledge and Power in Morocco: The Education of a Twentieth-Century Notable* (Princeton, NJ: Princeton University Press, 1985).

officials and policy makers in the U.S. government, including the president, the vice president, and the secretary of state. Donald Rumsfeld asked in an October 2003 memo to his inner circle, "Are we capturing, killing or deterring and dissuading more terrorists every day than the madrasas and the radical clerics are recruiting, training and deploying against us?"[3] Major U.S. and British newspapers, between December 2000 and June 2004, published 42 articles on madrasas in Pakistan alone, many characterizing them as threats, and many giving inaccurate or unverifiable figures concerning the number of madrasas and the scope of their enrollments.[4] The publicity that Islamic schools have attracted has shaped public perception and debate about these schools, often in a decidedly negative way.

Concerns about the role of Islamic schools are not limited to those in the West. For example, the president of Pakistan, Pervez Musharraf, has taken action to restrict madrasas and subject them to greater government scrutiny, partly in response to concerns/pressure from the West. *Al-Ahram Weekly* reported, "Forced to react to international and domestic pressure after the 7/7 attacks [in the London subway], President Musharraf made a televised address to the nation on Thursday, 21 July. . . . On the subject of madrasas, Musharraf promised that all religious schools in the country would be registered by December 2005."[5] The Yemeni Minister of Education stated in 2004 that private religious schools needed to fall under the framework of the ministry or face closure. In February 2005, the *Yemen Times* reported that 4,000 religious schools were being closed by the government.[6]

It is important to acknowledge, before going further, that there are some Islamic schools—a miniscule percentage of the overall number—that do seek to indoctrinate students with a one-sided, narrow-minded, and often pro-violence understanding of Islam. This relatively small number of Islamic schools that do promote violence have an explicit political agenda, and they promulgate it among their students through sermons, lectures, and conversations both inside and outside of school. However, too often the distinctions between the mission of these schools and that of the majority of Islamic schools are overlooked, and all Islamic schools are characterized as being in some way connected to the promulgation of violence and the growth of radical Islam.

The lack of appreciation of the distinction between radical and ordinary Islamic schools is due to a lack of understanding of the underlying assumptions and related practices of education in Islam. A key source of this mis-

[3] D. Moniz and T. Squitieri, "After Grim Rumsfeld Memo, White House Supports Him." http://www.usatoday.com/news/washington/2003-10-22-defense-memo-usat_x.htm.

[4] Tahir Andrabi, Jishnu Das, Asim Ijaz Khwaja, and Tristan Zajonc, "Religious School Enrollment in Pakistan: A Look at the Data," *Comparative Education Review* 50, no. 3 (2006): 446–77.

[5] I. Idris, "Suspect Schools," *Al-Ahram Weekly*, no. 754, August 4–10, 2005.

[6] *Yemen Times* 13, no. 815, February 10, 2005–February 13, 2005.

understanding concerns the role that memorization plays in relation to knowledge, learning, understanding, and reasoning, all of which have nuances in Islamic education that do not inhere in Western conceptions of these words. Without an appreciation of the purpose of memorization in the educational process and with the media images of children rocking back and forth, memorizing the Qur'an and reciting it in unison under the watchful eyes of stern-looking teachers, the basic mission of Islamic schooling has become confounded in the West with ideas of promoting violence and terrorism or inculcating a particularly radical, extremist, or militant view of Islam. Thus, the other purposes of Islamic schooling have not been highlighted.

Drawing on data from field research in Morocco, Yemen, and Nigeria, I suggest that Qur'anic memorization is a process of embodying the divine—the words of God—and as such is a far more learner-oriented and meaningful process than is typically described. I argue, furthermore, that the mission of contemporary Qur'anic schooling, with Qur'anic memorization at its core, is concerned with developing spirituality and morality as well as with providing an alternative to public education, when the availability and quality of public schooling is limited.

Sources of Data

As noted above, data from Morocco, Yemen, and Nigeria inform this article. However, the Morocco research was much more in-depth, due to its duration, and constitutes the bulk of the examples used to support the assertions in this article.

Morocco Fieldwork

In 1998 I spent 11 months doing dissertation fieldwork in the small town of Chefchouan, located in the Rif Mountains of northern Morocco. This research focused on understanding and describing the dynamics of teaching and learning in Qur'anic schools as well as understanding the role that these Qur'anic schools played in the lives of their communities. I conducted a total of 96 interviews, broken down as follows: 19 Islamic school teachers, 34 students, 28 parents, 4 experts, 8 Islamic school sponsors (members of an association running several schools in Chefchouan), and 3 local representatives of the Moroccan government. In addition to the interviews, I conducted approximately 180 of hours of classroom observation in several *kuttabs* and approximately 80 hours in one of the town's two remaining (at the time) *msids* (more traditional Qur'anic school).[7] In general, I would visit the *msid* in the morning, from 9:00 to 11:00 a.m., and the *kuttab* in the afternoon, from 2:30 to 5:00 p.m. In addition, I was a participant in community life in

---

[7] Helen N. Boyle, "Qur'anic Schools in Morocco: Agents of Preservation and Change" (doctoral dissertation, University of Pittsburgh, 2000).

Chefchouan, living there and interacting with community members, especially the Qur'anic school teachers, for a period of 11 months.

Yemen Fieldwork

In 1997, I spent 3 months in Sana'a, Yemen, carrying out a small pilot ethnographic study of two Islamic schools, one for males and one for females, with a colleague from Sana'a University.[8] This study was a precursor to the Morocco research described above. The purpose of the study was largely descriptive—to learn about the features of the schools, especially their teaching methods, and to better understand their significance in the lives of those associated with them. We conducted interviews and observed in classrooms over a 2 month period. Specifically, those interviewed included Qur'anic school students (four boys and four girls) and teachers (two male and one female), three parents of Qur'anic school students, one Qur'anic school alumnus, one faculty member from the College of the Holy Qur'an in Sana'a (an "expert"), and two members of Qur'anic school associations in Sana'a (those organizations that organize and run Qur'anic schools). We were not allowed to tape-record interviews with the female teachers and students, and thus took notes during these interviews. All other interviews were tape-recorded with the permission of the interviewee, transcribed, and translated.

Classroom observations were conducted continually over a period of 2 months in a boys' school, approximately 3 days a week, and in a girls' school for 1.5 months, once a week. (This time disparity is due to the difficulty of locating and securing permission for access to the girls' school.) Field notes were recorded by both observers, primarily in English, over the course of 20 school visits of at least 1 hour each. For classroom observations and interviews at the girls' school, a Yemeni female university student and/or a Yemeni female English teacher accompanied me in collecting the data.

Nigeria Fieldwork

In 2002 and 2003, I designed two small, principally descriptive, studies as part of a USAID-funded international development project (the Literacy Enhancement Assistance Project, or LEAP) in Nigeria.[9] The focus of the project was on improving English language literacy and numeracy acquisition in approximately 330 schools in three states in Nigeria (Kano, Lagos, and Nasarawa). Seventy-eight of the schools involved in the project were Islamic schools (frequently called *Islamiya* schools in Nigeria).[10]

[8] Helen N. Boyle and Abdullah Othman Abbas, "Contributing to the Health and Well-Being of the Next Generation" (paper presented at the World Congress of Comparative and International Education Societies, Cape Town, July 12–17, 1998).

[9] Helen Boyle, "Islamiyyah Schools' Parents' Attitudes and Perceptions toward Education" (LEAP Islamiya School Study no. 1 for USAID, January 2004); Helen Boyle and J. T. Zakariya, "Nigerian Qur'anic Schools: Characteristics and Needs" (LEAP Islamiya School Study no. 2 for USAID, September 2004).

[10] The decision to focus on Islamic schools was made by the USAID mission in Nigeria pre-9/11/01, because of an expressed concern about the quality of education in the ever-growing number of private Islamic schools.

The objective of the first study was to understand parental attitudes and preferences in selecting private *Islamiya* schools over the public schools for their children. This study was conducted in a random sample from among the 78 schools served by the project, specifically 10 schools in Kano state, 8 schools in Nasarawa state, and 8 in Lagos state. An oral questionnaire was administered to 131 parents (83 fathers, 43 mothers, and 5 parents for whom no gender was recorded).[11] In addition, more in-depth, open-ended interviews were conducted with 52 parents (2 per school).

The objective of the second Nigeria study was to learn more about the characteristics and needs of traditional Qur'anic schools in the same three states and to inform the government, donor organizations, nongovernmental organizations, and local communities in formulating appropriate strategies to assist them in meeting and even expanding their educational goals, especially those that relate to literacy, numeracy, and life skills. Data consist of oral questionnaire responses from 133 parents, 36 school proprietors, and 69 teachers across 36 different schools.

Islamic Educational Institutions

Islamic educational institutions can be situated on a continuum, from the most traditional one-room schoolhouse to the very modern Islamic high school, complete with the latest technology. However, the archetype of a traditional Islamic school (preuniversity level) is still that of a one-room school with a strict but learned master who teaches children (mainly boys) to memorize and recite (depending on the students' talents) some or all of the Qur'an, the holy book in Islam. The class encompasses children of different ages and levels. The master works one-on-one with the children and has the older or more accomplished students work with and coach the younger and less accomplished ones. The school year is flexible; students leave school and return, depending on the labor needs of their families. Students progress in the course of their studies at their own pace, according to how fast they master or memorize the particular material they are working on. There are no examinations or grades. If a student learns all he can from one teacher, he will get an attestation that he has studied with that teacher and perhaps go out and seek another teacher. Generally, these archetypical schools are supported by the community and the teachers—a *mu'allim* or *malam* or *fqih* or sheikh, depending on the area of the Islamic world—are also engaged and supported by community members. The curriculum is the Qur'an at first and then other Islamic religious texts, Arabic grammar, and perhaps some numeracy. As Islam spread from the Middle East to Asia and Africa, so too did this model of schooling, although it intermingled with existing educa-

---

[11] The lower number of female respondents is due to the difficulty of accessing females, especially in the conservative north.

tional structures and models. Thus Islamic schools, while retaining a core of commonality, took on features of the traditions and practices associated with their localities.

This archetypal model is growing less and less common across the Islamic world, as more and more children attend public schools and thus study a wider variety of subjects, including local language, foreign languages, science, mathematics, and social studies. Public schooling is commonly perceived by parents, teachers, and students themselves as offering more options for economic advancement through university enrollment or employment. Indeed, many traditional Islamic schools have closed as their student population has diminished.

However, a large number of Islamic schools in Morocco, Yemen, and Nigeria, as well as many other countries, have not remained dormant in the face of public school competition. In fact, they have proven quite able to evolve and change in response to local demands, despite their (somewhat undeserved) reputation as being quite conservative and unchanging.[12] For example, in Morocco many traditional Islamic schools have transformed themselves into preschools. In many urban and semiurban areas, a traditional Qur'anic school is now something students attend in the years before going to public school. Within traditional Qur'anic preschools, there have been many modifications to the form of the school itself. One noticeable change is the introduction of female teachers. While not as learned as traditional scholars who have memorized the whole Qur'an, these girls are taught to correctly recite many verses, which they teach to children in a friendlier and less authoritarian manner than the traditional male *fqih*, or scholar. These "new" Moroccan Qur'anic schoolteachers instruct rows of small children (ages 3–6), who sit crowded on straw mats on the floor, boys on one side, girls on the other, dutifully reciting, collectively repeating after the teacher, sometimes individually coming to the blackboard to write a letter, sometimes standing in front of the group or the teacher for individual recitation.

In Sana'a, Yemen (as well as Morocco and Nigeria), there are also a plethora of Islamic schools that have come to offer "after hours" instruction. These schools function in the late afternoon and early evening hours, after the public schools are closed, and sometimes during the summers, when public schools are not in session. In so doing, they are able to attract students who attend the public schools but whose parents want to make sure that they also receive some elements of a traditional Islamic education.[13] In Sana'a, the Qur'anic school teachers we interviewed mentioned how they operated after public school hours so as to enable students to attend both schools, mentioning that they even helped students with their public school homework. They instruct mixed-aged groups of boys (or girls) for a couple of hours

---

[12] Boyle, "Qur'anic Schools in Morocco."

[13] For a discussion of these basic varieties in these countries, see ibid.

a day, usually between the sunset and evening prayers, rarely using whole-group instruction but rather working with individuals and small groups, listening to recitation, making corrections, and occasionally meting out sharp slaps on the hands with wooden sticks (for those boys who misbehave). It should also be noted that in areas of rural Yemen, Qur'anic schools might be the only option for some communities, where rough terrain and distance impede students from getting to public schools. Hence, those schools would operate on a longer schedule than the urban ones described immediately above.

In Nigeria, especially in the north, there is a booming private Islamic education sector. These private schools offer a high concentration of Islamic studies, including Qur'anic memorization, but they also offer a range of secular subjects as well. By retaining their core mission but expanding their curricula, they have managed to offer an alternative to the public schools and thus retain their relevance to Muslim families in Nigeria. Indeed, the government is moving to register these schools and assist them in an attempt to achieve some standard of quality akin to the public schools, so that the students enrolled in the Islamic schools can be counted toward helping Nigeria achieve its Universal Primary Enrollment goals. These schools have multiple teachers, crowded into tiny, "hole-in-the-wall" classrooms, with large numbers of eager students ranging from grades 1 to 6, usually crowded three or four to a desk designed for two. Boys sit on one side, girls on the other, with each of the girls having her hair and upper body covered by a long scarf, but not her face. In theses schools, in contrast to the others described above, students study a variety of subjects—not just the Qur'an or basic writing—during the school day.

While Islamic schools vary widely across the Muslim world, as illustrated above, they still have certain defining traits in common. First, Islamic schools focus on promoting the acquisition of knowledge and are modeled on the educational practices of the Prophet Muhammad and his companions. Second, and most important, Islamic schools have as a central feature and goal the facilitation of Qur'anic memorization.[14]

Knowledge in Islam and Islamic Schools

Knowledge (*'ilm*) is referred to in the Qur'an 750 times, ranking it the third most used term, behind God (Allah, 2,800 references) and Lord (Rabb, 950 references), thus testifying to the centrality and importance of knowledge in the religious tradition.[15] However, there are two types of knowledge in Islam: (*a*) revealed knowledge, which comes from God, and (*b*) knowledge

---

[14] See Bin Omar, "In Quest of an Islamic Ideal of Education," and Eickelman, *Knowledge and Power in Morocco*.

[15] Franz Rosenthal, *Knowledge Triumphant* (Leiden: E. J. Brill, 1970), 20–21.

derived from reason, which comes from the physical universe, the human mind, and history or study of societies, both local and foreign.[16] Revealed knowledge is held to be of a higher form than knowledge based on reason because "it comes directly from God, is unique in certitude, and has a fundamentally beneficial nature. . . . All true knowledge or science should help us to understand and realize the meaning and the spirit of divine knowledge in its widest sense, for personal and social development."[17] Humans need knowledge derived from human reason to understand and interpret revealed knowledge. The Qur'an emphasizes the importance of reasoning in confirming and expanding existing knowledge. The Qur'an itself is the perfect example of revealed knowledge for Muslims, since it is considered to contain the actual words of God.

In part, because of the importance of revealed knowledge in Islam, the approach to knowledge acquisition in Islamic schools contrasts with that associated with Western educational systems. While Islamic education has a narrower initial focus and broadens over time, Western education begins with a broad focus and moves toward narrower specialization. In the Islamic tradition, children start with the very specific (i.e., the Qur'an) and, throughout the course of their studies, increase their focus to include a broader and broader range of topics. Conversely, in the West, children tend to start out with a wide variety of subjects to study—science, math, language, gym, art, music, social studies—and specialize as they get older, during their high school and/or university education. Thus, as figure 1 indicates, the whole approach to education that was typical in precolonial Muslim societies (and still exists in Islamic schools in certain contexts) is very different from that of Western countries.

Memorization as an Instructional Method

Memorization is a methodology that is used extensively in Islamic educational institutions, whether they be Islamic preschools (*kuttabs*), such as one finds in Morocco; full-fledged Islamic primary schools, such as are common in the largely Muslim north of Nigeria; or simply Qur'anic schools that serve students after hours, as one can find in the busy city of Sana'a, Yemen. Memorization is a purposeful pedagogical choice for Qur'anic study in particular. While memorization may have evolved into a catchall methodology employed for a growing number of school subjects over the past few centuries,

---

[16] Bin Omar, "In Quest of an Islamic Ideal of Education."
[17] Ibid., 29.

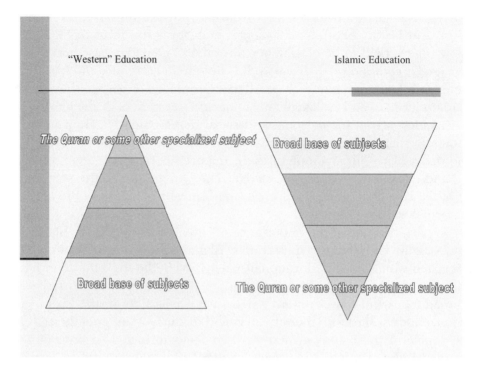

FIG. 1.—Comparison of curriculum structure between Islamic and Western education

it was not conceptualized this way when the principles and methods of Islamic school pedagogy were evolving in the first several centuries of Islam.[18]

Given its increased role in Islamic education over the past several centuries, particularly since the decline of the Arab empire, memorization in Islamic schools, especially when it comes to religious education, has generally been looked upon in the West as a process whose purpose is to indoctrinate the memorizer into the practices and beliefs of Islam.[19] However, this notion is too simple and does not accurately represent the role of memorization in

[18] It should be noted that memorization was not used as the only means of fostering learning in early Islamic schools. Islamic philosophers in the early days of Islam wrote quite thoughtfully about teaching and learning; memorization of the Qur'an was not a default method due to the lack of other ideas or insights on instruction. Early philosophers debated the merits of memorization vs. deductive reasoning, e.g., and opined how best to organize instruction. See Sebastian Günther, "Be Masters in That You Teach and Continue to Learn: Medieval Muslim Thinkers on Educational Theory," *Comparative Education Review* 50, no. 3 (2006): 367–88.

[19] See D. B. MacDonald, *Aspects of Islam* (New York: MacMillan, 1911); E. Michaux-Bellaire, "L'enseignement indigène au Maroc," *Rev. du nomade musulman* 15 (1911): 422–53; G. D. Miller, "Classroom 19: A Study of Behavior in a Classroom of a Moroccan Primary School," in *Psychological Dimensions of Near Eastern Studies*, ed. L. C. Brown and N. Itzkowitz (Princeton, NJ: Darwin, 1977); A. Talbani, "Pedagogy, Power, and Discourse: Transformation of Islamic Education," *Comparative Education Review* 40, no. 1 (1977): 66–82; N. Zerdoumi, *Enfants d'hier, l'éducation de l'enfant en milieu traditionnel Algérien* (Paris: François Maspero, 1970).

Islamic schooling. Understanding the role of memorization in Islamic schooling requires attention to learning, understanding, and reasoning.[20]

Memorization and Learning in Islam

Memorization as a practice was initially related to the preservation of the Qur'an in its exact form, as revealed to Mohammed. On a basic level memorization of the Qur'an is associated with knowledge of the Qur'an, although not in the Western sense of being able to understand and explain it, but in the sense of being able to recite it.[21] While the various groups and ages of learners I observed in the three countries were generally unable to explain what they had memorized, they did "know" some of the Qur'an in the primary sense of being able to recite parts of it. Memorization of the Qur'an, then, is synonymous with learning the Qur'an for many Muslims and as such is very important to Muslim communities worldwide.

Indeed, in the three countries cited in this work, national decision makers, local experts, teachers, and parents all want children to memorize some of the Qur'an, even though Qur'anic memorization in the contemporary schools is often much abridged from what it was in the past. To cite one example, in the second Nigeria study, 50 percent of the teachers of traditional Qur'anic schools surveyed and 50 percent of the school proprietors surveyed (18 out of 36) said that Qur'anic memorization was the primary objective of their school.[22] Likewise, a majority of parents interviewed in the same study said that the learning of Qur'anic recitation was the primary reason for their choice of a Qur'anic school for their children. Thirty-three percent of parents (44 out of 133) cited Qur'anic recitation as their main reason, while the next highest reason, gaining Islamic knowledge, was cited as the main reason by 18 percent of parents (24 out of 133).[23] These interviews expressed the clear link that parents, teachers, and school proprietors saw between memorization, Muslim identity, and learning to live life as a good and observant Muslim.

Data from Yemen (and Morocco) reflect the same commitment to and concern with Qur'anic memorization. A father in Yemen, after attesting to the importance of memorization, was asked whether Qur'anic schools are thus important institutions in Yemen. He said, "Yes, I can see that they are very, very important because without teaching the holy Qur'an the other sciences will not be acquired properly. We regard the Qur'an as the father of the other sciences, the element that could develop our kids mentally,

[20] Eickelman, *Knowledge and Power in Morocco*, 57.

[21] Ibid., 64.

[22] Other things listed included training of students for Islamic propagation, Islamic teaching, becoming a better citizen, and becoming a good Muslim.

[23] Boyle and Zakariya, "Nigerian Qur'anic Schools." Acquiring Islamic knowledge, quality of instruction, and moral education are among other reasons cited by parents. This was an open-ended question, and the variety of responses had to be grouped. Gaining Islamic knowledge could indeed refer to memorizing the Qur'an, but I restricted that category to responses that actually named memorization or recitation.

physically, spiritually and intellectually. Moreover, the holy Qur'an encourages people to go behind [i.e., go deeper into] knowledge." In sum, parents and teachers in varying contexts link memorization to knowledge, to the process of learning (beyond religious subjects), and to personal development in a variety of ways, beyond simply being able to say one's prayers.

Memorization and Understanding

Memorization and understanding are often considered to be opposites. Memorization without comprehension is mindless rote learning, and comprehension is not automatically associated with prior memorization. However, in Islamic education memorization of the Qur'an is generally considered the first step in understanding (not a substitute for it), as its general purpose was to ensure that sacred knowledge was passed on in proper form so that it could be understood later. Daniel A. Wagner quotes the most influential Muslim jurist, theologian, and Sufi al-Ghazali who pointed out almost a millennium ago that memorization of the Qur'an, as a first step to learning, did not necessarily preclude comprehension later on: "The creed ought to be taught to a boy in the earliest childhood, so that he may hold it absolutely in memory. Thereafter, the meaning of it will keep gradually unfolding itself to him, point by point, as he grows older. So, first, is the committing to memory; then understanding; then belief and certainty and acceptance."[24] Thus, memorization of the Qur'an (and other sacred texts) is meant to be the first step in a lifelong enterprise of seeking understanding and thus knowledge. The objective is not to replace understanding with dogmatism but to plant the seeds that would lead to understanding. As Sebastian Günther explains: "Al-Ghazali makes it very clear that, for him, true knowledge is not simply a memorized accumulation of facts but rather 'a light which floods the heart.'"[25]

These same ideas are echoed by historiographer Ibn Khaldoun, cited as part of a project report on *kuttab* innovations. "Ibn Khaldoun suggests that this system [Qur'anic memorization] took advantage of children's submissiveness in order to teach them what they would only be able to understand later: 'Only children are capable of learning a text that they don't understand now and will understand later,' he wrote."[26] The idea that memorization did not preclude understanding or enlightenment but was a precursor to both is an important distinction, because much of the criticism of traditional Islamic education centers on its emphasis on memorization. If memorization leads to understanding of the Qur'an, of divinely revealed knowledge, it is not surprising (and not threatening to the West) that Muslim parents and

---

[24] Wagner, "Rediscovering Rote."

[25] Günther, "Be Masters in That You Teach and Continue to Learn," 382.

[26] K. Bouzoubaa, "An Innovation in Morocco's Koranic Pre-schools" (Working Papers in Early Childhood Development no. 23, Bernard van Leer Foundation, The Hague, 1998), 3.

communities, regardless of how liberal or conservative they are, want their children to memorize at least some of the Qur'an.

Memorization and the Exercise of Reason

Furthermore, Qur'anic memorization can be seen as being associated with the exercise of reason, as were other mental processes involved in being a good Muslim. "Reason is popularly conceived as man's ability to discipline his nature in order to act in accord with the arbitrary code of conduct laid down by God and epitomized by such acts of communal obedience as the fast of Ramadan."[27] "Thus a firm discipline in the course of learning the Qur'an is culturally regarded as an integral part of socialization. . . . In Moroccan towns and villages, the discipline of Qur'anic memorization is an integral part of learning to be human and Muslim."[28] Reason is equated with discipline, and memorization is a form of discipline. In the above quotation, Eickelman is speaking of traditional *msids* from the early part of the twentieth century. Still, his observation rings true for today's *kuttab* students as well. The process of memorization of the Qur'an is a demonstration of behavior that involves mental and physical discipline. This in turn is a manifestation of behavior based on reason and is considered praiseworthy in Islam. Discipline is important in Islam, hence it is not surprising that Muslim parents who hope to send their children to the best universities in the West nonetheless want their children to memorize some of the Qur'an.

Memorization as a Process of Embodiment

Qur'anic memorization's traditional association with knowledge, understanding, and the demonstration of reason notwithstanding, there remains the question of how one can reconcile the ongoing significance accorded to memorization in today's world (and by implication the schools that facilitate it) with the reduced practical need for memorization as a way to demonstrate or even acquire any of the above. In the early days of Islam, Qur'anic memorization was a way of preserving the Qur'an and sharing it, as it was not initially written down. When it was written down, it was not widely available in print, such that everyone could obtain a copy, and literacy rates were very low so that people could not read it, even if they could obtain a print copy. Today, the Qur'an is widely available in print; it can be heard on cassettes, CDs, on the radio, and on TV. It can simply be read, given rising literacy rates, and referred to as needed, given the rising availability of print materials, without necessarily being memorized. Likewise, while Qur'anic memorization is conceived of as a manifestation of reason, it is certainly not the only such way to demonstrate reasonable or disciplined behavior. However, today, even

[27] Eickelman, *Knowledge and Power in Morocco*, 130–38.
[28] Ibid., 62–66.

as memorization might not be necessary, strictly speaking, in order to demonstrate Qur'anic knowledge or necessary as a first step to future understanding, or even necessary as a manifestation of reasonable behavior, memorization as the primary methodology for Qur'anic learning continues unabated. This article suggests that memorization of the Qur'an retains ongoing significance to Muslim communities, not only because it is associated with knowledge, understanding, and reason, but because this form of learning has the lasting effect of embodying the revealed knowledge of the Qur'an in the beings of the students.

The Concept of Embodiment

Maurice Merleau-Ponty and Pierre Bourdieu, the great precursors of embodiment as an anthropological concept, problematized the body as a perceptual setting in relation to the world or the site of unconscious practice (habitus), respectively.[29] Both Merleau-Ponty and Bourdieu conceptualized the body as a crossroads for cultural production and not simply as an object to be acted upon. Medical anthropologists took up the topic of embodiment, suggesting that the body is a site for moves of political power and social control, using examples of torture, anorexic and bulimic women in today's society, and debates over reproductive rights. In so doing, they identified even more explicitly the body as a subject, not simply an object, of cultural production.[30]

Thomas Csordas, in his work among charismatic Christians, extends the concept of embodiment beyond medical anthropology or anthropology of the body to the domain of religious practice. Csordas refers to the body as "the existential ground of culture," in this case the site and mediator of religious practice.[31] Finally, A. J. Strathern, elaborating on these ideas, offers the following more concrete or applied definition of embodiment: "Embodiment has to do with the body, but it implies that it is something else, other than or added to the physical body itself, that is, embodied, and such a "thing" often turns out to be an abstract social value, such as honor or bravery. Embodiment thus has to do with values that in some ways are also disembodied or may be thought of separately from the body itself. *Embodiment*, in other words, is a term that belies itself by combining the abstract and the concrete together."[32]

---

[29] Maurice Merleau-Ponty, *Phenomenology of Perception*, trans. Colin Smith (London: Routledge & Kegan Paul, 1962); Pierre Bourdieu, *Outline of a Theory of Practice* (Cambridge: University of Cambridge Press, 1977).

[30] Margaret Lock and Nancy Scheper-Hughes, "The Mindful Body: A Prolegomenon to Future Works in Medical Anthropology," *Medical Anthropology Quarterly* 1, no. 1 (1987): 6–41.

[31] Thomas Csordas, "Embodiment as a Paradigm for Anthropology," *Ethos* 18 (1990): 5.

[32] Andrew J. Strathern, *Body Thoughts* (Ann Arbor: University of Michigan Press, 1996), 195.

Qur'anic Memorization as a Process of Embodiment

In relation to Islamic schools, the "thing" that Strathern refers to in the quotation above is the divine—the revealed knowledge of the Qur'an. By memorizing the Qur'an (or parts thereof), students embody, or possess the words of God within their very beings, where they can physically reproduce it, share it, and refer to it, ideally over the course of their lifetimes. While memorization plays a role in the practice of other religions and their related educational traditions, it is not the exclusive pedagogy or mode of learning, as it is in the first few years of Islamic schooling. In addition, memorizing the whole Qur'an is a task of some magnitude in terms of time, effort, and discipline, in comparison to the scope of memorization in other traditions. Thus, in Islam, memorization has a deeper significance in the learning process because it allows children to embody the Qur'an.

Further, I would not characterize any and all memorization as leading to embodied knowledge. The Qur'an is uniquely significant in that it is thought to contain the exact words of God. As some Christians swallow a wafer that they believe, through transubstantiation, has become the body of Christ, so too do Muslims embody the Qur'an because they believe it to be the exact and immutable words of God. Memorization is a useful learning tool in many disciplines, but the memorization of knowledge coming from reason is not the same for Muslims as memorizing and embodying the revealed knowledge of the Qur'an. Knowledge coming from reason is not fixed—it can change and therefore does not need to be embodied or engraved upon the mind (or the heart) of the memorizer. The Qur'an, as something divinely created, is fixed and will not change. Hence, I use embodiment as a framework to describe Qur'anic memorization because it allows us to describe the significance of the act of memorization in a way that better captures its meaningfulness to Muslims and allows us to characterize Qur'anic memorization as a learning process, not simply as a mindless rote exercise or a form of indoctrination.

Interview respondents (in Morocco, in particular, but also in Yemen) often used bodily expressions to convey the mental process of memorization in very concrete terms. Typical were references to the Qur'an's "presence" in the mind or the heart or blood of the memorizer. For example, two different fathers from Morocco commented,

1. Now, it is still the beginning. The child's mind is empty when he is small, and it can record anything either bad or good [hence the need for the child to record the good, i.e., the Qur'an];
2. He will benefit from that [the *kuttab*] as far as religion is concerned. That will help him even when he becomes a young man, since the Qur'an can't be forgotten. It is good to have the Qur'an in one's heart.

A father, whose appreciation for the *kuttab* was mainly as means of preparing his child for primary school by teaching reading and writing, stated

3.   But, religious subjects are good as well. I cannot deny them. As soon
as a child learns them and puts them in his mind, they remain there.[33]
All of these parents suggest in one way or another (recording on the mind,
having the Qur'an in the heart, putting religion in the mind) the permanence of the process of grafting the abstract (the Qur'an) onto the physical
(the body).

Similarly, a Moroccan school headmaster, known for his religious knowledge, states that he views memorizing the Qur'an as making it part of one's
blood: "The child imitates his parents while praying or while reciting the
Qur'an; this is in our blood. Hence learning the Qur'an in an early age,
conserving it and relying on it while asking forgiveness, all these are in the
Moroccan blood and in the blood of all Muslims. . . . You know, we wake
and we live by the Qur'an, and the Moroccans declined when they deviated
from it and when they left off memorizing the book of God, since it is the
reason behind the existence of the 'umma."[34] These sentiments, which were
commonly expressed in all three countries, particularly by parents, illustrate
a belief in the memorized Qur'an being physically linked to the body and
to the receptiveness of the young mind—that is, embodied.

The Embodied Qur'an as a Moral Compass

Embodiment casts Qur'anic memorization in a decidedly more positive
light than referring to it as mindless rote learning that leads to a blind
acceptance of certain ideas and tenants. However, embodiment of revealed
knowledge through Qur'anic memorization was not an end in itself. Parents
spoke of memorizing the Qur'an as giving direction, helping children to find
or come closer to God, and helping them to become good citizens. In this
sense, parents and community members to whom I spoke looked on the
embodied Qur'an as having a salutary effect on the development of their
children because it acts as a sort of moral or ethical compass for them.

Even without comprehension, the embodied Qur'an is believed to provide
moral direction by virtue of its being the word of God, thus sacred and holy.
A person carries it, and it provides direction, much like a compass. A compass
is an apt metaphor for the embodied Qur'an. A compass will seek north
because of its magnetic attraction; one orients oneself with a compass by
finding north. However, one can go in any direction. Like a compass, the
embodied Qur'an does not negate free will and the process of making choices
about which direction to follow. Rather, it provides a point of reference from
which to make choices. With a compass, the pull toward magnetic north can
be interfered with by other magnets—smaller ones perhaps that pull the
compass needle in the wrong direction away from magnetic north. Likewise,

---

[33] He is referring to the Qur'an when he mentions "religious subjects."

[34] Note how this headmaster speaks of the decline of Moroccan society as resulting from diminished
memorization.

the Qur'an, because of its magnetic attraction, which comes from its divine essence, will pull the learner in the right direction as he or she grows; it is stronger than other magnets, although other magnets can interfere and lead one off course. It is possible that the student will go astray, but learning the Qur'an is one way of giving the child a compass—a moral compass—to help him/her find the desired path.

As Aisha, a Moroccan mother, describes Qur'anic memorization, "It is good, since it teaches human beings to go in God's path. When a boy or a girl learns religion, they follow God's path and they know what is between them and God; they know what is in this life. If a child learns at [public] school, he/she will reach a certain level, get angry and leave. This is not the case with the Qur'an. The more children learn it, the more it gets into their hearts." In addressing the question about the relative benefit of children attending public versus Islamic schools, a father from Yemen said, "The teachers in public schools do not care about the students' behavior. I mean whether he behaves in [an] Islamic manner or not. . . . Teachers in public schools focus more on providing knowledge to students but do not have time to focus on practices, such as learning how to pray, because there are hundreds or thousands in public schools. Students in Qur'anic schools learn how to read and memorize [the] Qur'an besides learning Islamic morals and [the] Islamic way of life. Such practicing is very rare in public schools." Similarly, a Qur'anic teacher from a boy's school in Yemen discussed the benefits of attending a *kuttab*: "They will be able to read [the] Qur'an and memorize it in an appropriate way. Furthermore, they will be able to use and practice what they learn in their lives. They learn Islamic morals and practice them. . . . Students try to practice what they learn. To move from theory to practice or to put into practice what you learn is appropriate for a Muslim person. Quranic schools work hard to raise students to be good persons in the society."

The Embodied Qur'an and Spirituality

In Yemen, which was closed off from much of the outside world for so long, spirituality—as fostered by embodying the Qur'an—is still seen as a legitimate focus of education, even a necessary part. Spirituality is not perceived, however, as simply a result of "religious education," as the passing on of doctrinaire knowledge. It is seen as fostering an awareness of the presence of God in daily life, of divine mystery, of life and death, of transcendence and peace. This starts with memorizing, with embodying the Qur'an. Spiritual wellness, emanating from the embodied Qur'an, then, is seen as a sort of preventative medicine, leading to emotional strength to deal with life's hardships and disappointments by fostering a sense of inner security, a sense of identity, and an appreciation of one's importance in the universe as a human being.

For instance, a Yemeni parent expressed it this way: "There are so many advantages [of sending our kids to Qur'anic schools] and the most important is that they are taught to know their religion with being in contact with Allah. [And] because we can find our needs addressed, whatever they are, mentally, physically, spiritually . . . in the Qur'an." A female teacher from Yemen described her views about facilitating Qur'anic memorization in a similar manner: "I am proud of that for [several] reasons. One of them is that I am in contact with Allah through his holy book. Another reason is that I feel that I achieved some of my duties and I am very happy when I teach the Qur'an." For this educator, at least, spirituality is related to being a healthy person in terms of social interaction as well: "Moreover, the child will receive a good education, especially in the spiritual aspect. So, he will be a good member in the society." And a parent, also from Yemen, indicated that the embodiment of the Qur'an, which comes from memorization, serves the individual well, not only during one's life but after the judgment day as well: "I see Qur'anic learning and memorization for my kids [as] very important. I prefer my son to memorize the whole Qur'an more than obtaining [a] PhD because I understand that such learning and memorization will benefit him in his life and the hereafter." Similarly, a female Yemeni student said that she feels reading and memorizing the Qur'an "ha[s] many benefits for people in this life and on the day of judgment."

Concluding Thoughts

Islamic schools serve complex purposes in Muslim countries and cannot be reduced to a simple description of religious education through memorization. In the Islamic tradition, memorization of sacred, revealed knowledge is an appropriate first step in the process of learning, understanding, and in developing reason and discipline. Learning, understanding, and the development of reason and discipline are, in turn, ultimately meant to lead the student to greater knowledge of God and the world. Using the anthropological concept of embodiment, furthermore, allows us to analyze the process of Qur'anic memorization as a process whereby the learner comes to possess the sacred (in the Qur'an) in a physical way. Conceptualizing Qur'anic memorization as a process whereby the Qur'an is embodied allows us to capture its significance as a form of learning and not merely a pedagogy of last resort. The embodied Qur'an provides a source of guidance—a moral compass— for the memorizer, possibly in a direct and literal sense as the meaning of the Qur'an unfolds in the mind of the memorizer, but also in a metaphorical sense by its very sacredness becoming inscribed on the body of the memorizer. The embodied Qur'an deepens students' spirituality and offers comfort and security as it increases their awareness of the presence of God.

Islamic schools serve other purposes, in addition to the facilitation of Qur'anic memorization. As Islamic schools have managed to adapt to the changing times, they have managed to fill evolving educational niches. In many cases, parents look to Islamic schools for more than religious education, but for pragmatic reasons as well: parents perceive that the schools are often of better quality than the public ones.

For example, in Yemen, parents, as well as teachers and students, felt that memorizing the Qur'an helped students to do well in Arabic in the public schools. They talked of the benefits that children get in Arabic language proficiency through studying the Qur'an. All of the "experts" interviewed who had a Qur'anic education as their sole form of early instruction spoke of their being advanced when they finally attended public schools (sometimes in Saudi Arabia) and of skipping grades. And in Nigeria, parents of *Islamiya* school students in the study would not be pinned down into choosing "secular" or "Western" subjects as more important than the other. In the interviews Nigerian parents tended to view the two as mutually interdependent—one knows the world through knowing God, and one knows God through knowing the world, roughly speaking. Finally, in Morocco, parents stated quite explicitly that Qur'anic schools prepared their children for primary school. Although hard data on this were not available, many Moroccan interviewees (parents as well as teachers) took this as accepted wisdom.

Parents in all three countries also had high aspirations for their children. Many cited professional careers and/or future, higher academic study as their goals for their children and indicated that they were confident that their children could realistically pursue those dreams by completing elementary school at the *Islamiya* school. Nigerian parents, in the interviews, cited graduates from their *Islamiya* school who went on to higher studies or professional jobs as proof that the school was helping them to realize their hopes for their child.

It might seem counterintuitive to think that parents select Islamic schools with often very secular goals in mind for their children, such as learning secular subjects, pursuing university education, and achieveing government employment. Parents in the three countries seemed to see the role of the Islamic school more broadly than might have been previously thought. Far from trading in anti-Western discourse, many Islamic school stakeholders I observed and interviewed seemed intent on both memorizing the Qur'an while also working toward future advancement, public school success, career achievement, and economic prosperity. This in turn helps to engender a clearer view of the multiple purposes of Qur'anic schools, which generally include fostering knowledge, spiritual development, moral guidance, and reinforcement of some public school subjects (mainly in Arabic-speaking Muslim countries) and not, perforce, indoctrination into radical Islam, which is commonly but generally incorrectly associated with them.

Qur'anic Education and Social Change in Northern Morocco: Perspectives from Chefchaouen

SOBHI TAWIL

Background and Rationale

Throughout the course of the twentieth century, educational development in Morocco had been characterized by "chronic crisis."[1] At Morocco's independence in 1956, national authorities had to deal with the heritage of educational fragmentation, an externally imposed segregated schooling structure, and marginalization of traditional Islamic education. Since then, the multiple symptoms of educational crisis have ranged from the lack of qualified teaching personnel in the early years of independence to linguistic and cultural dualism, incomplete access to primary schooling and to basic literacy, low levels of educational participation and attainment, poor adaptation of learning content to the needs of the labor market, brain drain, and graduate unemployment on a dramatic scale.

Notably, despite the constantly high share of public expenditure allocated to education in Morocco as compared to other countries in the Middle East and North Africa region, there was a disturbing pattern of decline of absolute primary enrollments observed during the 1980s. While this regressive pattern was halted in the early 1990s and significant progress has been made in expanding access to primary schooling in recent years, inequalities in participation persist, and the continued high dropout rates observed point to a serious crisis of quality of public schooling in Morocco. While primary net enrollment ratios were at 70 percent nationwide in 1998–99, they were under 55 percent for children belonging to the poorest families (income quintile 1), 46 percent for girls from the poorest families in both urban and rural areas, and only 43 percent for children from the poorest households in rural areas (see table 1). Such inequitable patterns of school enrollment constitute an important source of reproduction of adult illiteracy and explain why the national average was only slightly over 50 percent overall and only under 20 percent for women belonging to the poorest households.[2]

This article thus builds on prior analysis of patterns of participation in primary schooling in Morocco. Macro policy analysis of public expenditure

The views expressed in this article are mine and not those of UNESCO.

[1] The term "chronic crisis" was used in a speech delivered by King Mohammed VI on October 8, 1999, and is reproduced in the preface of the national charter on education and training adopted in 1999.

[2] Moroccan Household Living Standards Measurement Survey, 1998–99, data reported in Direction de la Statistique, *Education, formation, et niveau de vie*, vol. 2, *Annexes statistiques* (Rabat: Direction de la Statistique, 2002).

190

TABLE 1
NET PRIMARY (7–12) ENROLLMENT RATIOS (%): MOROCCO 1998–99,
DISTRIBUTION BY INCOME QUINTILE

| | Income Quintile | | | | | |
	1	2	3	4	5	Total
Total	53.9	66.9	75.5	81.9	86.0	70.2
Urban	80.6	85.3	86.6	88.7	87.1	85.2
Rural	43.1	55.1	59.4	63.2	71.0	56.7
Boys	63.7	76.9	84.3	88.1	89.8	76.4
Girls	46.1	65.7	72.6	77.6	83.6	63.4

SOURCE.—Data are from Moroccan Household Living Standards Measurement Survey, 1998–99.
NOTE.—Income quintile 1 = lowest; quintile 5 = highest.

in education suggests that inequitable access to, and exclusion from, primary schooling between 1960 and 2000 can be explained through dualistic development policies and urban bias in educational investment. This is clearly reflected in inequitable (and inefficient) public spending patterns observed until at least 1995.[3] Beyond policy issues, however, household demand for education has also been shown to be central to any understanding of patterns of primary education attendance. Thus, focusing on out-of-school children can be useful in understanding inequitable patterns of participation in primary education.[4]

According to the 1991 Moroccan Household Living Standards Measurement Survey data, the overwhelming majority of 7–12-year-old, out-of-school children had never been enrolled in primary school and had never taken up any Qur'anic education; a much smaller proportion of these children (over 15 percent) had dropped out of primary school, and some 8.5 percent were actually involved in formal Qur'anic education as an alternative to primary schooling.[5] In rural areas, 8 percent of all boys in the 7–12 age group were attending Qur'anic, rather than primary, schools. Three clusters of factors have been identified by heads of households to explain the non–take-up of primary schooling: (1) the inadequate provision of schooling in rural areas, particularly at the lower secondary level, which affects household demand by increasing the real or perceived costs and by lowering the perceived

[3] Sobhi Tawil, "Education et développement régional au Maroc: Stratégies éducatives et logiques sociales," in *Education et développement économique dans le monde arabe et en Europe*, ed. Rainer Biegel and Youssef Alouane (Tunis: Konrad Adenauer Foundation, 1997), 34–64.

[4] The Moroccan Household Living Standards Measurement Surveys (1990–91 and 1998–99) collected data on a variety of household characteristics including health, education, employment, consumption, income, and housing conditions. The 1990–91 survey (Direction de la Statistique, *Enquête nationale sur le niveau de vie des ménages* [Rabat: Direction de la Statistique, 1991]) collected data from 3,400 households across the country, while the 1998–99 survey (Direction de la Statistique, *Enquête nationale sur le niveau de vie des ménages* [Rabat: Direction de la Statistique, 1999]) was based on a sample of some 5,180 households.

[5] Sobhi Tawil, "Household Demand, Basic Education, and Exclusion: Focusing on Out-of-School Children in Morocco," in *Basic Education for All: A Global Concern for Quality*, ed. L. Malmberg, S. Hansén, and K. Heino (Vasa: Abo Akademi University, 2000), 137–55.

benefits of primary schooling, particularly for girls; (2) income poverty and the inability of poorer households in both urban and, more frequently, rural areas to cover the direct and (especially) the indirect costs of schooling; (3) attitudinal and value resistance related to negative attitudes toward schooling, to low perceived immediate and/or future benefits, and to lack of interest in schooling.

What, then, is the relationship between Qur'anic education and the inadequate provision of schooling, of household poverty, and of attitudinal resistance in explaining nonparticipation in primary schooling? Beyond considering national-level data that have been analyzed elsewhere, we need to examine in specific local contexts how demand for, and supply of, basic education—both traditional religious and primary school education—interact and are shaped by economic and local cultural realities.[6] This article documents patterns of take-up of traditional religious and primary school education in Chefchaouen, one of the most disadvantaged provinces in Morocco located in the impoverished northwestern region of the country.

First, I provide some background on the socioeconomic and cultural characteristics of the province of Chefchaouen, including the growing role of cannabis production in the local economy, as well as the significant heritage of traditional Muslim education. Next, I examine contemporary patterns of take-up of Qur'anic education in Morocco, highlighting (*a*) the disarticulation of the traditional system of Islamic education, the gradual integration of the postelementary levels of learning, and the marginalization of the elementary levels of the *kuttab*, as well as (*b*) how the difference between modern and traditional *kuttab* is generally overlooked, and thus a population of learners (7+ years of age) participating in traditional *kuttab* remain statistically "invisible" and consequently excluded from conventional analyses.[7] Then, I explore how Qur'anic education functions as an alternative to public schooling, satisfying the demand of poorer rural households, which cannot bear the direct and indirect costs of schooling or whose children are pushed/pulled out the schooling system as a result of academic failure. Subsequently, I discuss the impact of the expansion of cannabis production on social demand for education in Chefchaouen and the way in which increased opportunities for child work to supplement family income is increasing the indirect costs of schooling, particularly at the level of the lower secondary cycle. Finally, I reconsider the issue of resistance in education within the context of rapid social change, focusing on the negative perceptions of public

---

[6] Sobhi Tawil, "Basic Education, Exclusion, and Development: Change, Crisis, and Reform in Moroccan School Education" (PhD diss., University of Geneva, 2004).

[7] *Kuttab*, or *maktab* (as used in other parts of the Muslim world), represents the elementary level of traditional Muslim education. In Morocco this institution is also known as *msid*. Completion of this elementary level is determined by the complete recitation, transcription, and memorization of the Qur'an. Teaching also includes hygiene and rituals associated with prayer.

school teachers and the declining perceived utility of public schooling among members of certain rural communities.

The Province of Chefchaouen in Northern Morocco

The province of Chefchaouen is situated in the western half of the chain of the Rif mountains and is inhabited by the Jbala or Ghomara.[8] With a predominantly rural population (80 percent in the Rif as a whole and 90 percent in the province of Chefchaouen), it is also the region with the highest population density in the national context with 130 inhabitants per square kilometer. By tradition, it has been a region of out-migration representing the main source of national emigration in the 1960s and 1970s.

A Context of Socioeconomic Marginalization

Much like the rest of the Rif and the former Spanish-controlled northern region of Morocco, Chefchaouen has been associated with socioeconomic disadvantage and marginalization since independence in 1956. This marginalization results from a combination of factors including a tradition of rebellion and nonsubmission to the authority of the central government, or *makhzen*, characteristic of all regions habitually referred to as *bled el siba*, or regions of institutional dissidence.

It is also the result of an absence of any significant socioeconomic rural development strategy during the Spanish colonial period in the first half of the twentieth century. Apart from a crafts industry in the provincial center of Chefchaouen, the economy is overwhelmingly agricultural, characterized by generally difficult farming conditions with small land plots and very rugged and rough terrain. The fragile, largely subsistence and rain dependent, farming production is supplemented by temporary or permanent migration and illicit trade, including the production of cannabis, or *kif*. Finally, it is important to stress the general neglect of the entire Rif region during the reign of King Hassan II (1960–99), even if the situation has changed significantly since 1999 with the historic visit of King Mohammed VI to the impoverished provinces of the north in 1999 and the February 2006 visit to the city of Chefchaouen.

The combination of these factors largely explains why the province of Chefchaouen is one of the poorest and most disadvantaged regions in Morocco. With average literacy rates reported to be 44.4 percent, and as low as 26.1 percent for women, the province of Chefchaouen ranks among the

---

[8] The chain of the Rif Mountains spreads across the provinces of Tetouan, Chefchaouen, Al Hoceima, and Nador. Ibn Khaldûn refers to the Ghomara as a confederation of tribes to which the Jbala belong. See Ibn Khaldûn, *Al-Maqaddima—Discours sur l'histoire universelle*, vol. 1 (Paris: Sindbad, 1968), 317, 675, 680.

lowest nationwide in terms of literacy and school enrollment ratios.[9] More-over, 45 percent of the children in the 7–12 age group in the region were estimated to be out of school in 1994, with some having been enrolled and dropped out but most never having gained access to primary schooling.[10] And such low levels of educational participation and attainment continue to be recorded in Chefchaouen, despite strategic interventions as part of the Social Priorities Programme launched in the 1990s.[11]

The Expansion of Cannabis Production

The province of Chefchaouen is also unique by way of its marginal ag-ricultural economy that increasingly involves the production of cannabis. Indeed, the production of cannabis is the main agricultural activity in the Rif, and Morocco is considered to be the world's largest hashish exporter. According to the World Customs Organization, 70 percent of the European hashish market is supplied by Morocco, and according to Interpol, 90 percent of the almost 1,000 tonnes of hashish seized in Europe in 1999 originated in the Moroccan Rif.[12]

A traditional zone of production in the central Rif, Al Hoceima was the main region of production in the Rif, with cannabis occupying at least a quarter of the crop surface in each plot in 14 out of its 16 constituent communes. During the 1980s, cannabis production spread westward to the province of Chefchaouen, particularly in the southeast areas of the Ghomara and along the Ouad Lao areas. This expansion has continued with, for the first time in 1999, communes of Mokhrisset and Zoumi beginning to produce cannabis. In addition to the two traditional provinces of cannabis production of Al Hoceima and Chefchaouen, production has also recently spread to the province of Tetouan to the north, Larache to the west, and Sidi Kacem to the south. In the south, production is being extended to good quality irrigated

---

[9] Self-reported literacy figures reported in the general population census of 2004 (Haut Commis-sariat au Plan, *Les résultats de la population légale issue du recensement général de la population et de l'habitat [RGPH], 2004* [Rabat: Haut Commissariat au Plan, 2005]).

[10] Preliminary results of the 2004 census were being processed at the time of the writing of this article. Note that data available to the planning department are unreliable, being based on projections and estimations of the population of 6-year-olds to be admitted at the start of each school year; thus, the figures that serve as denominators for enrollment ratios are highly questionable given local de-mographic changes observed since the last population census in 1994. The situation is further com-plicated because of migration: (*a*) in rural communes affected by declining demographic growth rates, official enrollment figures may often be substantially underrepresentative of actual enrollment situations, and (*b*) in urban communes such as the municipality of Chefchaouen that often represents an initial stage of out-migration to Tetouan or abroad, enrollment figures may be grossly inflated as the actual population of primary school-age children is higher than those estimated on the basis of the 1994 census.

[11] Barnamij al Aoulauoiate al Ijtimaia (Social Priorities Programme), 1996–2002, combined basic education and basic health projects in 14 of the most disadvantaged regions of Morocco, including Chefchaouen.

[12] For the World Customs Organization data, see James Keterrer, "Networks of Discontent in Northern Morocco: Drugs, Opposition, and Urban Unrest," *Middle East Report* 218 (2001). For the Interpol data, see A. Labrousse and L. Romero, "Maroc: La production de cannabis dans le Rif," *Drogues: Traffic International—Bulletin Mensuel* 13 (2002): 1–4.

land being rented by farmers in Bab Berred and Ketama.[13] A 2003 study undertaken in the northern provinces of Al Hoceima, Chefchaouen, Larache, Taounate, and Tetouan reported that some 800,000 persons—or 66 percent of rural households—were involved in cannabis production and that the province of Chefchaouen has now become the main cannabis-producing region, representing over half of total production in the northern region.[14]

The illicit character of cannabis production and the large and growing consumption demand in Western Europe largely explain the fact that the attractive income generated from cannabis production far outstrips income that may be generated from legal subsistence or commercial agricultural production. Indeed, "non-irrigated fields cultivated in cannabis generated seven to eight times more revenues than those cultivated in barley, and twelve to sixteen times more when they were irrigated."[15] Moreover, some estimate at $2 billion the value of profits generated by the production of cannabis, which were reinjected into the Moroccan economy in 1997. This far exceeds the $750 million resulting from textile exports, $460 million of foreign investment, or even the $1.26 billion generated through tourism.[16] Others have suggested that the "turnover of smuggling activities in Morocco allegedly reached USD 3 billion in 1994–95, the equivalent of the domestic industrial output or 33% of GDP," thus becoming the first source of foreign currency in Morocco.[17]

It is in such a context that Chefchaouen, much like Ketama and Al Hoceima to the west, has become an important *kif*-producing region. While the relative weight of this agricultural activity is growing within the local and regional economy, it is paradoxical that the lucrative production of *kif* largely remains a subsistence strategy and that the revenues generated do not appear to be contributing to local regional development. Income generated from *kif*, much like that resulting from the remittances of migrant workers, does not appear to be invested in productive activities within the local economy. The income generated does not generally appear to contribute directly to the improvement of the family situation and is most often used in "sumptuary" forms of spending. This pattern of consumption of cannabis-generated revenue explains the fact that many Rifis own real estate in Tetouan or Tangiers. As status symbols, these properties remain unexploited, except for short stays several times a year. Despite these spending patterns, the production of *kif*

[13] Ketterer, "Networks of Discontent in Northern Morocco"; Labrousse and Romero, "Maroc"; Observatoire Géopolitique des Drogues (OGD), *La géopolitique mondiale des drogues: Rapport annuel, 1998–1999* (Paris: OGD, 2002), 9.

[14] UN Office on Drugs and Crime (UNODC)/Agence pour le Développement des Provinces du Nord (APDN), *Morocco Cannabis Survey* (Rabat: UNODC/APDN, 2003).

[15] Ibid., 7.

[16] Pascual Moreno, a Spanish agricultural scientist who has undertaken research on the subject for the European Union, quoted in Labrousse and Romero, "Maroc," 2.

[17] OGD, *La géopolitique mondiale des drogues.*

is increasingly a part of local economic strategies, and certain segments of the population do indeed raise their living standards through the income that such activity generates.

A Rich Heritage of Religious Scholarship

Although the province of Chefchaouen has been associated with the stigma of marginalization and socioeconomic disadvantage during the second half of the twentieth century, the region of Chefchaouen testifies to a rich heritage of traditional religious scholarship. Indeed, the mountainous region of the Arabic-speaking Jbala was at the historical crossroads of both sea and land routes between the intellectual and trading center of Fez and the cities of Andalusia. Given its strategic location, Chefchaouen served both as an advanced post for Islam and as a bastion of resistance to European penetration, with the Jbala developing a spirit of jihad.[18] Taken in its largest acceptation, jihad was an all-encompassing driving force through which Islamic scholars became "theoreticians of jihad," while warriors came together around marabouts who acted as fervent indoctrinators in a world of peasants, traders, and craftsmen.[19]

Being both a combative and a spiritual society, honor and *baraka* (God's grace), acquired through an ascribed status defined by the order of filiation with the prophet (*shorafa*), and the status of *fqih*, acquired through the quest for knowledge, were of prime importance within Jbala society. Indeed, the density of local scholars, or ulama; doctors of law, or *fuqaha*; and saints, or *shorafa*, and their role in the perpetuation of tradition has undoubtedly been the most striking characteristic of local society. However, with the end of Muslim control over Andalusia and the Strait of Gibraltar, the region of Chefchaouen, along with the entire Mediterranean facade of Morocco, was progressively marginalized, becoming a dead end at least in the south-north axis. Moreover, despite the fact that the region has become economically and politically marginal within the Moroccan nation, there continues to be a very dense network of *foqaha* (teachers at traditional centers of learning). The *foqaha* have been referred to as "one of the main export resources in the region,"[20] and each village continues to have one or more *msids* despite the progressive introduction of government primary schools.

[18] J. Vignet-Zunz, "Montagne et société: Les Jbala dans la problématique Riff-Tell," *Abhath* 4 (1994): 64.

[19] M. Mezzine, "Jihad au pays Jbala (XVIème et XVIIème siècles): Effervescence et régulation," *Jbala—Histoire et Société* 1 (1994): 63. According to Dale Eickelman (*Knowledge and Power in Morocco: The Education of a Twentieth-Century Notable* [Princeton, NJ: Princeton University Press, 1985], 24), "Maraboutism was the prevalent popular belief that certain persons, living or dead, possess a special relation toward God which makes them particularly well placed to act as intermediaries and to communicate God's grace (*baraka*) to their clients. This implicit belief was in uncomfortable tension with Islam as understood by educated Moroccans and many townsmen."

[20] Vignet-Zunz, "Montagne et société," 64.

Contemporary Patterns of Qur'anic Education: The Invisible Learners of the Traditional *Kuttab*

Following the 1968 Operation Écoles Coraniques that encouraged participation in Qur'anic schools as a form of preprimary education, the new *kuttab* model emerged, representing a wide range of adaptations of the original religious model to the modern conception of the (private) preschool. Although governmental supervision of Qur'anic schools was theoretically initiated at the end of the 1970s—at least in urban areas—the community-based schools did not receive any form of assistance or support from the government to take on this new role. On the contrary, very little adaptation actually took place in traditional *kuttab*. Rather, private "modern" Qur'anic (i.e., preprimary) schools sprang up to meet the challenge and growing demand for preschool education and preparation for entry into grade 1. And the modern Qur'anic preschools differ entirely from their traditional counterparts, not only with regard to curriculum content and pedagogy but also with regard to the role and profile of the educators, how the schools are managed, the clientele that they cater to, and the nature and source of their legitimacy (see table 2).

While "modern" (preschool) *kattatib* are private institutions based on fixed tuition, "traditional" Qur'anic schools are community-based institutions in the classical sense. The locale used is most commonly an annex to the

TABLE 2
"MODERN" AND "TRADITIONAL." *Kuttab*

Criterion	Type of *Kuttab*	
	Modern	Traditional
Management	Private: supervision by Ministry of Education (MOE)	Community based
Source of legitimacy	Official authorization required from MOE: modern pedagogy and curriculum as effective preparation of grade 1	Social contract, or *shart*
Learning content	Complete or partial implementation of national preschool curriculum: preliteracy skills	Partial or complete study of the Qur'an through dictation, recitation, and memorization
Target age group	5–6-year-olds: boys and girls	All ages, no restriction: predominantly boys, particularly at more advanced levels
Profile and role of educator	High school education or more; teacher/instructor	*Fqih*, or *taleb* (pl. *tolba*): product of traditional education system; teacher, prayer leader, arbitrator, and pious social model

local mosque or to a local *sharif*'s tomb.[21] The modern *kuttab* teacher is a product of the public education system and employed in the private sector, although the traditional *taleb* or *fqih* is a product of the religious learning tradition, working within a community-managed institution and depending on a number of community sources for his livelihood.[22] This fundamental distinction is officially overlooked, and all Qur'anic schools—be they traditional community-based institutions or modern preschools—are referred to as *kattatib*.[23]

Although integrated into the national education system at the preprimary level, Qur'anic schools are either private preschools or, as is the case for the vast majority in the province of Chefchaouen, community-based rural schools that are not part of the public school system. Available figures on enrollment patterns are approximate, and national researchers largely acknowledge that official figures are a gross underestimation of the number of traditional Qur'anic schools, particularly in more remote rural areas.[24] There is a striking contrast, for instance, between the estimated 1,300 Qur'anic schools reported in official statistics for 1995 and the estimated 14,000 schools cited 15 years earlier by Attilio Gaudio.[25] Nevertheless, the available data reflect three important patterns that emerged: (1) the overwhelming majority of *kuttab* institutions among the predominantly rural population of Chefchaouen are of the traditional variety (over 95 percent); (2) with the exception of the more developed provincial capital and urban center of Chefchaouen where numerous modern *kattatib* provide preschool education to the children of the sizable population of civil servants, enrollment in traditional *kuttab* is overwhelmingly male with young girls attending only for short periods of 1–2

[21] *Shorafa* (sing. *sharif*) claim descent from the Prophet Muhammad and are believed to be endowed with divine blessing (or *baraka*).

[22] Community compensation includes (*a*) *shart*, or annual contracts for the services of the *fqih* to the community, e.g., teaching, calling to prayer (muezzin), leading prayer, and arbitrating; (*b*) lodging at the local mosque or an annex; (*c*) meals provided on a rotating basis by students' families; (*d*) payment of a share of the proceeds from the collective land (which varies with overall agricultural production); (*e*) a small weekly cash or in-kind contribution brought by children each Friday; and (*f*) fees received for attending to religious rites and ceremonies, e.g., marriages, circumcisions, and funerals.

[23] This is the case, e.g., for the 1993 study of some 600 schools selected from across seven regions undertaken jointly by UNICEF and the MOE. The term *préscolaire coranique* is used in the study in reference to all Qur'anic schools, including the traditional community schools as defined above. Although differences between modern and traditional *kuttab* are briefly described, no distinction is made between the two in the collection of data, and findings are presented only in terms of urban/rural differences. See MOE/UNICEF, *Etude évaluative des actions du ministère de l'education nationale pour le développement du préscolaire coranique* (Rabat: MOE/UNICEF, 1993).

[24] The provincial Office of Preschool Education collects data annually on the number of modern and traditional *kuttab*, teachers, and students enrolled in the province of Chefchaouen. Although the data are said to be based on systematic on-site visits to all communes within the province conducted during a 4-week period each autumn by a team of 10–15 inspectors, the reliability of the data collected through this mechanism is questioned by the MOE regional planning department. Moreover, interviews with preschool inspectors confirmed that the figures they reported were often gross approximations, because it is extremely difficult and time consuming to visit schools in many remote *douars*, or villages.

[25] Attilio Gaudio, *Maroc du nord: Cités andalouses et montagnes berbères* (Paris: Nouvelles Editions Latines, 1983).

years; and (3) the total number of pupils attending the *kuttab* includes children that are age 7 or more, although at present, no data exist on the proportions of children in the 7–13 or 14–16+ age groups who are studying at traditional Qur'anic schools (see table 3).

Despite the fact that public schooling has become the main route to literacy acquisition in Morocco during the second half of the twentieth century, alternative traditional paths still do exist. At the beginning of the 1990s, an average of 6.6 percent of the national literate population—and over 16 percent of literate males in rural areas—still acquired literacy through traditional forms of Islamic learning and not through public schooling or adult literacy programs (see table 4).[26]

Alternative Basic Education for the Children of the Rural Poor

The available evidence does not support the traditional argument that the *msid* plays a substitution role, attracting children who would not otherwise attend school because of an inadequate supply in rural areas. For instance, an examination of regional disparities at the preprimary and primary levels in the late 1980s indicated that high rates of enrollment in traditional elementary Islamic education were not correlated with a deficient supply of primary schooling.[27] Three of the provinces with the lowest primary school enrollment ratios—Chefchaouen in the north, as well as Tarouddant and Tiznit to the south of Marrakech—did not demonstrate particular deficiency in the provision of public schooling relative to the national average. Moreover, indices of preprimary education in these three provinces were among the highest nationwide. What, then, is the nature of this demand for traditional education? What is the interplay of economic and cultural factors in shaping such demand?

The persistence of traditional Qur'anic schooling in rural areas and small

TABLE 3
DISTRIBUTION OF PRESCHOOLS, 1994–95: PROVINCE OF CHEFCHAOUEN

Administrative Circle	No. of Schools			No. of Students	
	Modern	Traditional	Total	Total	Girls (%)
Chefchaouen	14	10	24	1,092	44.5
Bab Taza	21	257	278	5,187	1.0
Baberret	5	461	466	9,041	1.4
Bou Ahmed	7	282	289	5,520	1.4
Mokrissat	7	232	239	2,871	4.8
Total	54	1,242	1,296	23,711	3.7

SOURCE.—Unpublished statistics made available at the Regional Delegation of Preschool Education, MOE, Chefchaouen.

[26] Moroccan Household Living Standards Measurement Survey, 1990–91.

[27] Bouthaïna Azami-Tawil and Sobhi Tawil, "Les disparités régionales dans l'enseignement primaire au Maroc et le rôle de l'education traditionnelle" (master's thesis, University of Geneva, 1988).

TABLE 4
LITERACY ACQUIRED THROUGH TRADITIONAL ISLAMIC LEARNING
(as a Percentage of the Total Literate Population)

Gender	Urban	Rural	Total
Male	5.7	16.7	9.9
Female	.5	1.9	.8
Total	3.5	13.2	6.6

SOURCE.—Based on data from Moroccan Household Living Standards Measurement Survey, 1990–91.

urban centers may be attributed to poverty and to the precarious subsistence living conditions that are the dramatic reality of so many families: conditions that make the direct and indirect costs of schooling unbearable. According to the UNICEF-MOE 1993 study, many parents preferred Qur'anic schooling because of their lower direct cost as compared to primary schooling. A study of the dynamics between primary and Qur'anic schooling in a small village in the High Atlas Mountains found a pattern of dropping out prompted by economic constraints on the community and the inability of households to cover the costs of schooling. In response to these conditions, families migrated from rural to urban areas or sent their children to Qur'anic schools.[28] These observations are corroborated by field observations in the rural communities of Chefchaouen, where the increasingly harsh subsistence constraints resulting from years of drought (1993–95 and again in 1999–2001) led to increased school dropout.

An examination of the growth of absolute preprimary enrollment over the 1980s and 1990s (see fig. 1) reveals paradoxical patterns. Figures for Qur'anic preschool education during the 1980s indicate an increase in enrollment at a time when primary school enrollment patterns were stagnating and declining. The increased incidence of poverty documented during that period, particularly in rural areas, adversely affected the take-up of primary schooling at a time when the direct and indirect costs of schooling became increasingly difficult for households to bear. It may therefore be argued that some children from poorer households attending *msids* did not transfer to primary schooling upon reaching age 7. Moreover, other children returned to the *msid* after having dropped out or after having been pulled out by the head of the household.

Nonenrollment in and dropout from public primary schooling along with an increased participation in Qur'anic education among children (both boys and girls) was the pattern in the 1980s. However, in the 1990s, when the regressive pattern of public primary enrollment was halted and progressively reversed, Qur'anic education continued to increase. It therefore becomes clear that the *msid* responds to educational demand that cannot be met by

[28] Ali Amahan, "Dix ans d'évolution dans un village du Haut-Atlas," *Bulletin Economique et Social du Maroc* 159–61 (1987).

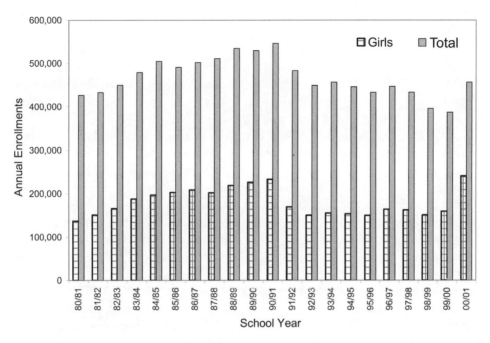

Fig. 1.—Growth in absolute Qur'anic preschool enrollments distributed by gender (Morocco, 1980–2000).

primary schooling, not because of a lack of schooling infrastructure but because of household poverty and exclusion (push out) from schooling as a result of repetition and/or failure.

As many as half of all primary school-going–age children in the province of Chefchaouen attend traditional Qur'anic schools. Students of 18–20 years of age sometimes study alongside younger children. The Ussala al Kadima Qur'anic school in the heart of the provincial center of Chefchaouen, for instance, is typical of the age range that may be found in *kuttab* in the province. Out of 20 students observed, half were of the preprimary age (under 7 years old), one-quarter were of the primary age group (7–13 years old), and one-quarter were of a postprimary age (14, 15, and 17 years old).[29] The second half of the students, ranging in age from 7 to 17, constitutes the "invisible" segment of youth attending traditional community-based religious education, although they are officially considered to be out of school.

Muhammad (age 14) and Abdellatif (age 13), whose father is a construction worker who attended both a *kuttab* and a primary school and whose mother had not participated in either formal religious education or in primary schooling, have been studying the Qur'an at Al Ussala al Kadima for the past 8 years. The boys, like their older sisters (now aged 8, 13, and 15), enrolled in grade 1 of primary school after having completed approximately

[29] Based on field observations conducted in the province of Chefchaouen during the period 1995–97.

2 years of study at the *kuttab*. However, unlike their older sisters (who continued within the public schools at the primary and lower secondary levels), both boys dropped out in their first year and returned to the *kuttab*, where they continue to pursue their formal education to this day. Muhammad now combines Qur'anic studies with an informal learning of the leather trade through a 2-day-a-week apprenticeship in his uncle's business, as well as looking after their home and his 3-year-old sister.

The fact that both these boys dropped out of primary schooling while their three sisters remained at school has a number of important implications. First, despite the very low level of formal education of the parents, there is a clear demand for schooling for the children. Second, the fact that the two boys are attending Qur'anic schooling is in no way an indication of any type of cultural resistance to the public schooling model—be it in terms of content, methods, or organization. Indeed, not only had both boys transferred to grade 1 after completing the equivalent of a preschool Qur'anic education but their sisters are all pursuing primary or lower secondary schooling. The question as to why the two boys are attending Qur'anic education appears to have to do with the need for the children to be involved in supplementing family income, both through the meager present and the more substantial future returns of the informal learning of traditional trades.

Deschooling and the Expansion of Cannabis Production

The low patterns of take-up of primary schooling in the province also are related to significant changes in the structure of economic production and associated opportunities for employment and income generation. How does the development of cannabis production affect educational enrollment in the region? In addition to the development of a sense of individualism and the spread of corruption associated with illicit trade, as well as the shift in power structures from the traditional authority of village and tribal notables to that of the economic power of the emerging class of drug smugglers, local education officials confirm that the extension of cannabis production is also having a negative impact on social demand for education. The emergence of cannabis production as an important source of revenue in the early 1980s appears to have reduced family demand for the schooling of children, particularly of older children and adolescents within the province of Chefchaouen.

Examining the impact of the increasing weight of *kif* production in the local economy on the development of education is a difficult endeavor, in part because of the difficulty of obtaining qualitative or quantitative data related to this illegal activity in Morocco. While the 2003 UNODC/APDN study is a new and welcome initiative by the government, the evidence I discuss here is mostly anecdotal or inferred indirectly from educational data that do not address the issue explicitly. This evidence suggests that the extension of the *kif* economy affects both the supply of, and demand for, education in a number of ways:

1. Heightened value of real estate and consequently higher cost of establishing new public primary school units[30]
2. Increased opportunities for child work and increased indirect cost of schooling[31]
3. Out-migration and declining latent demand for education
4. Resistance to the establishment of public schooling perceived as a form of intrusion of central governmental authorities feared to be engaged in the surveillance of the illegal activities of producing *kif*.

While no evidence is available on the relationship between attrition at the level of the second cycle of basic schooling and the development of employment and income-generating opportunities in the *kif*-producing sector, it is possible to infer a relationship between communes that are most affected by patterns of school dropout and the preponderance of *kif* production in those same areas. Indeed, as *kif* production spreads within and beyond the confines of the administrative limits of the province, it is possible to see how communes adjacent to the province of Chefchaouen, which are also known for their involvement in the production of *kif*, are also affected by the phenomenon of deschooling.

In a much more indirect fashion, it is possible to refer to studies on the perceptions of schooling among youth, heads of households, and community leaders. At the national level, heads of households sampled in the Moroccan Household Living Standards Measurement Survey (1998–99) provided the following reasons for dropping out at the levels of the first and second cycle of basic schooling: (*a*) provision of schooling, (*b*) economic constraints, (*c*) repetition or failure, (*d*) child's lack of interest, and (*e*) parental attitudes (see table 5). What is most striking about the data presented in table 5 is that the overwhelming reason in both urban and rural areas for dropping out of both cycles of basic schooling is the parent's perception that the child lacks interest in schooling (varying from 38.3 to 53.7 percent). This is a clear signal about the lack of perceived utility of schooling and the low relevance for both the

[30] The sparse residential patterns observed in the province of Chefchaouen pose genuine challenges in terms of educational planning and the provision of primary schooling in view of ensuring access for all children. In Chefchaouen, as in rural Morocco more generally, the strategy has been to bring small schools as close as possible to children's homes, rather than build schooling centers for multiple villages with accessory services, e.g., school canteens, dormitories, and so forth. The strategy of building many small schools, particularly, is affected by the cost of land.

[31] The growth of employment opportunities related to the production of cannabis affects more particularly on the education of girls who are often reputed to be more efficient for tasks related to the tilling of the land, irrigation, and the separation of male and female plants. For both boys and girls, the opportunity cost of schooling rises sharply as opportunities to earn up to DH 100/day (or some $10 per day) working in the range of activities related to the production of *kif* also increase. Such incomes are highly competitive when compared to incomes that school graduates may hope to earn should they be able to secure employment, e.g., as lower-level civil servants.

TABLE 5
DECLARED REASONS FOR DROPPING OUT OF THE FIRST AND SECOND CYCLES OF
BASIC SCHOOLING, 1999: DISTRIBUTION BY RESIDENCE

	Urban		Rural		National Average	
Reason	First Cycle	Second Cycle	First Cycle	Second Cycle	First Cycle	Second Cycle
Provision of schooling	2.9	3.5	12.2	19.2	9.1	12.0
Economic constraints	31.5	21.4	28.1	20.6	29.2	20.9
Repeat/failure	15.1	13.4	6.2	3.0	9.3	7.8
Lack of interest	41.6	38.3	41.1	53.7	41.2	46.7
Parental attitudes	3.1	21.6	5.1	3.5	4.4	11.8
Other	5.8	1.8	7.3	.0	6.8	.8
Total	100.0	100.0	100.0	100.0	100.0	100.0

SOURCE.—Based on Moroccan Household Living Standards Measurement Survey data (1998–99).

NOTE.—The first cycle of basic schooling concerns children in the 7–12 age group, while the second cycle (middle school) concerns children aged 13–15. Factors related to the provision of schooling include distance to school, climatic conditions making access difficult or impossible during certain seasons, and lack of schooling in the vicinity. In the case of the primary cycle, this also includes lack of equipment. Factors grouped under "economic constraints" include the need to assist parents in their professional activities, the need for children to work, and a lack of financial means to cover the direct costs of schooling. The category "parental attitudes" in the case of the first cycle also includes the original Moroccan Household Living Standards Measurement Survey category of "family difficulties."

present and perceived future realities of children, which in Chefchaouen may be at least partly shaped by the increasing availability of attractive income-generating opportunities offered by the production of *kif.*

Reconsidering Value Resistance in a Context of Rapid Social Change

The rich religious and scholarly heritage that characterizes Chefchaouen may explain forms of resistance to the introduction of primary schooling on the part of rural communities. Cherifa Alaoui (1994), for instance, cites the key question of the negative image that many rural communities have of the primary school teacher, who is usually of urban origin, single, an outsider to the local community and its culture, often unmotivated, and frequently absent.[32] These negative perceptions that rural communities often have of the primary school teacher reinforces the *fqih*—an essential constituent element of local culture and perfectly integrated into the social life of the local community—who may, out of his own interests, resist primary schooling in an attempt to ensure attendance of children at the Qur'anic school for as long as possible. Because the livelihood of *foqaha*, or traditional teachers, depends on the size and wealth of the community, as well as on the volume of their clientele (in terms of number of children), they may resist the establishment of a nearby primary school, which is often perceived as a potential competitor.

The negative image that rural communities often have of the primary school teacher is increasingly combined with the low perceived utility of primary schooling as an effective means of upward social mobility, particularly

[32] Cherifa Alaoui, "Obstacles à la scolarisation des filles en milieu rural," in *Femmes et education: Etat des lieux*, ed. Cherifa Alaoui et al. (Casablanca: Editions le Fennec, 1994), 91–92.

in the absence of easily accessible opportunities to pursue schooling at the postprimary level. The lower the perceived returns of household investment in primary schooling, the higher the opportunity costs, including those associated with forgone learning in terms of both traditional farming and other vocational skills, as well as religious knowledge. A rural child that does not continue schooling at the postprimary level will have "neither learned the Qur'an from a young age, nor learned how to farm."[33]

The data generated through an examination of regional disparities in preprimary and primary education in Morocco suggest a degree of incompatibility of public primary schooling to the local value system in certain peripheral rural regions. Field research in smaller farming communities suggests that primary schooling has often contributed to its own social isolation by neglecting to consider networks of traditional education as institutional expressions of local culture and customs, thus reinforcing its image as an assimilationist institution.[34]

In such an analysis, it is important to recall that the regions of the western Rif in the north, the central and southern High Atlas, and the Anti-Atlas in which high rates of take-up of traditional elementary education have been observed are all regions that correspond to the historical territories of *bled el siba,* or tribal zones that were traditionally considered to be in "institutional dissidence" and extremely defensive of their autonomy with regard to the central government, or *makhzen.* In this perspective, the subsistence of the *msid* may be interpreted as a local expression of resistance in the context of the introduction of public primary schooling seen as an exogenous institution introducing a form of submission to central authorities. Refusing to submit to state control and domination, the autonomous local institution of the *msid* became an expression of a local desire to maintain control over mechanisms of social reproduction. Data collected from provincial services of the Ministry of Education (preschool and planning units) suggest forms of resistance. It is such resistance that explains attitudes of noncooperation and even of hostility on the part of *fqihs* encountered and reported by supervisors and surveyors from the Chefchaouen regional office of preschool education when they conduct their annual rounds of data collection.

However, it would appear that the function of cultural resistance attributed to *kattatib* in peripheral regions can only partly explain their coexistence with primary schools. A study conducted in the mid-1980s in a Berber village of the High Atlas suggested that the *taleb* was only playing part of his traditional role, and he was maintained by the village in a "false occupation" in an attempt by the local community to convince itself that its institutions and values were being preserved and reproduced. The process of traditional learning of the

---

[33] Interviewee quoted in Alaoui, "Obstacles à la scolarisation des filles en milieu rural," 91.

[34] See Ahmed Zouggari, "L'école en milieu rural," *Bulletin Economique et Social du Maroc* 159–61 (1987), and *L'école en milieu rural* (Rabat: El Maarif al Jadida, 1996).

kuttab in the High Atlas (much like the Friday sermon at the mosque) is to be seen as a rite. Arguably, participation in the collective Friday prayer, much like participation in formal Qur'anic teaching/learning, reinforces group cohesion more than the actual content and message of the sermon delivered by the *fqih* in Arabic to Berber-speaking communities.[35]

The results of a survey conducted by M. Echhab (1981), however, indicated that only a small minority of rural households (4 percent) chose the *msid* for the elementary education of their children rather than primary schooling. This would suggest that the hypothesis of cultural resistance—at least in the region of the High Atlas—is not a satisfactory explanation. Indeed, what is most surprising about the findings is that over half of the *foqaha* interviewed had themselves chosen to send their children to primary schools rather than to traditional *msids*.[36]

This clearly reflects a changing social order in which the nature and function of formal education is rapidly changing and in which individual literacy acquisition becomes an objective of modern formal education. While the base of traditional Islamic education was historically large, the elementary education of the *kuttab* or *msid* was not necessarily associated with literacy acquisition, which remained a collective social resource fully possessed only by a small minority of ulama, while "restricted traditional literacy" was more broadly distributed. This explains the fact that, while literacy in rural Morocco during the first half of the twentieth century necessarily implied formal religious education, formal education did not necessarily imply literacy.[37] The traditional function of restricted literacy acquisition through Qur'anic learning has been overshadowed by the more generalized and efficient development of reading and writing skills through public primary schooling. The growing recognition of the need for literacy skills and the greater efficiency of primary schooling in ensuring literacy acquisition is confirmed by many *tolba* or *foqaha* themselves and explains the results of Echhab's survey.

Data for the 1990s indicate, furthermore, that although participation in traditional Islamic learning is negatively correlated with income in urban areas, the correlation observed in rural areas is positive (see table 6). This would appear to support the idea that Qur'anic schooling continues to be a socially valued educational path despite the spread of government schooling. However, participation rates in rural Qur'anic schools among the younger generation (7–12 age group) mark the opposite trend, where the take-up of Qur'anic schooling is highest for boys from the poorest families (see table 7). Clearly then, intergenerational participation rates reflect the process of social

[35] Ahmed Zouggari, "Le taleb dans le village: Etude de cas de Ounien" (paper presented at the World Archeological Congress, Southhampton and London, September 1–7, 1986), 8–9.

[36] M. Echhab, "L'école et la société en milieu rural au Maroc" (PhD diss., University René Descartes, 1981), 109.

[37] Eickelman, *Knowledge and Power in Morocco*, 59.

TABLE 6
PARTICIPATION IN TRADITIONAL ISLAMIC EDUCATION (as a Percentage of the Total Population):
DISTRIBUTION BY RESIDENCE AND INCOME QUINTILE

Residence	Income Quintile				
	1	2	3	4	5
Urban	7.5	6.1	3.0	3.1	3.1
Rural	6.2	6.8	9.5	7.8	11.7
Total	6.5	6.7	6.8	4.9	4.9

SOURCE.—Based on data from Moroccan Household Living Standards Measurement Survey, 1990–91.
NOTE.—Income quintile 1 = lowest; quintile 5 = highest.

change in rural communities and the weakening of the traditional role and status of Islamic learning as a means of social promotion. This corroborates the findings of V. Lavy, J. Spratt, and N. Leboucher on changing patterns of illiteracy in Morocco based on their analysis of 1991 Household Living Standards Measurement Survey data.[38]

Despite these changes, however, there often appears to be a degree of ambivalence in that the increased recognition of schooling as a more effective educational strategy for rural children in a changing world is often associated with a continued respect for the *msid* as a social and cultural institution and resource.[39] In contrast, research in other regions has indicated that cultural resistance may indeed be an important factor in understanding low primary enrollment and the subsistence of the *msid*. This is the case in Chefchaouen where, in addition to factors such as scattered habitat, inadequate communications infrastructure, and household poverty, the causes of low primary enrollment rates have also been attributed to the antagonism between modern and traditional schooling.[40]

This is particularly true of the Jbala, who, as we have seen, are reputed to have a rich heritage and a dense network of *tolba* who deliver to the rural population an elementary education that supplements the scholarly and spiritual role of the *shorafa* (holy men) or ulama who provide postelementary Islamic learning. As M. Mezzine (1994) points out, Jbala society is characterized by a dense network of scholars and an extensive network of *zawias* that function as cultural and spiritual centers.[41] This tradition continued well into the 1990s where the reputation of the Jbala was unequaled. Chefchaouen welcomed students from both distant regions and from the numerous quality

[38] V. Lavy, J. Spratt, and N. Leboucher, "Changing Patterns of Illiteracy in Morocco: Assessment Methods Compared," Living Standards Measurement Survey Working Paper no. 115 (World Bank, Washington, DC, 1995).

[39] Echhab, "L'école et la société en milieu rural au Maroc," 114.

[40] Gaudio, *Maroc du nord*, 99. Resistance to the establishment and spread of primary schooling documented in the course of the development of the national school system within northern Morocco reflects the type of educational and cultural resistance that was often encountered in the colonial period. In referring to the period of Spanish occupation of Chefchaouen, Gaudio notes that a number of families obstinately refused to send their children to primary schools.

[41] Mezzine, "Jihad au pays Jbala," 64.

TABLE 7
PARTICIPATION RATES (7–12 Age Group) IN QUR'ANIC EDUCATION:
DISTRIBUTION BY RESIDENCE AND INCOME QUINTILE

Residence	Income Quintile					Total
	1	2	3	4	5	
Urban	.0	2.9	2.9	2.2	.5	1.50
Rural	6.1	5.6	5.1	2.9	2.9	4.60
Total	5.3	5.0	4.6	2.5	1.2	3.36

SOURCE.—Based on data from Moroccan Household Living Standards Measurement Survey, 1990–91 ($n = 104$).
NOTE.—Income quintile 1 = lowest; quintile 5 = highest.

religious schools that prepared students for higher education provided at the Quarawiine University in Fez. The Chefchaouen *tolba* themselves were in great demand elsewhere and constituted a modest but nonnegligible source of regional income in a rather difficult agricultural economy.[42]

Ulama, or traditional scholars, are now rare in the rural areas outside of the provincial capital of Chefchaouen. The region continues, however, to produce a small number of *foqaha*, although they too are many fewer than in the past. Indeed, the reproduction of this generation appears to be in crisis. This concern with changing modes of social reproduction is echoed in fundamental existential questions about life and death: "Who will wash and bury our dead?"[43] Such concerns are symptomatic of the tensions associated with times of rapid social change and the threat of anomie as established norms and rituals are no longer properly being reproduced and in a context where new forms of social reproduction have not fully taken root.

Demand for traditional religious education and resistance to primary schooling remain important factors in understanding inequality in participation in schooling as experienced in poorer marginal regions such as Chefchaouen. Although traditional education has receded in many areas, it remains dominant in certain rural areas. Many communities continue not to trust the public school institution that is perceived as detaching their children from local cultural traditions, and resistance to schooling is often expressed in an antagonism with the teachers' behaviors considered to be inappropriate to local norms and customs.

[42] Vignet-Zunz, "Montagne et société," 151.

[43] A concern expressed by the head of the planning department at the regional delegation of the Ministry of Education in Chefchaouen. The preoccupation with the continued social treatment of biological life cycles of birth and death according to local custom and tradition are curiously similar to the protest expressed by segments of rural Turkish society during the 1940s in reaction to the violent modernization of Kemalist Turkey and the 20-year ban on religious training centers in the Turkish countryside. See F. Rahman, *Islam and Modernity: Transformation of an Intellectual Tradition* (Chicago: University of Chicago Press, 1982), 92.

Concluding Remarks

The challenges of educational development in Chefchaouen and the difficulties in ensuring equitable participation in primary schooling may largely be explained by a range of forms of resistance to schooling. Such resistance is not to be reduced to a narrow understanding of the historical forms of resistance to schooling that have been experienced in the transition from colonial domination to national independence and largely documented, for example, in societies with a strong and long tradition of Muslim scholarship. While this was also historically the case in Morocco at the national level, certain pockets of traditional scholarship have continued to resist the introduction and expansion of government-provided secular schooling, favoring the preservation of modes of transmission of knowledge and of social reproduction that have been central to the Moroccan tradition. This has been very much the case in Chefchaouen and in regions of southern Morocco with a similar heritage of reputed scholarship. While this continues to be the case nationally in certain peripheral regions of Morocco, resistance to schooling in present-day Chefchaouen appears to have as much to do with economic realities as with issues of preservation of local identity and cultural heritage.

This is perhaps most evident in the significant progress that has recently been made in expanding access to primary schooling within the province. Net enrollment ratios for 6-year-old children in the Chefchaouen province have gone up from 53 to 87 percent since 2000. This spectacular progress reflects renewed national commitment to Universal Primary Education goals and may be explained through a combination of factors, perhaps most notably (1) the program of distribution of dried foods, which has been an effective incentive for girls' schooling; (2) the dramatic expansion of primary school coverage as a result of the new impulsion of the Ministry of Education, the involvement of the Ministry of Interior, and the increased participation of local communities; and (3) the awareness-raising campaigns that involve the creation of commissions at the provincial, communal, and school levels.[44]

This article has examined the interaction between Qur'anic education and primary schooling in relation to the contradictions inherent to the rapidly changing social and economic regional context of Chefchaouen. The region is characterized both by geographical, economic, and political marginalization, as well as by a solidly rooted heritage of traditional religious learning. Qur'anic education in predominantly rural Chefchaouen is of the traditional variety, serving simultaneously as preprimary education for both boys and girls and as an alternative form of schooling for boys who either never enroll in primary school or who drop out because of a combination of failed school-

[44] Once a local community has prepared and proposed a locale for primary schooling, the MOE will deploy a teacher. As a result of these efforts, regional Ministry of Education officials report that all rural *douars* that have thus far been unserved by a primary school now appear to be covered.

ing experience (repetition/failure) and economic constraints and the subsequent need to contribute to the livelihood of the household. In the provincial center of Chefchaouen, boys of a primary school–going age or older who attend traditional *kuttab* tend to combine study of the Qur'an with nonformal apprenticeships in the crafts industry, as well as with assistance to the family in daily subsistence and income-generating activities. In the *douars*, study of the Qur'an is combined with domestic help and farm work.

Patterns of participation in *kuttab* suggest that religious education is generally not a substitute for a lack of accessible primary schooling but, rather, an alternative form of basic education that responds to several distinct logics. The *kuttab* caters primarily to poorer boys whose families are unable to cover the direct and indirect costs of schooling. Boys of 10–14 years of age interviewed in the city of Chefchaouen, for instance, have reported daily routines of up to 12 hours of combined Qur'anic study, participation in traditional apprenticeships, and work. Moreover, the increased attendance of *kuttab*—often associated with an increased pattern of "pull out" from primary school—observed in rural communities during periods of economic hardship is evidence of the alternative basic education that Qur'anic schools provide to the poor.

However, as a local, community-managed, and culturally appropriate institution, the *kuttab* is also an alternative form of basic education that responds either (1) to a (declining) educational demand based on traditional conceptualizations of learning seen as a pious pursuit of learning and an investment in symbolic capital or (2) as a form of resistance. Such resistance may be cultural, as expressed in the antagonism sometimes caused between the behavior of the primary school teacher, most often a stranger to the region, and the customs and values of the local community. But resistance to schooling may have more to do with the low perceived relevance of schooling and the intrusion of public administration in more remote areas where the economy is increasingly centered on illicit cannabis production.

The case study in Chefchaouen supplements macroanalysis at the national level in a crucial way, highlighting the importance of examining social, economic, and cultural dimensions of specific local contexts in order to develop a more subtle understanding of the interplay between demand and supply of both traditional religious and government primary education. The specific case of Chefchaouen also shows the difficulties in establishing clear patterns of educational strategies when confronted with the contradictions inherent to the process of rapid social change currently underway. This social change is being shaped by both external factors, such as the recent expansion of schooling resulting from renewed political commitment of central authorities to basic education, and internal factors, such as the impact of the rapid extension of the cultivation of cannabis, the prospects of improved household income, and the consequent demand for children's work.

While the impact of the last is beginning to be seen in the declining pattern of demand and enrollment at the level of the second cycle of basic schooling (grades 7–9), its effect on the development of Qur'anic education remains to be seen. Existing data deficits at the level of the regional planning services of the regional delegation of the Ministry of Education can be partly overcome with more qualitative research on emerging patterns of dropping out at the level of the second cycle of basic schooling. Interestingly, this recent pattern of dropping out is associated with increases in grade 1 intake rates. This paradoxical pattern of participation in school education is perhaps indicative of the shift in the nature of the national crisis of the Moroccan education system from concerns about access to schooling to concerns about quality and the relevance of schooling to social and economic realities.

We have seen that it very difficult to determine the relative weight of supply- and demand-side factors in explaining educational and occupational patterns within the region. The issues of (*a*) the current and future role of traditional religious education and (*b*) the development and expansion of an agricultural economy based on the production of cannabis are politically sensitive. This is particularly so given the risks of political turmoil and instability that underlie the "networks of discontent," or the objective alliance observed in the north among traditional drug barons of Rifi origin, opposition forces, including those of political Islam, and those who experience a popular urban unrest, particularly in Tangiers.[45] It must nevertheless be emphasized that the attitude of governmental authorities in the early years of the twenty-first century reflects much greater transparency to sensitive and often controversial social issues, including the long-standing taboo issue of cannabis production. The international research findings published in 2003 on the extension of cannabis production in northern Morocco are a clear indication of this shift.[46]

[45] J. Ketterer, "Networks of Discontent in Northern Morocco: Drugs, Opposition, and Urban Unrest," *Middle East Report* 218 (Spring 2001).

[46] UNODC/APDN, *Morocco Cannabis Survey.*

Index